CODE RED:

Computerized Election Theft

and

The New American Century

Election 2016 Edition

Jonathan D. Simon

www.CODERED2016.com

Praise for *CODE RED*:

Jonathan Simon's *CODE RED* is unique, timely, easy-to-understand, and vastly important. The book uses an innovative Q&A format to enable readers to comprehend why computerized elections fraud represents an unprecedented challenge to democracy. The author has been a pioneering expert in this research, which has been widely ignored by traditional watchdog institutions and the political media. His book provides a convenient news-peg for them to start doing their jobs instead of continuing the go-along, get-along game.

Andrew Kreig, Justice Integrity Project director and author of
Presidential Puppetry: Obama, Romney and Their Masters

CODE RED: Computerized Election Theft and The New American Century by Jonathan Simon, co-founder of Election Defense Alliance, is not a fun read. Nor was it fun to write, Simon admits. But that doesn't make it any less important. Simon sees our nation heading over a cliff, democratically speaking; hence, his sense of urgency. He is desperate for us to get active and do something, but without the facts we are powerless. And without familiarity with computerized election history, there is no context in which to comprehend what has happened in recent electoral contests.

As Simon says, in his Foreword, "The Big Picture of American politics has become an ugly one and one that will only get uglier with time and inaction. So let's take an unblinking look at what the hell is happening to America and what we still just might be able to do about it." He dives in with a question-and-answer section that puts the major facts out there for people to examine and evaluate for themselves. We owe it to ourselves and the tattered system we hold dear to do that. The sooner the better.

Joan Brunwasser, OpEd-News

In 2004 Jonathan Simon downloaded state-by-state CNN screenshots of the first-posted exit polls. It was the seminal event which fueled the efforts of election analysts to investigate the mathematical probabilities of the one-sided exit poll-votecount disparities. But now we know that 2004 was not unique; many elections in what Simon refers to as "The New American Century" have deviated sharply from the unadjusted exit polls—and virtually always in the same direction. It is solid mathematical evidence of systemic election fraud. Were it not for Jonathan's foresight, it is unlikely that any of this information would have come to light.

But 2004 was just the beginning. Jonathan analyzed the 2006 midterms in which the Democratic landslide was denied; the 2008 presidential election in which Obama's true margin was reduced drastically; Martha Coakley's strange "loss" in the Massachusetts special election for the US Senate seat previously held by the late Ted Kennedy; and the bizarre national election that followed in November 2010. He now has taken on the even more bizarre 2014.

Jonathan writes in a clear, compelling and dramatic style—as befits his passion for the truth and the urgent need for an observable vote-counting system, as opposed to the sham that has corroded our reputation as the world's greatest democracy.

This book cannot be more highly recommended.

Richard Charnin, author of **Matrix of Deceit**

CODE RED lays out the case that election fraud has been occurring via the targeting and manipulation of computerized voting equipment across America.

Dr. Simon supports his conclusions with detailed and extensive data-gathering and analysis. He asks why we continue to entrust our voting process to this inherently non-transparent and vulnerable equipment. And he shows us how we can restore an observable process and reclaim ownership of our democracy.

As a professional statistician, I found *CODE RED*'s data, analyses, and conclusions compelling.

Dr. Elizabeth Clarkson, Statistician, National Institute for Aviation Research, Wichita State University

A spirited, data-driven argument that our computerized voting system is frighteningly vulnerable to corruption. In his first book, Simon brings his considerable experience on voting matters to bear; he is the executive director of Election Defense Alliance, a nonprofit voting rights watchdog. He argues that what at first appears to be a triumph of progress, the widespread application of new voting technology, actually generates myriad opportunities for partisan sabotage. ...[T]he allure of greater convenience comes at the price of transparency: newly secretive elections basically take place in the "impenetrable darkness of cyberspace." ... The scope of the book is broad, covering related topics like campaign finance and gerrymandering, and includes an instructive discussion of exit polls and Internet voting... Much of the work is written in a "Q&A format," which makes for highly readable prose, ... an often rigorous account of an important issue.

Kirkus Reviews

On one level, *CODE RED* is straightforward and refreshingly direct. No punches are pulled. But that doesn't make it easy to absorb. So many things I used to believe have to be re-thought. Amid the upheaval, I remind myself of a profoundly optimistic consequence of all this gut-wrenching shift in perspective.

I had thought democracy had just failed. People are too stupid, too easily manipulated. The power of money to corrupt politicians and to buy propaganda has just overwhelmed our democratic machinery.

But now I see we may not have given democracy a chance. Before we give up on majority rule, let's try counting the votes in an open and verifiable process. Before we talk about a revolution or a new Constitutional Convention, let's dust off the Constitution we've got, exercise the rights it gives us, and see how far it can take us.

Josh Mitteldorf, PhD
Co-author (with Dorion Sagan) of **Cracking The Aging Code**

Jonathan Simon has provided an important public service. *CODE RED* must not only be widely read and distributed among people who care about the integrity of our elections, but should provide enough fodder for a comprehensive investigation of ballot counting procedures. Such an investigation needs to happen soon and it cannot be conducted by Congressional or other political leadership. Simon's research is thorough and his case is more than compelling.

John Zogby
Founder of the Zogby Poll

To the memory of my parents, Ruth and Saul, who taught me to look into things; and to my daughter Emily, to whom it seems to come naturally.

Holly says tell folks the truth and they will sooner or later come to believe it, and Aaron says the same.

— *Mark Harris,* The Southpaw

TABLE OF CONTENTS

VII. EVIDENCE AND ANALYSIS

10010101 (149)

VIII. FOR FURTHER REFERENCE

11111111 + 00001110 (269)

FOREWORD to ELECTION 2016 EDITION

The saddest aspect of life right now is that science gathers knowledge faster than society gathers wisdom.

-- Isaac Asimov

THIS is still, as it was two years ago, a book for everyone who has been wondering what the hell is happening in America and in American politics.

And it still tells the story of how America's electoral system has been corrupted in the most direct and fundamental of ways: vote counting, the bedrock protocol of our democracy, has been computerized, outsourced, and made unobservable. In the darkness of cyberspace, common sense and the experts tell us, the vote count is vulnerable to manipulation—hacking by outsiders, rigging by insiders. And the forensic evidence indicates that the vulnerability has been exploited.

None of this is new. So why a new edition for *CODE RED*?

Election integrity and security is, as news anchors put it, a *developing story*. The "R-word" is being thrown about by, among others, a major-party presidential nominee. Serious articles in our "newspaper of record" warn of potential foreign interference with the vote counts of American elections. Things are moving, and moving fast.

Whatever one's opinion of Donald Trump as an avatar of electoral integrity, it was only a matter of time before *someone*, whether from a place of fairness or from one of self-interest, called into question a vote counting system that cannot be seen. This emperor has been walking around naked for 15 years now and the real mystery is why it has taken that long for *anyone* to mention the obvious. Nor is Trump the only one speaking publicly of rigging and hacking: the forensically bizarre 2016 primaries triggered such allegations, lawsuits, and a wave of distrust from millions of supporters of the Sanders candidacy.

However you feel about such stirrings, you can sense that the political and electoral environments have undergone a sea change. Our electoral system has failed badly in the translation of public will into electoral outcomes and representative government, and the result has been a rapidly metastasizing politics of disgust and distrust.

Whether and how this may come to a head in November and beyond remains to be seen, but it is hard to imagine a restoration of trust in our elections and our political system without the restoration of an observable vote counting process. The new chapters **"E2014: What Democracy Doesn't Look Like"** and **"E2016: The Chickens Come Home"** address our recent rapid descent into this hole; **"The Way Forward"** crucially offers a plan of action for digging ourselves out.

We are in a strange and difficult but by no means a hopeless place. We will have to work to restore our democracy and reclaim our sovereignty—work together with grit and tenacity. It begins with becoming informed, then trusting our common sense, communicating, organizing, moving mountains. The inertias are great but so is the strength of a people acting together to overcome them. We possess that strength and we owe it to ourselves and to the future to find it and use it.

Jonathan D. Simon
August 19, 2016 – Felton, California

FOREWORD to POST-E2014 EDITION

It was the best of times, it was the worst of times, it was the age of wisdom, it was the age of foolishness, it was the epoch of belief, it was the epoch of incredulity, it was the season of Light, it was the season of Darkness, it was the spring of hope, it was the winter of despair.

— *Charles Dickens,* A Tale of Two Cities

THIS is a book for everyone who has been wondering just what the *hell* **is happening in America and why American politics has become so increasingly warped as this new century has unfolded.**

It is a book for everyone who has wondered what is behind the gridlock in Washington, and the political hyperpolarization everywhere in America.

It is a book for everyone who has been scratching his or her head as election results show voters seeming to be voting against their own interests and contrary to virtually all measurements of their opinions, in the process transforming America into a harsh, mean, and baffling land.

And it is a book for those who cannot quite believe this is the real America they are seeing—who say to themselves, and increasingly to each other, "There's something wrong with this picture."

This is also a book I'd rather not write and it is one that I believe most Americans would rather not read. The story it tells is grim and a 'happy ending' will depend on an exercise of public will not seen in America within living memory. Yet, if America is to be rescued from the slow-rolling coup that is turning our nation into an unrecognizable place, this book *must* be written and *must* be read, and such an epochal exercise of will *must* rapidly become a reality.

The grim truth that is so hard to tell and so hard to swallow is that America's electoral system has been corrupted in the most direct and fundamental of ways: the computers that now count virtually all of our votes in secret can be—and, the evidence indicates, *have been*—programmed to cheat. To override the will of the voters and change the outcome of elections. To steal and hold power that could not be gained and held legitimately. Ultimately to reshape America more effectively than could a junta rolling tanks down Pennsylvania Avenue. The junta would, by its very visibility, at least provoke resistance.

I can only wish it were a fantasy, a fiction, the fevered invention of easy-to-dismiss, get-a-life "conspiracy theorists." I can't blame anyone for reflexively wanting to write it off as such, for asking, reasonably, "If this is happening, why aren't election administrators all over it? If this is happening, why aren't the losing candidates and/or their party all over it? If this is happening, why isn't the media all over it?" And I can't blame some for saying, with great indignation, "America is the world's Beacon of Democracy—this is the *one thing* that could *never happen here*!"

To which I can respond only by asking you to set that cherished, comforting, and dangerous vision of Exceptional America aside as we take a hard look at the core danger of computerized vote counting and the evidence that its vulnerability to wholesale fraud is being exploited to alter the very nature and direction of our country against the will of the majority of its people. Yes, it will most likely ruin your day. It will, if you're anything like me, leave you angry. Beyond angry. And I hope therefore ready to act, and determined to keep acting, until we Americans have our democracy back.

I've chosen to present a good part of this book in a Q&A format. I believe it makes things clearer and gets down to brass tacks quicker. There is so much about elections, vote counting, computerization, polling, and media coverage of each of these that is generally unknown or not well understood. Once the questioning process is begun, each question tends to lead to another, until the whole picture seems to take shape. The Q&A precedes an examination of the current state of affairs and an appendix presenting forensic evidence and analyses, and finally an ample bibliography for readers who feel the need to explore further before swinging into action mode.

I am well aware that, much as in the aftermath of the 2008 election ("E2008"), the Obama/Democratic victory in E2012 left the vast majority of potentially skeptical observers believing that *nothing* is rotten in Denmark (if the Right *could* rig, why *wouldn't* it? and if it *did* rig, why would it *lose*?) and that it's perfectly safe to go back in the water. We address this tragically misguided belief and answer those perfectly logical questions. We will see that there is nothing safe about the water and that the Denmark of American vote counting is rotten to its unobservable core.

The Big Picture of American politics has become an ugly one and one that will only get uglier with time and inaction. So let's take an unblinking look at what the hell is happening to America and what we still just might be able to do about it.

Jonathan D. Simon
December 21, 2014 – Arlington, Massachusetts

I. INTRODUCTION

There's something going on here and you don't know what it is,
do you, Mr. Jones?

– Bob Dylan

Who among us would trust an election where the ballots were handed to a man, dressed in a magician's costume, who took them behind a curtain and emerged some time later, claiming he had counted and then shredded them, to tell us who won?   What if the man were wearing a "So-And-So For President" button or some other partisan signifier?   And what if the results of key and close elections—elections that shaped American politics by determining the balance of power in statehouses and in Congress or by setting the field for November in presidential contests—kept going *that same way*?   How many, and what overall pattern of, strange results would it take before we insisted on going behind the curtain with him, or at least sending a trusted representative of our interests, to observe the count?

Nothing should be more self-evident than the simple statement that for an election to have *legitimacy* the counting process must be *observable*.   If the votes are counted in secret "behind a curtain," it does not matter how or by whom, no one other than the counter can really know who won and the results therefore lack legitimacy. *If you do not accept this basic statement, you may as well save yourself the time and put this book down now, because nothing else I have to say will make much of an impression.* Please take a moment, indeed as much time as you need, to think it through and decide for yourself. Would you shrug, say "Ah, what the hell," and simply trust the man behind the curtain with the fate of our nation and, given our nation's position in it, much of the world? Or would you take Democracy seriously enough to demand a vote count that could be observed?

Now let's look at our "real" elections, the ones that determine the leadership and direction of our towns, states, and country. The ones where we rely upon the media to tell us who won (and why). We have long employed the secret ballot process and for most of our nation's history an open, public counting process was the norm. Votes cast in private, counted in public. Makes sense.

But that is no longer the case. In 21st-Century America, aside from a few tiny pockets where ballots are still counted observably in public by humans, vote counting is an entirely secret enterprise, taking place on chips and memory cards concealed inside computers or, worse yet, in servers arrayed along a network, often far distant from where the votes are cast, in the full, impenetrable darkness of cyberspace.

The first alarm sounded by this book is that these elections are in practice no different from the charade of the man in the magician's costume "counting" behind the curtain. Not one of these elections— from presidential to congressional to dog-catcher to referendum— warrants the trust necessary to claim legitimacy. And an electoral system so untrustworthy that it cannot claim legitimacy, whether in a Third-World nation or here in the touted Beacon of Democracy, makes a mockery of the democratic process in which we take such reflexive pride.

Why would a nation install, and why would its people acquiesce in, such a patently untrustworthy process for making its most critical decisions and for transforming the public will into leadership, policy, and direction?

We will return to this question often in the course of this book; it has a number of disturbing answers. But for the moment we think it fair to observe that we live in a time and a place where *convenience is king*. Every improvement in speed, each yet slicker technological "advance," is embraced with reflexive zeal. Our cultural impatience ("Faster connection time! Faster downloads! Faster everything!") seems to know no bounds.[1] After all, isn't it obvious that, as the too-cute kids seated at the table with the friendly corporate suit kept reminding us in that brilliant and ubiquitous TV ad for the latest happiness-bestowing smartphone, *"faster is better?"* Moreover, we seem to have a collective affinity for that which *looks* sophisticated—sleek, digital, graphic, multi-layered, multi-colored, rapid and impeccable. Isn't a glistening iPad, quite apart from its utility, also a comforting symbol to us of how far removed and safe we are from the raw, naked dangers of the pioneer's cabin, the medieval hut, the prehistoric night?

This hi-tech, hi-speed ethos is, of course, not entirely new, but the grip that speed, convenience, and sit-back-and-enjoy-the-show choreographed entertainment now hold on our culture is tight and getting tighter every minute. "Progress," so defined, has become a *habit* and appears to be inexorable. Thus when it comes to elections, there is, in effect, a mandate that virtually every one be decided within hours, if not minutes, of poll closing, and that, in our major biennial elections, the direction that America will be taking be brilliantly and artistically laid out in a mélange of pie-charts, blue and red blinking states, and punditory consensus, all before it is time for bed. This is such a *fait accompli,* such a *ritual,* that it is hard to remember that it wasn't *always* this way and, when it comes right down to it, isn't really *necessary*—much less to contemplate the price paid for our convenient and entertaining experience.

The price is simply that we as citizens have no basis for trusting it. Behind this festive TV extravaganza—reassuringly presented as "Decision 20XX"—are those vote-counting computers and computer networks, *not one of which is one iota different from the magician behind the curtain*, a faith-based enterprise where votes are counted

---

[1] Perhaps the only real exception to our pan-cultural haste is our embrace of video review in our various sports (now trickling down even to the high school level). We accept these delays because of the importance we have come to place on accurate athletic outcomes and sports justice: i.e., because "football matters."

in secret and results announced (and accepted) with the straightest of straight faces. In fact, it is as a prop to this media production and its programmed primetime-slot narrative that the vote counting computers are deemed "indispensable."

How long this irrational situation has been going on is open to question. Computers in one form or another (initially mainframes using punch cards) have been employed in vote counting since as early as the 1960s, and there is some evidence that they were sporadically being used to manipulate electoral results almost from their first deployment. So even in the "good old days" when the nation watched the votecount numbers rolling up behind such trusted icons as Walter Cronkite or David Brinkley, it did so without any real assurance that there wasn't a thumb (or two or ten) on a scale somewhere in the pipeline where computers could be programmed to add, delete, or shift votes.[2]

What has happened since then, however, is that with rapidly advancing technology it has become *infinitely easier* to alter far more election results, with far greater effect, efficiency and precision, and far less risk of exposure. What was once labor-intensive, requiring a good-sized crew to hack punch cards or cover up falsified lever machine check-sheets machine by machine in a single contest, can now easily be accomplished by a single insider or hacker, even one working from outside our borders anywhere in the world. A single individual can change the results of dozens, indeed hundreds of elections, with virtually no risk of detection. With the help of a tiny staff, such an individual can essentially stage an undetectable rolling coup. The system is *that* vulnerable, a piece of red meat lying unguarded in a yard full of salivating dogs.

---

[2] See Collier J, Collier K: *Votescam: The Stealing of America,* Victoria House Press 1992, at http://www.amazon.com/dp/0963416308, for the history of electoral manipulation and its cover-up in the early computer age, before the passage of the Help America Vote Act opened the floodgates in 2002.

Too dramatic? Too purple? Study after study, by the most prestigious researchers and institutions, tells us that we can be sure about the red meat, the vulnerability.[3] But is it paranoid to imagine the *dogs*, hungry and willing to exploit it? In other words, given the opportunity, who would *want* or *dare* to steal an election, or a nation, that was lying unguarded in the yard? Who would set their sights so high and sink so low?

To answer this, we need first to make a quick sketch of our era, and the ethics of our time. Author David Callahan has done much of this work for us. In his 2004 best-seller *The Cheating Culture: Why More Americans Are Doing Wrong to Get Ahead*,[4] Callahan is hard-pressed to find a nook of competitive endeavor where cheating or rigging to achieve some goal has not become commonplace. From students, to job applicants, to athletes at every level, to financiers, to corporations, to public officials—Callahan takes us on a grand tour of what has been happening where and when no one is looking in today's 'just win, baby' America. It is not pretty. And at every turn the vast majority of us have been, at least initially, very reluctant to believe the extent of the rot, the malignancy of the tumor.

When 500-foot home runs were flying off the bats of Mark McGwire and Sammy Sosa, we desperately wanted to believe that healthier diets and better workout regimens could account for it. Few were willing to give any credence to former major-leaguer Jose Canseco's

---

[3] See, e.g., http://brennancenter.org/dynamic/subpages/download_file_39288.pdf, http://itpolicy.princeton.edu/voting/ts-paper.pdf, http://www.blackboxvoting.org/BBVtsxstudy.pdf, http://www.blackboxvoting.org/BBVreport.pdf, http://www.gao.gov/new.items/d05956.pdf. It is of interest that the comprehensive reviews undertaken by the states of California and Ohio have been removed from the official websites and are no longer available to the public.

[4] Callahan D: *The Cheating Culture: Why More Americans Are Doing Wrong to Get Ahead*. New York: Harcourt, 2004. See also, Michael Lewis, "Extreme Wealth Is Bad for Everyone—Especially The Wealthy," *The New Republic*, 11/12/2014 (reviewing West D: *Billionaires: Reflections On the Upper Crust*. Brookings, 2014), in which copious research is presented showing the propensity to cheat to be correlated with increasing wealth.

claim that these new supermen were juiced.[5] Something did seem wrong with that picture—as something seemed wrong with Bernie Madoff's Ponzi scheme, with credit default swaps, with the anthrax in the vial at the U.N. and the supposed WMD's in Iraq—but it was not something that as a culture we were willing to acknowledge. All that taint was just too much to face, *until we were forced to*. Until we were *made* to look hard at how our high stakes "games"—from Wrigley Field to Wall Street to the White House—were actually being played.

The question we are compelled to ask—by all that once was holy; by Major League Baseball and the Tour de France; by the state-doped and Rio-banned Russian Olympians; by Bernie Madoff and Lance Armstrong and A-Rod; by the signaling cheaters exposed at the top of the impeccably-mannered contract *bridge* world;[6] by the ring of computer hackers charged with the theft and use of 160 million credit card numbers from the likes of Citibank and NASDAQ;[7] by the fraudsters at Volkswagen who programmed the computers in their cars to cheat on emissions tests, got caught, and have agreed to pay $14.7 billion in settlement to US consumers alone;[8] by the apparent foreign-state cyber-incursion manifest in the "Sony" hack and of course the "DNC" hack of 2016;[9] by the plethora of hacking and rigging

---

[5] Canseco J: *Juiced: Wild Times, Rampant 'Roids, Smash Hits, and How Baseball Got Big.* New York: William Morrow & Co., 2005. *Publishers Weekly*, in describing *Juiced* as "poorly written, controversial," was typical in doubting whether Canseco "really knows anything about the problem beyond his own use." Canseco's next book, written three years later when events and investigations had borne him out, was entitled *Vindicated: Big Names, Big Liars, and The Battle to Save Baseball.*

[6] See http://www.newsweek.com/big-rich-cheaters-bridge-world-rocked-top-players-busted-375414.

[7] See http://www.bbc.com/news/technology-23448639. One of the ring's members, Mikhail Rytikov, is charged with having the sole role of covering up the ring's tracks. By 2016 such massive cybercrimes have become rather ho-hum, barely generating headlines. Among them the cybertheft of what appears to be the entire US national voter database.

[8] See http://www.nytimes.com/2016/06/28/business/volkswagen-settlement-diesel-scandal.html.

[9] As Ajay Arora, CEO of cybersecurity firm Vera, put it in warning that the DNC hack might be the new normal: "This is a bellwether of things to come. The techniques are advancing. There are strategic attacks, and then there is tactical warfare. There are parties out there now thinking, 'hey, let's affect outcome of whole election.'"

schemes that are now accepted as commonplace—is how a computerized US election, vital and vulnerable as it is, could *not* be a target for skullduggery?

Are the stakes anywhere in any endeavor in the entire world ever higher than in a biennial American election? We know of no pot of gold—home runs, capital, fame, power, policy—that can compare to that at stake in American elections.[10] Winning elections confers the power to reward friends and punish enemies, along with the opportunity to set policies that can engender enormous profits. But, just as dogs of many different breeds might find the unguarded hunk of beef irresistible, so those moved to rig elections may be of different breeds and driven by different hungers. Besides the obvious yearning for practical power and profit, there is the "true belief" of the political extremist and, at the other end of the spectrum entirely, the climb-Everest-because-it's-there lure for the conscienceless "pure player," one who, not necessarily in the service of any genuine conviction but just for the "rush" (and of course the money), would be the human god, the Master of the Dance who from an unseen perch alters politics on the grandest scale—and with it the course of history.

Some true-believers—who now abound in American politics, have made an apparently successful bid for control of the Republican Party, and (as we shall see) dominate the upper echelons of the voting computer industry—are so strongly motivated and inspired by an outcome vision (whether fundamentally religious or secular in nature)

(http://www.aol.com/article/2016/07/26/the-worst-might-be-yet-to-come-with-the-dnc-email-hack/21439542/). Presumably those "parties out there" have grasped that "whole election" includes the part where the votes are counted.

[10] Although it is hardly possible to quantify the "net worth" of an election, it bears mention that more than $7 billion was spent to win federal office alone in E2012 (http://www.politico.com/story/2013/01/7-billion-spent-on-2012-campaign-fec-says-87051.html), and, with "dark money" taken into account, E2014 was by far the most expensive midterm election in American history. With lobbyists enjoying a "return on investment" rate of better than 100-to-1, it is not hard to see that, even calculated in cold monetary terms, the value of an election—which of course is concentrated in the relatively few key contests that determine control of the governmental apparatus at various levels—is astronomical.

that they can thoroughly rationalize an ends-justify-the-means approach to their activities. From the standpoint of such a true-believer, there *are* no ethics as compelling as that true belief. And from the standpoint of a pure player, there are no ethics, period: if you ain't cheatin', you ain't tryin'.

Thus an individual or group might feel justified in, say, sending "Vote Wednesday" informational flyers or making "Vote Wednesday" robocalls to the homes of opposing voters when the election is Tuesday. In fact they *have*, repeatedly.[11] Is there a bright line, we must ask, between behavior so blatantly unethical and, say, a more efficient gambit—simply offsetting the zero-counters on the memory cards of voting computers to +X for the candidate you favor and –X for the candidate you oppose, so that at the end of the day (as explained in the next chapter) the vote totals will reconcile with the poll tapes recording the number of voters, the election administrator will see and certify a "clean" election, and you will have stolen a net of 2X votes per machine so rigged? Indeed, it would be hard to resist if you were a "Vote Wednesday" kind of true-believer who happened to have access to those memory cards, or to the cyber-networks on which millions of votes are now "processed." And just another day on Mt. Everest for a pure player.

In light of this we must ask a hard question: lip-service aside, just how sacred *are* elections and just how sacrosanct *is* the counting of the votes?[12] And a follow-up: How does the democratic process *per se* stack up against a burning true belief or a boatload of money? Just how deep and abiding a respect for democracy itself, how much pure *principle*, would it take to overcome the tremendous temptation to palm a card or two and *have things your way*, alter the course of

---

[11] See http://www.motherjones.com/politics/2012/11/election-dirty-tricks for a record of this and other dirty tricks recently relied upon to gain electoral advantage.

[12] Because a major election is virtually *never* decided by a single vote, the value we place upon a single vote *in actuality* tends to be a good deal lower than our exalted rhetoric would have it. It may be that this low pragmatic value assigned the individual vote in turn colors our laissez-faire attitude toward the voting and vote counting process as a whole.

history, and create (as George W. Bush was praised for doing) your own reality?[13] Having made a realistic appraisal of the behavior, mindset, and character of some of the political actors and operatives now on the scene,[14] do we really believe that such deep and abiding respect vests in every player in the game of "democracy" as it is currently being played in The New American Century?

Many observers have begun to question, and often deplore, the "new madness" of American politics.[15] Taking in the current hyperpolarization, the intransigent hyper-radicalism of the Right and what seems to be its poll- and explanation-defying endorsement at the ballot box by a traditionally moderate electorate, many have wondered what is happening in America. Witness Thomas Mann's and Norman Ornstein's 2012 bestseller, *It's Even Worse Than It Looks*.[16] Many explanations are offered up, from clever messaging to voter suppression and gerrymandering to the role of money. Pundits, after all, are not paid to be stumped. But there remains a nagging disquiet, a sense that all these explanations don't quite explain enough. There's still something happening that defies not only conventional political wisdom but plain old common sense, as if the Political Universe had been taken over by some new asymmetrical non-

---

[13] There is a chilling and revealing testament to none other than Karl Rove's fervent embrace of this approach to political action, as captured in an October 17, 2004 article written by Ron Suskind for *The New York Times Magazine*, as part of which Suskind interviews the at-the-time anonymous Rove:

> The aide [subsequently identified as Rove] said that guys like me were "in what we call the reality-based community," which he defined as people who "believe that solutions emerge from your judicious study of discernible reality. . . . *That's not the way the world really works anymore*," he continued. "We're an empire now, and *when we act, we create our own reality. And while you're studying that reality—judiciously, as you will—we'll act again, creating other new realities, which you can study too, and that's how things will sort out. We're history's actors ... and you, all of you, will be left to just study what we do.*" [emphases added]

[14] And adding, with a nod to the likely perpetrators of the 2016 DNC hack and leaks, states and political actors and operatives anywhere in the world who might have more than a rooting interest in American electoral outcomes.

[15] See, e.g., *New York Review of Books*, 9/27/2012, cover headline: "OUR WEIRD POLITICS NOW," featuring separate pieces on the theme by Andrew Hacker, Ezra Klein, Jacob Hacker, and Paul Pierson.

[16] Mann TE, Ornstein NJ: *It's Even Worse Than It Looks: How The American Constitutional System Collided with The New Politics of Extremism*. New York: Basic Books, 2012.

Euclidean geometry. There seems to be a missing force, an X-factor analogous to cosmic dark matter or dark energy, that is needed to explain what is happening here in America.

We will present comprehensible and compelling evidence that the X-factor is the electronic manipulation of votecounts and that, all other factors notwithstanding, what is happening here in America would *not* be happening in its absence.

For anyone persuaded by the evidence, presented in the chapters that follow,[17] that the electoral process in America has been subverted, or even that it is merely vulnerable to and perhaps teetering on the brink of such subversion, our predicament takes on a nightmarish quality— one of those dreadful dreams where you are running without moving while the locomotive speeds on to its inexorable impact with the child who has wandered onto the tracks.

Virtually everything about the situation is surrealistic and absurd. Election integrity activists are told to produce "a smoking gun," when all such "hard evidence" materials are strictly off-limits to investigation; statistical evidence, no matter how copious and consistent, is received with a dismissive shrug; reform proposals such as hand-counted paper ballots for federal and statewide elections are shot down as ludicrous nonstarters; "rogue" journalists and whistleblowers are cowed, exiled, silenced, or ignored. America seems hell-bent on sticking with its faith-based election system, no matter how vulnerable it is shown to be and no matter how weirdly distorted our politics becomes.

And yet . . . and yet, America is one examined memory card (however obtained), one white-hat real-time election hack ("Mickey Mouse gets 4 billion votes!"), one open and honest recount, one "Opscan Party"

---

[17] Election forensics is not, for better or worse, the stuff of soundbites; but neither does it have to be eye-glazingly abstruse and obscure. I have sought to balance comprehensiveness with clarity and have provided links and references for additional exploration as appropriate.

(where citizens form a ring around an optical scanner and demand a public, observable count of the voter-marked ballots within), or even one serious article in the *New York Times* or *Washington Post* away from *critical mass*, from the sudden explosive recognition that something thought too ghastly to imagine (even *worse* than the idea that *baseball* was not the wholesome Norman Rockwell game it seemed) will *have* to be imagined and then dealt with.

Given how unimposing the civic duty of public, observable vote counting is in actuality,[18] the problem can be dealt with easily enough. The real challenge is not in the dealing with, but in the collective imagining.

There are some indications that the American *people* at least—after a generation-long embrace of the private, and rejection of the public, sphere—are ready once again to invest in the common good, and perhaps even to part with a few of the expedients and conveniences that are now being seen to do us individual and collective ill.[19] There is an emerging, priority-reordering, "anti-seduction" culture that could come to support a demand for reform of our voting system and could be mobilized to let our representatives know that we are ready to serve and determined to protect our democracy.

Yet there continues to be a great political disconnect and realistically, *absent a galvanizing catastrophe or a complete media about-face*, there have been few signs that such reforms are in the offing. In this, vote counting reform is not alone: think gun safety, climate change. *At least as now represented by our elected leaders*, we are a

---

[18] It has been calculated that hand counting the federal and statewide races would require a *maximum of four hours per lifetime from each American voter*, a civic burden far less onerous than jury duty, one that Americans of previous generations assumed and one that Canadians, Germans, and Australians, among others, perform today.

[19] Apart from the bevy of books and blogs blasting Wal-Mart culture and its corporate-serving anomies, we can look around us and see the regrowth of participatory communal foci such as farmers' markets and food co-ops. While alienation, speed, convenience, and self-interest clearly remain the dominant cultural modes, it appears that a turning point may finally be in sight.

conservative nation, reactive rather than pro-active, simultaneously smug and insecure, paradoxically hubristic yet with a fragile self-esteem giving rise to much denial.

If, in one way or another, a massive electoral theft *were* exposed beyond all cover-up and forced upon the public consciousness, it would of course be technically and pragmatically possible to quickly restore hand counting or at least a comprehensive and effective auditing protocol. Neither is beyond our capacities and both cost a tiny fraction of what we have recently spent bringing "democracy" to foreign soils.[20]

Whether it would be *politically* possible would remain to be seen. If by that point majority control at critical levels were held by those who had achieved that control through years of systemic fraud, could they be expected to willingly institute honest elections and so inevitably surrender power and go gentle into that good night? Or even if a majority of officeholders thought quite reasonably, "Why mess with a system that has worked for *me* by putting me in office?" What form and intensity of public pressure would it take to move our successfully elected lawmakers and officeholders? Would marches and sit-ins and massive demonstrations persuade our leaders to restore our sovereignty or would these simply be ruthlessly suppressed in the name of security and domestic tranquility? Would it come down to massive voting boycotts and general strikes? Would the simmering subliminal battle between the newly awakened public and its newly exposed oppressors come shockingly to a turbulent and violent head?

---

[20] It is perhaps worth recalling here that our wars in Iraq and Afghanistan will end up costing the United States a total of about $5 trillion (see http://time.com/3651697/afghanistan-war-cost), an *average* of nearly $7 billion *every week* (www.costofwar.com) since their inception. A *single month* worth of those wars would pay (at $20/hour per counter) for hand counting our *American* ballots for a minimum of 45 biennial election cycles, or fully *three generations*.

Why, it must be asked, can't we do this? Why, for that matter, is our computerized voting equipment, in addition to being so corruptible, also aged into obsolescence and dysfunction? Why are we so lavish with our *global* democracy-promotion follies and so ridiculously, and it would appear intentionally, cheap with our *own* democracy?

It is grim to speculate on these scenarios. *But I think it is fair to say that the later in the game this critical mass of public awareness and outrage is reached, the less likely that a political remedy will be possible.* So the first thing to be done is to engender awareness, and that right soon. Thus the urgency of this writing. It is a CODE RED.

I'd like to think this story will have a happy ending, that history will review in appreciative terms the struggle of a few activists— Cassandras really—to prod leaders and public alike to scale the towering Never-Happen-Here Wall Of Denial so that they can then act together to restore the essential process of observable vote counting to our nation. Most truths eventually come out. All we can do is keep trying in every way possible to help this one find its way into the light.

We will, in the series of questions and answers to follow, examine computerized election theft from many angles, and explore motive, means, opportunity, and, of course, the evidence for such a ghastly criminal enterprise. We will also explore why it continues to remain hidden, the quintessential Big Lie corrupting our nation and its democracy. We will look unblinkingly at democracy down and ask realistically whether there is any chance that it can get back up. We will ask *you* to override the powerful "naaaah" reflex and be among the first to scale with us that towering Never-Happen-Here Wall Of Denial.

It will be a rough ride we are taking. For ourselves, our children, and the life that shares the Earth with us, it will be a lot rougher if we refuse to take it.

II. QUESTIONS AND ANSWERS

In searching out the truth, be ready for the unexpected,
for it is difficult to find and puzzling when you find it.

— Heraclitus

Q: In 100 words or so, tell me what you believe is happening with American elections.

A: Computerized vote counting has opened the door wide, over the past 15 years, to large-scale fraud and election theft. Virtually all the vote counting equipment is produced and programmed by a few corporations with right-wing ties. There is strong and pervasive forensic evidence that votecounts are being shifted to the right, altering key election outcomes. Mystifyingly, political intransigence is being electorally rewarded rather than punished. As a result, even as the pendulum *appears* to swing, American politics has veered inexorably and inexplicably to the right. This amounts to a rolling coup that is transforming America while disenfranchising an unsuspecting public.

Q. Haven't there always been attempts to steal elections? Why is now any different?

A: Yes, political history is full of skullduggery. But, as IT expert Chuck Herrin memorably put it, "It takes a long time to change 10,000 votes by hand. It takes three seconds to change them in a computer."[1]

---

[1] Herrin, a Republican, was interviewed in Dorothy Fadiman's 2008 documentary *Stealing America: Vote by Vote*, http://www.stealingamericathemovie.org/. He

What computerized elections have brought us, along with speed and convenience, is the opportunity to alter electoral outcomes strategically, surgically, massively, and covertly. And, because of selective access stemming from partisan control over the equipment itself, it is not equal-opportunity rigging—the evidence has shown that it virtually always goes in the same direction.

The "retail" fraud of the past, although unfortunate, was inefficient, rather overt, and tended to wind up a net wash overall, as it was a game played by both sides. The "wholesale" fraud of computerized rigging is a far more potent and incomparably more dangerous phenomenon.

Q: How do you *know* the computers on which we vote are so susceptible to fraud?

A: There is virtual unanimity among the experts who have studied electronic voting that insiders or hackers can change the results of elections without leaving a trace—at least not the kind of trace that any election administrator is likely to find. These studies have come from institutions such as Johns Hopkins, Princeton, the University of Michigan, The Brennan Center for Social Justice at NYU, the states of California and Ohio, and even the US Government Accountability Office.[2] White-hat hackers such as Harri Hursti and Alex Halderman

---

concluded, "I think the most appropriate technology is what we should be going for, instead of the latest and greatest."

[2] See, e.g., California Secretary of State: *Top to Bottom Review (TTBR) of Voting Systems.* As of July 16, 2008, all 14 TTBR reports linked at http://www.sos.ca.gov/elections/elections_vsr.htm; Feldman A J, Halderman J A, Felten E W: *Security Analysis of the Diebold AccuVote-TS Voting Machine*; Princeton University, Center for Information Technology Policy and Dept. of Computer Science, Woodrow Wilson School of Public and International Affairs, September 13, 2006, http://itpolicy.princeton.edu/voting/ts-paper.pdf; Ohio Secretary of State: *Project EVEREST (Evaluation and Validation of Election Related Equipment, Standards and Testing).* As of July 16, 2008, all 13 *EVEREST* reports linked at http://www.sos.state.oh.us/SOS/elections/voterInformation/equipment/VotingSystemR eviewFindings/EVERESTtestingReports.aspx; Hursti H: *Security Alert: Critical Security Issues with Diebold Optical Scan Design*, Black Box Voting, July 4, 2005, http://blackboxvoting.org/BBVreport.pdf.

have demonstrated how quick and easy it is to swap memory cards in voting machines (inserting cards with malicious code) or break into the networked vote-counting computers increasingly in use.[3]

The level of security of all this equipment is orders of magnitude *below* that found at major banks, corporations, and governmental institutions, and yet all of those *high-security* enterprises have been hacked and compromised repeatedly over the past several years, with increasing frequency.[4] How much easier when the "hacker" is working from the *inside* or has been let in the door by someone who lives in the house.

Why, on what basis; *why*, by what logic; *why*, according to what understanding of human nature; *why*, from what view of history, politics, and the way high-stakes games are played by those high-rollers for whom, in Vince Lombardi's words, winning is the *only* thing; *why*, *why*, *why* do we collectively and so blithely *assume* that hundreds of millions of votes counted in secret, on partisan produced and controlled equipment, will be counted honestly and that the public trust will be honored to the exclusion of any private agenda, however compelling?!

Why and how, in the face of this level of *risk*, can we just rest easy that all is going well and fairly in the depths of cyberspace where our

---

[3] The "Hursti Hack" was demonstrated in the 2006 film *Hacking Democracy*, Simon Ardizzone director, http://tinyurl.com/8vqrd6u.

Halderman, a professor of engineering and computer science at the University of Michigan, was invited, on three days' notice, to attempt to penetrate the security of the new Washington D.C. internet-based voting system; within 36 hours of the D.C. system's launch, Halderman and a group of three student assistants had not only penetrated the system's security, but had gained "almost total control of the server software, including the ability to change votes and reveal voters' secret ballots;" they also found evidence of other attempts to breach the system's security originating from IP addresses in China, India, and Iran. See https://jhalderm.com/pub/papers/dcvoting-fc12.pdf.

[4] See, e.g., http://www.wired.com/threatlevel/2012/02/anonymous-friday-attacks/; also http://about.bloomberglaw.com/legal-news/5-hackers-charged-in-largest-data-breach-scheme-in-u-s/; and http://www.informationisbeautiful.net/visualizations/worlds-biggest-data-breaches-hacks/.

choices have all become 1s and 0s dancing by the trillions in the dark? That dance is the embodiment of our sovereignty. It is from that dance that our future emerges and whoever programs the computers calls the dance. *Setting aside for a moment all evidence of fraud*, how can we possibly be OK with *that*?

Q: If you wanted to alter the outcome of an election, give me an example of how you might do it?

A: It depends upon the type of computer, but there are many ways to manipulate votes. One very basic scheme, where optical scanning voting computers ("opscans") are in use,[5] would be to set the "zero counters" on the memory card in each machine to, say, +100 for the candidate you want to win and -100 for the one marked for defeat.[6] At the end of the day the positive and negative offsets are a wash, so the total of ballots recorded by the opscans matches the total of voters signing the log books, the election officials are satisfied that the election was "clean," *and you have shifted a net of 200 votes on each machine so rigged*, PDQ.

This takes just a few lines of programming out of the hundreds of thousands of lines of code on the memory card.[7] It would be detectable only by a very painstaking examination of the card and its code, but the cards are regarded as *strictly corporate property*,

---

[5] Opscans—which use sophisticated spatial programming to scan, and record as votes, marks made by voters on paper ballots—counted approximately 56% of the ballots nationwide in 2012; see
http://votingmachines.procon.org/view.resource.php?resourceID=000274.

[6] The "zero counter" refers to the number assigned to the first vote recorded for a given candidate or proposition; i.e., where the count begins. Logically that number is "1" and if you were counting ballots by hand "zero" would be the bare table. But in a computer there *is* no fixed starting point known as "zero." A single line of code can be inserted into the 500,000+ lines already on the memory card to start a candidate's count at *any* number, positive or negative.

[7] The memory card, which both controls how the computer "reads" the ballots and tallies the votes cast, is produced in such a way that code containing the rig can easily, in fact automatically, be replicated onto however many cards necessary to shift the total number of votes projected as required to alter a targeted contest's outcome.

completely off-limits to public inspection; in fact, not even election administrators are allowed to look. The command to alter the zero counters can be written not to take effect until actual vote counting begins on Election Day so that the opscans pass any pre-testing that election administrators might perform, and it can also be written in self-deleting code so that literally no post-election trace remains.

None of this is difficult or beyond the skills of even a high school-level programmer. Nor, for that matter, are rigs that instead work by shifting every n^{th} vote or simply capping one candidate's vote total and assigning all subsequent votes to her opponent. And, since opscans are programmed to "read" the marks voters make on ballots "geographically," it is easy enough to alter the code in the ballot definition files to flip votes by reading the area for Candidate A as a Candidate B vote, and vice versa, or to be more or less sensitive to inevitable stray marks on the ballot, so as to selectively void more ballots in precincts known to be strongholds of the candidate(s) targeted for defeat.[8]

Where "touchscreen" (also known as Direct Recording Electronic or "DRE") computers are in use, their programming can be altered to cause the screen button pushed for "A" to record instead a vote for "B." DREs that print out a "receipt" for the voter to "verify" (the vaunted "paper trail") are of little help, as it is a trivial step to program

---

[8] It has recently come to light, through the investigative and analytic work of election integrity advocates Bev Harris and Bennie Smith, that in the 25% of US voting equipment that uses the GEMS operating system, a "fractional vote feature" is embedded, such that votes are recorded not as integers (1,2,3 . . .) but as decimal fractions of 100 (0.75, 0.47, 1.29 . . .).

According to Harris and Smith, this strange feature can be used to "invisibly, yet radically, alter election outcomes by pre-setting desired vote percentages to redistribute votes. This tampering is not visible to election observers, even if they are standing in the room and watching the computer. Use of the decimalized vote feature is unlikely to be detected by auditing or canvass procedures, and can be applied across large jurisdictions in less than 60 seconds."

A detailed and chilling six-part walk-through of decimalized vote counting and its implications for votecount manipulation may be found at http://blackboxvoting.org/fraction-magic-1/.

the DRE to print a vote for "A" on the receipt while recording a vote for "B" in its cumulative count. While such a rig would lead to a disparity between the paper trail and the machine count, uncovering that mismatch would require a hand count of the paper-trail and the reality is that both the voter-marked ballots deposited into opscans and the "receipts" generated by paper-trail DREs are off-limits to public inspection and virtually never see the light of day, no matter how suspect an election's results.

Where the voting equipment is networkable (that is, as is often the case, equipped with a modem), votes can be added, deleted, and shifted *at will, as needed, in real time* on Election Night. Millions of votes are sent through IP networks off-site and often out-of-state for "processing." This saves manipulators from having to guess in advance how many votes they will need to shift, and so permits real-time-calibrated, "tidier" rigs—contests stolen with a smaller numerical footprint.

Q: How did we ever come to approve and accept such a dangerous system?

A: That is a difficult and complex question with answers rooted deep in our political culture and attitudes toward democracy, technology, public responsibility, the value of the vote, and time itself. But the short answer is that the highly publicized debacle of "hanging chads" in the presidential election of 2000 engendered a panic situation that was shrewdly exploited (if not in fact engineered) by those whose agenda it was to computerize American elections. The needs of disabled voters, which could have been effectively addressed without the introduction of computers,[9] were also cynically exploited by computerization's proponents. The Help America Vote Act (HAVA)

---

[9] Non-computerized devices, such as the VotePad, had already been developed to allow blind and mechanically disabled voters to mark ordinary paper ballots with their votes; see http://www.bradblog.com/?p=2330.

was passed in 2002, creating a powerful mixture of incentives and mandates for states to rapidly computerize their elections.

HAVA's Republican architects[10] secured Democratic cooperation by emphasizing that its passage would lead to increased voter turnout. This should have thrown up a glaring red flag since for over a century the GOP had done (and continues to do) everything in its power to *decrease* overall voter turnout. Given that they recognized that computerizing the voting process would likely promote ease of voting and increase turnout among marginal (i.e., predominantly Democratic) voters, and given that this goal was manifestly the *last* thing that they sought to see accomplished, we must ask just what HAVA's GOP promoters expected in the way of partisan *advantage* from computerization that would be alluring enough to outweigh that hefty partisan disadvantage.

In the climate of post-debacle panic, few thought to question the appropriateness and safety of computers, so much a part of our modern world, for the particular task of vote counting. And those who did were drowned out by a chorus of derision from well-financed promoters. The rush was on. Once the computers were paid for and deployed, it became a powerful *fait accompli* and any return to noncomputerized counting was written off as a ridiculous Luddite retreat.

Q: You say that the system is indisputably vulnerable and dangerous but what makes you think that it has *actually* been corrupted and elections have *actually* been stolen?

A: Introducing The Red Shift. When official votecounts come out to the right of other measures of voters' intent—such as exit polls, pre-

---

[10] HAVA's chief congressional sponsor was Bob Ney. A senior Republican representing Ohio's 18th Congressional District, Ney was convicted in 2007 on federal corruption charges (pleading guilty to conspiracy and making false statements to federal investigators) and served a 30-month term in federal prison. HAVA is widely regarded as Ney's signature legislative accomplishment.

election polls, post-election polls, and handcounts—forensic analysts refer to it as a "red shift."[11] Since 2002, when the computers took over the counting, the red shift has been *pervasive*: election after election, in competitive contests, the official votecount has been to the right of *every* baseline measure. We very rarely see the reverse, which we would call a "blue shift." There is a tremendous amount of data and it all points in the same direction.[12]

From a forensic standpoint, much of our work goes into determining whether those baselines from which the official votecounts keep diverging are themselves valid. Naturally *if you simply assume all votecounts are valid,* you then look for reasons to dismiss any data that disagrees with them. You could, for example, disparage all the incongruent exit polls as "off again" because they "oversampled Democrats." However, we have examined exit poll samples and other baselines closely and found that such is not the case—the problem is definitely *not* that all of these other measures of voter intent are chronically incompetent or corrupted. Yet that is precisely what would *have* to be the case if we are to justify steadfastly refusing to examine the validity of the votecounts and instead remain determined to give those votecounts and the concealed process that generates them a full faith-based free pass.

In 2006, for instance, we examined the national exit poll sample and found that it was actually to the *right* of every other measure of the

---

[11] The term "red shift" was in fact coined by this author (with apologies to Herr Doppler) in reference to the exit poll-votecount disparities favoring Bush in E2004; it has been adopted into general usage when describing such disparities.

[12] See Chapter VII for several evidentiary studies, including: *The 2004 Presidential Election: Who Won the Popular Vote? An Examination of the Comparative Validity of Exit Poll and Vote Count Data* (2004); *Landslide Denied: Exit Polls vs. Vote Count 2006, Demographic Validity of the National Exit Poll and the Corruption of the Official Vote Count* (2007); *Fingerprints of Election Theft: Were Competitive Contests Targeted?* (2007); see also, Charnin R: *Proving Election Fraud: Phantom Voters, Uncounted Votes, and the National Exit Poll*, AuthorHouse 2010, http://preview.tinyurl.com/8anvvbr, and *Matrix of Deceit: Forcing Pre-Election and Exit Polls to Match Fraudulent Vote Counts*, at http://www.amazon.com/Matrix-Deceit-Forcing-Pre-Election-Fraudulent/dp/1480077038.

national electorate. We knew, therefore, that the massive red shift we found in the 2006 election could not have been a function of a faulty (i.e., left-skewed) exit poll baseline, leaving mistabulation of the votes as the only explanation for the shift that could not be discounted.[13] We went further in 2006 (and again in 2008) and, recognizing that competitive races are natural targets for rigging (high reward/risk ratio) while noncompetitive races are not (much higher risk factor: to alter the outcome you have to shift too high a percentage of votes to pass the smell test), we compared competitive with noncompetitive races relative to an identical baseline. We found that the more competitive a race the more likely it was to be red shifted—the correlation was clear.[14] In 2010[15] we were able to compare hand-counted to computer-counted ballots in a critical US Senate race and again found an outcome-altering red shift of the computer-counted votes, one that we were unable to explain by any factor other than strategically mistabulated votecounts. Most recently, in 2016, our analysis of the respective party primaries found that, while the exit poll results were consistently accurate throughout nearly all of the Republican primaries, they were wildly and broadly inaccurate in the Democratic primaries, exhibiting a pervasive intra-party "red shift" to the detriment of Bernie Sanders. It seems very unlikely that the same pollsters, employing the same methodological techniques and interviewing voters at the same precincts on the same days, would be competent and consistently successful with Republicans but somehow incompetent and consistently unsuccessful with Democrats.[16]

---

[13] Simon J, O'Dell B: *Landslide Denied: Exit Polls vs. Vote Count 2006, Demographic Validity of the National Exit Poll and the Corruption of the Official Vote Count* (2007), http://electiondefensealliance.org/files/LandslideDenied_v.9_071507.pdf.

[14] Simon J, et al: *Fingerprints of Election Theft: Were Competitive Contests Targeted?* (2007), http://electiondefensealliance.org/files/FingerprintsOfElectionTheft_2011rev_.pdf.

[15] Simon J: *Believe it (Or Not): The Massachusetts Special Election for US Senate* (2010), http://electiondefensealliance.org/files/BelieveIt_OrNot_100904.pdf.

[16] This pattern in the 2016 primaries will be explored in greater detail in Chapter V. See also the work of Theodore deMacedo Soares at www.tdmsresearch.com.

Exit poll-votecount and similar comparisons constitute an *extrinsic* analysis, comparing the votecounts with alternate measures of voter intent. Analysts have also, more recently, discovered a powerful tool of *intrinsic* measurement known as Cumulative Vote Share ("CVS") analysis, "intrinsic" because it measures and analyzes only the votecount itself.[17] A peculiar and consistent pattern has emerged from analysis of precinct-level votecount data from suspect elections: the cumulative vote share of the candidate who is the suspected beneficiary of votecount manipulation unexpectedly increases with increasing precinct size. This "CVS Upslope" does not appear to reflect either demographic or partisanship tendencies of the precincts. It does, however, fit perfectly with a highly rational tactical decision to shift votes in larger rather than smaller precincts: the "splash" made by a vote theft of equal size is correspondingly smaller and less noticeable the larger the pool from which the votes are taken.

I hope that you will take the time to examine these studies, included in the "Evidence and Analysis" chapter (VII) and all fully accessible to the non-statistician. For now, the key point is that it is not just a few instances or an equivocal pattern—it is pervasive. It is hard to look at all this data gathered together and *not* be gravely concerned that elections have been systematically manipulated.

Q: What about for those of us who don't "get" statistics and numbers? Are there any other signs of foul play? What about a "smoking gun?"

A: It is precisely because of the secretive nature of the American vote counting process and because the "hard" evidence—memory cards, programming code, server logs, and actual cast ballots—is all strictly off-limits to the public (and, in most cases, to election administrators

---

[17] See, e.g., the work of Wichita State University statistician Elizabeth Clarkson, at www.bethclarkson.com. See also "An Electoral System in Crisis," a recent paper by L. Friese'dat and A. Sampietro, in collaboration with Fritz Scheuren, former President of the American Statistical Association, currently accessible at http://www.hollerbackfilm.com/electoral-system-in-crisis/.

as well), that forensic investigation of election security and authenticity perforce has come down primarily to numerical, statistical, and pattern analysis. Following along after the election circus with a forensic pooper-scooper (only, as you will see, to have all such evidence ignored or ridiculed by the media and the powers-that-be) is a rather ridiculous way to try to insure democracy. But until the public reclaims its right of access to voted-on ballots and the counting process, *it just happens to be the only way we've got.*

That said, such numerical, statistical, and pattern analysis is relied upon routinely in fields ranging from aerospace to economics, climate study, epidemiology and disease control. It is also routinely applied, often with the sanction of the government of the United States, to elections pretty much everywhere on Earth *other* than in the United States, periodically leading to official calls for electoral investigations and indeed electoral re-dos.[18] Exit poll disparities—i.e., foreign correlates of the red shift—have factored in the overturning of elections from the Ukraine to Peru and are relied upon for validation of votecounts in western democracies such as Germany.[19]

There are also other, nonstatistical signs of manipulation. In 2004, for example, in several battleground states touchscreen voters who attempted to vote for Kerry found that the computers switched and recorded their vote for Bush. The pattern of reports of vote flipping was over 10-to-1 in that direction.[20] You don't need a course in

---

[18] See, e.g., Kharchenko N, Paniotto V: "Exit Polling in an Emergent Democracy;" *Survey Research Methods* (2010), Vol.4, No.1, pp. 31-42.

[19] On the other side of the fence, repressive regimes such as Uzbekistan have now seen fit to ban exit polls entirely, a nod to their utility as indicators of election theft. In 2016 the United States seems to have taken a page from the Uzbekistanian playbook, cancelling all exit polling for the remaining states, including critical California, after a long string of unidirectional embarrassments in the first two dozen Democratic state primaries (see http://www.democraticunderground.com/12512018534; a search of the NY *Times* and Washington *Post* databases revealed no coverage of the cancellation).

[20] See "Reports of vote switching from the 2004 national Election Incident Reporting System (EIRS)," at http://www.iefd.org/articles/evidence_for_vote_switching.php. The overt *display* of a switched vote makes most sense when seen as a manipulator's programming *error,*

statistics to recognize that unintentional "glitches" would *go both ways* and eventually (as the number of them increased) even out, 50 - 50 not 10-to-1.

In 2010 in a Democratic primary for US Senate in South Carolina, run on paperless touchscreen voting computers (a.k.a. "DREs"), a "phantom" candidate, who had never campaigned and didn't even have a website, *received 59% of the statewide vote*, beating a well-known opponent, a state judge who after campaigning vigorously had pulled within a few percentage points of the far-right Republican incumbent in the tracking polls anticipating their November general election match-up. The "losing" candidate brought his case—including the evidence that, where early and absentee votes were tallied on optical scanners (where, at least in theory, a paper ballot would be available for recounting), he had won handily—to the Democratic Party State Committee, which went into closed session and then voted overwhelmingly to shut down the investigation.[21]

The past decade and a half, inaugurating the New American Century of computerized elections, is strewn with such bizarre, shocking, and anomalous results, virtually all of them favoring the more right-wing candidate or proposition.[22] Election integrity advocates have routinely been told to produce a "smoking gun" as a *prerequisite* to the launching of any governmental or journalistic investigation. Since memory cards, software, code, voted-on ballots, and of course corporate correspondence are all regarded as strictly proprietary and off-limits to citizen investigation, this demand is an absurd Catch-22.

It really comes down to an inverted burden of proof. There is essentially an irrebutable "presumption of innocence" when it comes

---

in which case these reported incidents would likely be the tip of an iceberg of successfully concealed manipulations.

[21] The story of this bizarre election, presented in greater detail at pp. 61-62, is the subject of the 2016 documentary feature film *I Voted?* directed by Jason Grant Smith and co-produced by Katie Couric.

[22] See Chapter VII, Study VI, for a timeline of "anomalies."

to the secret process of vote counting in America. You would think that at *some* point and in *some* way the process itself, and those who control it and conceal its workings, would be asked to produce *some* persuasive evidence that it is functioning reasonably honestly and accurately to translate collective voter intent into electoral results. You would be wrong.

Q: What about whistleblowers? Wouldn't at least a few who were involved in such an enterprise come forward?

A: They have. With a couple of chilling exceptions, they have been ignored. Clint Curtis testified under oath in a Congressional hearing that, as a programmer, he was commissioned by the Republican Speaker of the House of Florida to write a program designed to "flip the vote" in south Florida.[23] Having twice passed a lie-detector test administered by the retired chief polygraph officer for the state, Curtis was ignored. Apparently not ignored, however, was the reporter actively investigating Curtis's allegations, Raymond Lemme, who was found to have committed suicide, evidently, according to forensic photographs, by the popular method of stabbing and beating himself to death.[24]

Mike Connell, known as Karl Rove's "IT guru," who had set up the off-site SmarTech servers (in Chattanooga, Tennessee) that processed the decisive Ohio presidential vote In 2004, was compelled to testify in a lawsuit challenging the improprieties in that election.[25] After giving a

---

[23] See "Testimony of Clint Curtis" at
http://www.iefd.org/articles/evidence_for_vote_switching.php.

[24] See http://journals.democraticunderground.com/Time%20for%20change/402 and http://www.bradblog.com/?page_id=5479.

[25] *King Lincoln-Bronzeville Neighborhood Association et al v. J. Kenneth Blackwell et al,* filed 8/31/2006 in US District Court, Southern District of Ohio. Reverend William Moss, the lead plaintiff in *Moss v. Bush,* an earlier legal challenge to Bush's 2004 election, died on August 2, 2005, following a stroke. While the death of Reverend Moss may best be filed in the "sometimes a cigar" drawer, the deaths of Lemme and, particularly, Connell have both the timing and the hallmarks of something more troubling.

sealed deposition and being informed that he would likely be compelled to provide further testimony, Connell was killed when the plane he was piloting crashed. The attorneys for the plaintiff in the case, who took seriously threats made by Rove against a wavering Connell, had requested but been denied FBI protection for their star witness. The official investigation of the crash was cursory at best, breaching standard protocol on several key fronts. It was left to Connell's *widow*, combing the crash site, to find the *earpiece* to Connell's notorious Blackberry, reputed to contain on its drive thousands of emails between Connell and Rove. The Blackberry itself vanished.[26] *It is not difficult to imagine other prospective whistleblowers getting the message.*

Another factor to bear in mind is that, although this election theft enterprise has a massive effect, its execution requires the participation of no more than a tiny cast of characters. This minimalism keeps the potential ranks of whistleblowers and leakers tiny as well. And finally, as the cases of Bradley Manning and Edward Snowden illustrate, whistleblowers whose revelations tarnish the revered patina of American democracy are apt to be treated, by officialdom at least, not as heroes but as criminals.[27]

Q: Why has there been so little response from the "immune system"—election administrators, Democrats, the media? You would think they would be all over this.

A: Yes, you would. It's always baffling when an entire system with all of its disparate players seems to acquiesce in a disaster that you would think any one of those players would step up to prevent. But it is

---

[26] See Worrall S: *Cybergate: Was The White House Stolen by Cyberfraud?* Amazon Digital Services, 2012, http://preview.tinyurl.com/98ntmc6.

[27] The Obama Administration has been especially and unexpectedly harsh in its treatment of whistleblowers, exceeding all prior administrations in its prosecutorial zeal. See http://www.counterpunch.org/2015/10/09/mouths-wide-shut-obamas-war-on-whistleblowers/ and http://www.washingtonsblog.com/2015/05/obama-has-sentenced-whistleblowers-to-31-times-the-jail-time-of-all-prior-u-s-presidents-combined.html.

hardly unprecedented. There was an array of institutions, for example, that witnessed the rise of the Nazis to power and—each for its own reasons, knowing better—stood passively and silently by.[28] There are fiefdoms to be protected and all else can appear rather abstract and distant to the individual and institutional players faced with a seemingly gradual progress toward what turns out only in retrospect to be a catastrophe.

---

[28] Although it is all-but-reflexive, when discussing contemporary politics, to eschew all parallels with the Nazi era as "offensive" or in bad taste, the lessons of that all-too-real history are there for the taking and should not be ignored for their unpleasantness. Human nature alters and "evolves" less than it would please us to believe and there is much to be gleaned, from close observation of that very dark chapter in human history, about how that nature may play out on the grand political stage.

Of the hundreds of present-relevant observations made by William L. Shirer in his classic chronicle *The Rise and Fall of The Third Reich* (Simon & Schuster, New York, 1990), we might consider these: "[Adolf Hitler's] plan was deceptively simple and had the advantage of cloaking the seizure of absolute power in legality." (p. 196) and "[P]art of [Hitler's] genius was that . . . he knew the mettle of his . . . adversaries . . . In this crisis [over Germany's abrupt withdrawal from The League of Nations], as in those greater ones which were to follow . . ., the victorious Allied nations took no action, being too divided, too torpid, too blind to grasp the nature or direction of what was building up beyond the Rhine. On this, Hitler's calculations were eminently sound, as they had been and were to be in regard to his own people." (p. 211) It should be noted that a world of rational actors continued to pursue normal relations with the Third Reich for years after it had revealed its unmistakable monstrosity for all to see in its first of many nights of mass public book-burning (May 10, 1933), roaring book-fed bonfires unseen on Earth since the darkest days of the Inquisition.

One need not accuse a contemporary political actor of *being* a Nazi or indeed sympathizing with them to recognize analogous calculations and strategies in contemporary translation, and chart to what end a failure to comprehend those calculations and strategies brought our not-so-far-removed predecessors. The will to absolute power and control—whether sociopathic, psychotic, or merely existential in its genesis—seems to be a recurrent pestilence of civilized humanity, something like a retrovirus in its periodic reemergence. When the driving goal is to establish anything as unnatural as a "thousand-year Reich" or, in less Wagnerian modern parlance, "perpetual rule," resistance will be met and will tend to grow in response to the increasingly harsh measures necessary to overcome it, until a point of crisis is reached, at which if the "Reich" is to survive all resistance must be crushed. It is not unlike a game of all-in poker that can proceed quietly enough only to explode into the highest drama at a critical tactical or strategic moment. Thus are totalitarianisms born and reborn (though not necessarily to the heavy tread of jackboots goose-stepping in torchlight parades) and it would be naïve to think that, fortunate enough to be born into an exemplary democracy but less than a lifespan removed from the Third Reich, we ourselves are utterly immune to one or another variant of such a dynamic.

Q: OK, but can we look at some specifics? What about the officials who actually run and certify our elections? If elections are being stolen, isn't it right under their noses?

A: Of the election administrators, Democrats, and the media, the behavior of the election administrators is probably the easiest to explain. Election officials at every level wish, first and foremost, to avoid controversy. When computers are doing the counting, vote totals magically appear at the end of the pipeline; humans with their potential biases and agendas have apparently not been involved; and at the surface everything looks clean and tidy. Election officials get to deal with a known and established vendor rather than with what amounts to an itinerant temporary labor force of vote-counters. Human counters need to be trained and supervised; computers need only to be programmed and, in the vast majority of cases, the corporate vendors take care of that.

The terrain is complex but it's not all that different from military contracting: often the official on the local level has little or no choice of which vendor will supply his or her equipment and technical services and, where there is a choice, the winning vendor will generally have done what vendors traditionally do to grease the wheels for the awarding of contracts and the unquestioning allegiance of the decision-making officials. The technical demands of programming and testing opscans and DREs are generally well beyond the capacities of the local officials who will be deploying them, so they have no real alternative to simply trusting the vendors and their technicians.[29]

This is all assuming, of course, that the election official is not himself more devoted to a private or partisan agenda than to the public trust. While the vast majority of election officials are almost certainly trying

---

[29] The state of Oklahoma, which programs its own equipment, is an exceedingly rare exception to this arrangement, one that, as we will explore in Chapter V, has profound implications for our analysis of the 2016 primaries.

to be, within their limited technical capacities, decent and fair administrators of their elections, we have also seen outrageous conflicts of interest, where such officials, as lofty as states' chief election administrators, have simultaneously been high-level *campaign* officials, most egregiously Katherine Harris in Florida 2000 and J. Kenneth Blackwell in Ohio 2004, not coincidentally the controversial and decisive states in each of those presidential elections.[30]

But the key point to recognize is that *it does not require corrupt, or even conventionally negligent, election administrators to certify a corrupted election.* They simply do not have either the incentive or the chops to dig deep enough to detect the exploits of non-administrative insiders or hackers.

Q: OK, how about the Democrats? They seem very reluctant to challenge or question even the most suspect electoral outcomes and have done little to promote serious reform measures even when they've had the power to do so.

A: A good way to liven up any gathering of understandably morose election integrity activists would be to ask everyone's view on why the Democrats have consistently acquiesced in highly suspect electoral defeats and been so unwilling to look into the role of computerized vote counting in the rightward veer of American politics. You will hear, in four-part harmony, explanations ranging from ignorance to naiveté to denial to intimidation to complicity, and of course stupidity. Frankly, it does boggle the mind. But let me contribute five observations that I hope will be of some help to our understanding:

---

[30] The spectre of administrative bias has reared its bipartisan head more recently in the 2016 Democratic primaries, where election officials from New York to Kentucky, Arizona, and California have faced well-supported allegations of procedural bias in favor of party-anointed Hillary Clinton.

1. There is enormous pressure on "losing" candidates to concede, move on, and permit the machinery of government to go forward. Consider the plight of Al Gore, who in 2000 was the national popular vote *victor* by over half a million votes (as tabulated), and yet was pilloried for "holding the nation hostage" while he challenged the *537-vote* official Bush margin in the state of Florida. If popular vote *winner* Gore could be so effectively painted as a "sore loser," what of other candidates in less sympathetic circumstances?[31] For many such candidates, challenging an election, however suspect the results, can understandably be seen as an act of political suicide.

2. As for the Democrats successfully elected and serving in office, it would take a rare politician to challenge, or even support a challenge to, the legitimacy of the very system that brought him or her to power.[32] Anyone who has strolled the marble corridors of Congress should recognize that, recent hyperpartisan politics notwithstanding, it has the feel of an elite club whose members coexist in a tradition of log-rolling cooperation and are *all alike* underwritten by the grandeur of high public office and the legitimacy of the electoral process that bestowed it upon them. There is great reluctance to rock the boat at a foundational level or indeed to bite the electoral hand that has fed you.

---

[31] John Kerry, still haunted a decade later by his prompt concession in E2004 (he had accepted $15 million in donations specifically earmarked for legal challenge of suspect electoral results), spoke candidly about these pressures in a remarkable 2015 interview with *The New Yorker* editor, David Remnick:
http://www.newyorker.com/magazine/2015/12/21/negotiating-the-whirlwind.

[32] I am waiting still for a *victorious* candidate to step to the podium for his or her acceptance speech and say something like the following: "I am grateful for your votes and the trust you have placed in me today. But if I am to serve you in good conscience I need to *know* that I was in fact your choice, and the secret vote counting system that has given me this apparent victory gives no such knowledge to you or to me. So I am requesting that, before this election is certified and before I take office, there be a full public hand count of the ballots" [impossible, of course, if DREs were part of the counting system], "and I am asking you as citizens and voters to consider this observable counting process to be your right and your duty in every election in our proud democracy." America's first *sore-winner*: a genuine elevation of the public trust over immediate political self-interest; a "Man Bites Dog" headline and a potent career booster to boot.

3. Democrats depend on and are obsessed with *turnout*, particularly among the marginal voting groups that make up much of their constituency. With good reason. If turnout levels among the rich, the white, the old, the suburban homeowners were equaled among the poor, the non-white, the young, the urban, US politics would scarcely even be competitive; it would be a Democratic rout. But these Democratic constituencies under the best of circumstances are reputed to need a lot more prodding to cast a ballot than do their Republican counterparts, and Democratic strategists fear that playing up any concerns about the honesty of elections and vote counting will discourage and lose these potential voters, many of whom are already deep-down skeptics when it comes to the fairness of "the system." And there is indeed evidence that massive turnout sometimes does overwhelm the rig, which only reinforces Democratic willingness to continue playing on a tilted table what is in the long run bound to be a losing game.

4. In virtually all cases and for obvious reasons, election rigging is *designed* to pass the smell test. Highly competitive elections are targeted, where a shift of just a few percent of the votes can reverse the outcomes. There are generally "benign" explanations for these outcomes—speculations about the role of money, endorsements, gaffes, voter turnout (now ironically including *overt* vote suppression via selective purges, diminished access, and restrictive Voter ID laws). For any given election it is ordinarily possible to find *some* reason, other than computerized manipulation, for disappointing and/or unexpected results. *It is the pervasive one-way pattern into which all these individual elections fall that is inexplicable without reference to rigging.*

Falsely reassured as they have been by the electoral victories of 2006, 2008 (which were both the results of bizarre 11th-hour *political* shifts that appeared to overwhelm the rig[33]), and 2012 (where credit appears to be due principally to covert intervention by Anonymous[34]), the Democrats have consistently ignored or dismissed this *pattern*, and that behavior remains to be explained. It is worth noting, however, that although Democrats could obviously be portrayed as the victims of election rigging in America, they are firmly entrenched in the corridors of power and would remain so even as a minority party under Karl Rove's projected "40-year dynasty" of Republican rule.

Election rigging, targeting primary as well as general elections and skillfully applied, can transform (and evidence suggests has already transformed) the American political spectrum, sliding it further and further to the right, *without in any way disturbing the two-party system and the power duopoly it bestows on Democrats and Republicans alike.* It is not at all clear that the Democrats would care to jeopardize that arrangement, opening the electoral doors to progressives, mavericks, and third parties.[35] *The true victims of election rigging in America are not the Democrats but the uninformed and disenfranchised American people and ultimately public sovereignty itself.*

5. Finally, there is religion. I don't mean here belief in a deity but rather a secular religion of equal intensity. To illustrate I'd like to recount an experience I had at a national conference on media reform in 2007. At a panel session I publicly asked Cornell Belcher,

---

[33] In 2006 the Foley and related GOP September sex scandals; in 2008 the mid-September collapse of Lehman Brothers and the subsequent market crash. Both dramatically altered the electoral dynamics: in 2006, for instance, the Democratic margin in the Cook Generic Congressional Ballot jumped from 9% in the first week of October to 26% the week of the election, a Republican free-fall of epic proportions; a similar fate overcame McCain in the wake of the economy's September 2008 collapse. Manipulations calibrated and deployed prior to these unexpected events would have foundered in the political sea changes.

[34] Explored in greater detail in Chapter III.

[35] Indeed, many are now accusing the Democratic Party establishment of employing a variety of hi-jinx to close the electoral doors to the campaign of a progressive candidate, Bernie Sanders, in the 2016 nomination battle.

at the time chief pollster for the Democratic National Committee, a question about poll-votecount disparities and the red shift. Having stated flat out that the red shift could not be attributable to any problem with vote counting (i.e., election theft), he then added this curious observation, which I give from memory: "You know, it's odd but we have the same problem with our own internal polling: in important races, when our polls show our guy [the Democratic candidate] up by 10%, we've learned that we need to regard the race as a dead-heat toss-up."

Well. What exactly is to be made of *that*? Such "internal" polls are designed not for political salesmanship but for *maximum accuracy*; they inform the party where support is needed, not needed, or likely to be wasted—where vital campaign dollars should and should not be spent. When such internal polls are consistently "off" in the neighborhood of 10%, all sorts of alarm bells should be ringing and ringing loud. It takes a religious belief in the sanctity of an entirely unseen process, and everything we so desperately want that process to stand for, to be deaf to those bells. After I pointed this out, Belcher then restated flat-out that the 10% disparity between his internal polls and election outcomes could not possibly be caused by election rigging. It felt like something out of *Inherit The Wind* or perhaps *Elmer Gantry*: "Brothers! Sisters! Do ye *believe*?!"[36]

---

[36] *Esquire* blogger Charlie Pierce has spoken brilliantly to this phenomenon, writing: "[G]iven that there is overwhelming evidence of a national campaign to suppress the potential vote through law, why should we not believe there is a parallel effort to influence votes after they are cast? Why should we believe that the national campaign to rig an election is purely legal, and not technological? The only reason is that *we don't want to believe it*. The will not to believe is the shifting sand beneath the unstable entire architecture of American Exceptionalism. Because our attachment to the idea is theological, and not empirical, we can look neither at our history nor our politics honestly. Eventually the lies pile up, one atop the other . . . Eventually, the elections become electronic Kabuki. 'Our elections must be honest, not because we make them so, but simply because they are *ours*. It will all work out right in the end because this is America, fk yeah, the shining city on a hill.' Faith eventually undermines reality. We start believing in spirits and incantations. And then we fall, hard." http://www.esquire.com/blogs/politics/american-exceptionalism-14056595#ixzz2AdeYV3y2.

Q: And the media? This is potentially the biggest story of their lives. Isn't the "Fourth Estate" traditionally one of the most important guardians of democracy?

A: Many of us retain a warm spot for the American press still left over from the days of Watergate, when Woodward and Bernstein, *The Washington Post, The New York Times,* and even the networks seemed to be among the big heroes. It wasn't that simple in reality, but the impression of both a heroic and a liberal press has been slow to fade, especially with the "liberal" label being flogged mercilessly by the right-wing media machine even as that machine took over talk radio and came to dominate network news and newspaper ownership.

Fast forward to 2014: the mainstream media (MSM) is almost entirely a subsidiary of mega-corporations, news budgets are slashed to the bone, opinions (often shouted) have displaced reporting and investigation, entertainment is the order of the day, and there are some insidious limits on the stuff that is, as the *Times* continues to put it, "fit to print." That said, it is still astounding how impervious the MSM has been to this story. We have it, off the record, from several top journalists that their employers have flat-out prohibited them from writing or speaking on the matter of computerized election theft or reviewing any of the evidence that it is occurring.

The MSM has what seems to be a "rule" on this: it's OK to make noise about the potential *vulnerability* of the machines in the run-up to elections (Lou Dobbs, for example, was all over this right up through Election Night in 2006; and we witnessed a virtual repeat in the days preceding E2012 and again this year[37]); but *following* the election,

---

[37] See, e.g., Zeynep Tufekci, "The Election Won't Be Rigged. But It Could Be Hacked," NY *Times* 8/12/16; Bryan Clark, "An easy-to-find $15 piece of hardware is all it takes to hack a voting machine," *aol.com* 8/11/16; Ben Wofford, "How to Hack an Election in 7 Minutes," *Politico,* 8/5/16; etc.: all excellent articles; all, by focusing exclusively on outsider hacking and ignoring vulnerability to insider rigging, missing the spot.

when evidence pointing to actual manipulation is made available, all coverage is *verboten*. *Omerta* is the word that comes to mind, an unwritten code of silence. In 2004, when this story was "fresh," Keith Olbermann had the temerity right after the election to start covering what had happened in Ohio, and actually began to dig into things a bit. He wrote to me that he was "very interested" in the statistical evidence that we had gathered. He devoted several powerful, widely-viewed, and very enthusiastically received segments to it and then . . . POOF! He was off on a two-week vacation of which there had been no prior mention. And when he came back . . . not another word, ever. The biggest story, by a factor of ten, of Olbermann's professional career and he walks away mid-sentence?! It should be obvious that there are some powerful forces at work here set on making sure this story never gets legs.

And I might as well add that it's not just the MSM. The *progressive* media—ranging from *The Nation* to *Mother Jones* to *The Progressive Populist*—have all taken a virtually complete pass. In their pages they continue to discuss—and bemoan—election dynamics and the "new politics" of the Tea Party era, without an iota of attention paid to even the possibility that these bizarre and troublesome results may have something to do with a digital thumb on the electronic counting scale, not so much as a hint that there may be something to question or investigate.

This is perhaps the most mystifying thing of all: watching the progressives of America commit political suicide, as their media buy into a rigged game and seem perpetually to be discussing their own culpability for the latest political setbacks or shocking routs, while their entire agenda goes DOA. As far as I can tell, apart from the Wall Of Denial itself, the fear in these quarters is *marginalization*, that even mentioning the possibility of actual electronic election rigging will forfeit their hard-earned place at the "serious journalism" table or, in the case of groups such as Common Cause or People For The American Way or the ACLU, the "serious advocacy" table. If that risk seems exaggerated, simply recall the fate of Dan Rather, a titanic media figure permanently exiled after stepping "out of bounds" regarding George W. Bush's National Guard records.   As with the whistle-blowers, even a single such demise sends a powerful and unambiguous message to the rest.

From his place of exile (*Dan Rather Reports* on the little-watched HDNet), Rather himself took on at least some of the story in a program that aired in October 2011.[38] But journalism is classic groupthink and, until you have *more than one* brave soul willing to step concurrently into the breach, the story generally dies on the vine. No one followed Rather's lead.   Jon Stewart once questioned the technology in his inimitable way on *The Daily Show,* Garry Trudeau in *Doonesbury,* Scott Adams more recently in *Dilbert,* and I hope they (and/or some of their colleagues) will come back to it. Sporadic eyebrow-raising and throat-clearing is better than total silence, but it goes only so far and that is not close to far enough given the massive inertias involved.

Ironically, among many in the progressive media, the attitude seems to be, "If there were anything seriously wrong, the *Democrats* would be all over it." This from the same people who regularly pillory the Democrats as political sellouts? So, in a classic and deadly illustration of Bystander's Syndrome (action is distasteful or risky and we can each convince ourselves that someone *else* will "call 911"), everyone sort of sits around waiting for someone else to stick out his or her neck. And about the only press willing to do that are web-based sites such as BradBlog and OpEdNews. They merit very high praise indeed for their persistence. But in America if a story doesn't make it to the *Times* or the networks, it's still a tin-hat conspiracy theory, no matter how well presented and documented. Look at how long it took us to take seriously allegations of performance-enhancing drugs in baseball. Look at how long, even after the whistle-blower Harry Markopolos had

---

[38] Dan Rather: *Das Vote: "Digital Democracy in Doubt,"* HDNetTV
http://www.huffingtonpost.com/dan-rather/digital-democracy-in-doub_b_774137.html
(see link to *iTunes* video download at end of article).

stepped forward, Bernie Madoff continued to operate his Ponzi scheme.

With elections the stakes are immensely higher and the fear that *everything will fall apart* if the truth is rigorously pursued is rather paralyzing. To put it slightly differently, investigation would lead to *knowledge* and knowledge would mandate *action*, an inexorable process once begun. But no individual operating within the vast system of American politics can imagine what action he or she might take—both the personal blowback and the national earthquake would be too catastrophic.[39] So the morally compelling but pragmatically daunting "action imperative" itself paradoxically operates to block the road of investigation at its very beginning.

To get back to the media, I wrote in 2004 that when the autopsy of American democracy is performed the cause of death will be given as media silence. What I've seen in the dozen years since only strengthens that prediction. To me, in fact, the American press and media are the most wretched villains of the piece. Those actually doing the rigging, whether it's a Rovean figure playing God or some cadre of true believers, are in a sense "doing their job," just like a lineman "holding" in football to protect the quarterback. The media's job is to *spot the foul*, get at and promulgate the truth. And *they* are the ones who are *not* doing their job. Individually by the hundreds, and collectively as a force, they have served as enablers. They appear to be either in deep denial, anaesthetized, or content with a sham

---

[39] It is perhaps instructive to compare the 544-day saga of "Deflategate," the national crisis that arose regarding the air pressure in Tom Brady's footballs. In 2016 America, football *matters*! The pounds-per-square-inch in the footballs used by Brady, and the possible impact of that number's manipulation on performance and wins and losses, was frequently the lead story not just of sports sections but of network news programs. Footballs were impounded (if they had been voting machines or memory cards, the argument that they belonged to the *Patriots* and could not be examined would have prevailed), as were cell phones emails, etc.; many $millions were spent investigating and litigating. It was fascinating; it was entertaining; it was "important" without being "too important," without threatening a 9.0 national earthquake. It was, in short, the perfect story.

democracy, which would of course suit their ultimate corporate masters just fine.[40]

I'm not sure how much intimidation is being meted out or even what quarter it's coming from, but it is time someone with a following found the courage to risk his or her job, or even his or her life, in service to the truth. That courage is surely not unprecedented in our nation's history and it is sorely needed now if what the courageous have fought and died for is to survive.

Q: Is it really possible, in a major election, to "count every vote as cast?"

A: In theory, yes; in practice, no. There is going to be a bit of "noise" in any system that attempts to count and aggregate large numbers. So "count every vote as cast" is a quixotic and misleading standard. "Noise" is not *The Problem* and neither are so-called "voter" frauds or genuine "glitches."   Computerized election rigging is not about miscounting a vote here and there, nor even about a few people voting twice or in the wrong district. Such exploits as double voting and impersonational voting are open to both parties, are at once low-yield and tremendously labor-intensive, virtually never alter electoral outcomes, and in the end, over time and space, wind up a wash. *You can't take over and hold onto America by hand.*

Nor will "glitches"—which, with the non-intentionality of a flipped penny, break 50-50, yielding no net advantage—turn that trick (indeed we would *accept* computerized counting if truly inadvertent "glitches" were the only problem). *Only deliberate systemic misrecording of votes and/or deliberate mistabulation at the aggregate level can do it, and only computers and their programmers have that power.*

---

[40] I suspect also that there is a shared Hamiltonian sneer among these highly educated professional elites who, subconsciously at least, regard public sovereignty per se—in an era in which so much of that public finds the NFL or the Kardashians infinitely more absorbing than the facts and nuances underlying policy debates—as not especially worthy of respect, trust, or electoral protection.

It is beyond ironic that Republican-controlled state legislatures throughout the country, many of which came to power via the highly suspect 2010 election, have in the past few years enacted restrictive Voter-ID laws, several of which have already been ruled unconstitutionally discriminatory by the courts, to deal with a putative epidemic of "voter fraud" that turns out to be virtually nonexistent.[41] Yet manifestly vulnerable secret vote counting by radically partisan corporations goes merrily on its unchallenged way, pervasive red-shift disparities notwithstanding.   There is a real Alice-In-Wonderland feel to it all.

Q: How does America stack up against other long-established democracies when it comes to electoral integrity?

Not very well. Indeed, in a joint study conducted by Harvard and the University of Sydney, the US elections of 2012 and 2014 scored *dead last* among the group of 54 long-established democracies.[42] Particularly revealing was each nation's electoral integrity score plotted against per capita GDP.[43] To a significant degree, electoral integrity follows national wealth; in essence, free and fair elections are a commodity that wealthier nations can generally better afford. In the graph of all the world's democracies, the US appears as an egregious outlier far below the wealth/integrity curve: a great deal of wealth *not*

---

[41] The gates were opened to this templated campaign of voter suppression by another in a series of 5-to-4 party-line US Supreme Court decisions. The 2013 holding in *Shelby County v. Holder*, gutting critical Section 4(b) of the Voting Rights Act of 1965, left states that sported a long Jim Crow history (ironically under mostly Democratic state administrations) free to install *new* Jim Crow laws and regulations without federal approval. See generally, Berman A: *Give Us the Ballot: The Modern Struggle for Voting Rights in America*. New York: Farrar, Straus and Giroux (2015); at https://www.amazon.com/dp/1250094720/ref.

[42] See "The Electoral Integrity Project: Why Elections Fail and What We Can Do About It" at https://sites.google.com/site/electoralintegrityproject4/projects/expert-survey-2/the-year-in-elections-2015 (also see https://www.dropbox.com/s/ziav8ce6c63lx0k/The%20Year%20in%20Elections%202015_pages.compressed.pdf?dl=0 for the full report).

[43] The Electoral Integrity Project (full report), p. 30.

being spent here on democracy, at least on its electoral component. This of course squares with the sadly dilapidated state of America's voting equipment and with the budgetary impracticality of beefing up the invitingly low levels of administrative scrutiny.

A recent foreign example serves to place in context the low standard of fidelity to which the process of counting votes is held in America. The Constitutional Court of Austria held, on July 1, 2016, that the mere possibility of irregularities in the counting process (counting in some places was begun before the prescribed cast of observers was present) was enough to void that nation's presidential election results and necessitate a new election.[44] It was not necessary for the challenger[45] to prove fraud or actual manipulation, merely a lapse of full transparency such that outcome-altering manipulation might have occurred unobservably. Quite obviously, if US elections were held to such a standard, our unobservable vote counting process would foster a continual string of electoral re-dos, until it was replaced with an observable process.

Q: Who are these corporations that count our votes? What makes you think they care who wins elections?

A: Democratic elections should by their very nature be a public trust. The fact that virtually the entire vote-counting process in America has been outsourced to a few private corporations that operate behind an impenetrable screen of proprietary legal and administrative protections is bad enough. The actual history of the shape-shifting electronic voting industry and the cast of characters that has

---

[44] See https://www.washingtonpost.com/15c1c843-368b-44a5-8d99-764fa88c52d8_story.html.

[45] That the challenger and beneficiary of the Court's ruling was an extreme right-winger may be food for cynical thought, but we would like to believe that the principles of electoral integrity and vote counting transparency were upheld by the justices without regard to partisan political impact.

controlled it is in no way reassuring.[46] Republican Senator Chuck Hagel owned a good part of the outfit that counted the votes returning him to the US Senate in Nebraska. Walden O'Dell, CEO of Diebold and an active Bush supporter, in 2003 penned a letter to potential donors in which he stated that he was "committed to helping Ohio deliver its electoral votes to the president next year." O'Dell was seen to be in a unique position to fulfill his commitment, as Diebold was the supplier and programmer of Ohio's voting computers in E2004. Right-winger Bob Urosevich, founder of Election Systems and Software (ES&S), was also the first CEO of Diebold Election Systems (a subsidiary of O'Dell's Diebold, Inc.); his brother, Todd, was Vice-President of ES&S.[47]

As of 2012 the vote-counting corporations had been whittled down to two principals—ES&S and the descriptively named Dominion Voting—which between them controlled the computers that counted the vast majority of the votes in America. When you trace the pedigree of these vendors, every road seems to lead back to the right wing: wealthy Texas oilmen, fanatical Fundamentalists, major Republican donors, and prominent Republican politicians. In fact, Hart Intercivic, a junior partner to ES&S and Dominion, has a board majority controlled by an investment firm known as H.I.G. Capital, which in turn boasts Mitt Romney, his wife, son, and brother as major investors through the closely-held equity fund Solamere.[48] Then there are the

---

[46] See https://www.verifiedvoting.org/resources/voting-equipment/ for a comprehensive cataloguing of voting equipment vendors and their products. See also http://blackboxvoting.org/reports/voting-system-technical-information/ for an examination of the activities, pedigree, and affiliations of the principal vendors. The cast of characters is highlighted in Victoria Collier's 2012 article "How to Rig an Election" (*Harper's* 10/26/2012, as reprinted at http://readersupportednews.org/opinion2/277-75/14198-focus-how-to-rig-an-election).

[47] See http://www.sourcewatch.org/index.php/Diebold_Election_Systems. Bob Urosevich turned up again more recently as Managing Director of Scytl, a Barcelona-based firm that has taken control of electronic databases in a number of states, including several where targeted electronic purges were alleged in the 2016 primaries.

[48] See Ungar C: "Romney-linked Voting Machine Company Will Count Votes in Ohio and Other Crucial Swing States," (10/26/2012) at http://www.salon.com/2012/10/23/romney_linked_voting_machine_company_to_count_votes_in_ohio/

satellite corporations that do much of the actual programming, servicing, and deploying of the machines—outfits like Command Central, Triad, LHS, and the late Mike Connell's own SmarTech—secretive to outright impenetrable.

All the self-promotion and self-congratulation on a sleek website like Dominion's cannot quite obscure the fact that what these Lords of Elections are really saying is, "You may as well trust us. You have no other choice." While the privatization of the vote-counting process gives rise to a situation in which electronic thumbs on the scale could in theory be sold to the highest bidder, the manifest partisanship of the outfits that program, distribute, and service the voting equipment is far more likely to translate in practice to *politically selective access* or, in the language of criminologists, opportunity and means. The consistently one-sided forensic evidence in the elections of the computerized era supports this assessment. It really *is* the man in the magician's suit with the "Vote For So-And-So" button, if not on his lapel then on the inside of his sleeve, who takes our ballots and disappears behind the curtain.

Q: You state that virtually all the anomalies, disparities, and shifts are in one direction, favoring the right-wing candidates and positions. But what about 2006, 2008, and 2012? Those were Democratic victories! Why would forces on the right rig to lose?

A: They didn't rig to lose, they rigged to win—or, more precisely, *to maximize winnings and minimize losses within bounds of acceptable risk of detection.* With a single very odd exception, to be discussed in the next chapter, *every* post-HAVA biennial election from 2002 through 2014 has exhibited a red shift both nationally and in the key states and districts.[49] The red shifts in 2006 and 2008 were in fact

---

[49] In E2002 the red shift could not be measured because the exit polls were withheld from public view. That it *existed* is clear from the fact that the plug was pulled on the exit polls because they were so far "off" that the networks could not come up with a plausible explanation for the magnitude of the red shift disparities in key races (e.g., Cleland/Chambliss in Georgia, Hagel/Matulka in Nebraska).

massive but, in both 2006 and 2008, unexpected 11th-hour events (in 2006 the lurid sex scandals and cover-ups enveloping Republican Congressman Mark Foley and several other prominent right-wingers; and in 2008 the collapse of Lehman Brothers, which ushered in the Great Recession the day after John McCain had proclaimed the economy "strong"), dramatically altered the electoral dynamics.

In 2006, for instance, the Democratic margin in the nonpartisan Cook Generic Congressional Ballot ("On Election Day will you vote for the Republican or Democratic candidate for Congress in your district?") jumped from 9% in the first week of October to 26% the week of the election, a Republican free-fall of epic proportions; a similar fate overcame McCain in the wake of the economy's nosedive on Bush's watch late in 2008. These leftward political sea changes likely swamped a rightward manipulation that turned out, in light of the unforeseen events, to be under-calibrated; and they came too late to permit rescue via recalibration and redeployment of tainted memory cards and malicious code.

The devil is in such details, but these red-shift red flags were ignored, trampled in the Obama victory parade. It is of course possible for Democrats and left-leaning candidates to win elections and there comes a point where, if the margin is large enough, reversing the outcome through computerized rigging, although technically feasible, would no longer pass the smell test. Nor is it necessary, after a certain point, for every vulnerable contest to be targeted for rigging: in bodies such as the US House and most state legislative chambers, a bare majority will suffice for practical partisan control and "padding" becomes a low-reward gambit. But it should be obvious that, in a finely balanced nation such as America, it is a long-term, indeed permanent, losing proposition to be required to poll supermajorities of 55% to 60% in order to eke out electoral victories. Even a relatively light thumb can effectively wreak havoc with the political scales.

It is now comprehended by strategists across the political spectrum that shifting demographic patterns have handed the Democrats a massive and growing electoral advantage nationwide. The radicalization of the Republican Party has only heightened that advantage.[50] To win general elections and hold onto power—barring massive scandals and other egregious political fiascoes—Republicans are now obliged to turn to *structural* strategies to offset their demographic and political handicaps. Thus we have witnessed a spate of restrictive Voter-ID laws ostensibly passed to combat a nonexistent "epidemic" of "voter" fraud; ruthless gerrymandering of US House and statehouse districts,[51] with emerging proposals to extend the gerrymander's cynical powers to the presidential contest itself;[52] the

---

[50] It is worth recalling what happened to the *Democrats* when they similarly radicalized (Eugene McCarthy, George McGovern) in the Vietnam era when votes were still being *counted* rather than *processed*. They were *crushed* and all-but-marginalized for a generation.

[51] The gerrymander is of course a tool available as well to Democrats, who have not shied away from its use. Demographics, however, give Republicans a significant advantage here: Democratic constituencies tend to cluster in large urban areas, which can be gerrymandered into near-100% Democratic districts, more effectively "consuming" Democratic voters within a given state than a pro-Democratic gerrymander can consume the less geographically-concentrated Republican voters. E2010 was a critical election at the below-the-radar statehouse level because their key state legislature victories gave Republicans control of the decennial redistricting process, based on the 2010 Census, for the US House and many key statehouses. The result has been and will continue to be, *at the minimum,* effective veto power over national (and key state) politics, without the necessity of winning a presidential election for years to come. A subtle beauty of this down-ballot strategy lies in the fact that voters can be expected ultimately to grow weary of gridlock and, given the very dim prospects for wresting the House from GOP control, could sooner or later be persuaded to turn to a (Republican) presidential candidate who "will be able to work with Congress."

[52] Apportioning presidential Electoral College votes by congressional district rather than the current statewide winner-take-all basis has the ring of fairness but would in actual effect subject the presidential election to the same ruthless gerrymandering process that has locked in 90% of US House seats and would allow a few successfully rigged down-ballot (i.e., state legislative) elections to deliver control, through that process, of *both* the US House and the White House indefinitely. Direct Popular Vote for the presidency (i.e., doing away with the Electoral College) would, unlike the congressional district apportionment scheme, be a genuinely progressive reform, *but only if coupled with the restoration of observable vote counting.* Under the current computerized system, doing away with the Electoral College and simply counting the national popular vote would make it possible for election riggers to shift votes with equal impact *anywhere in the country*, making it even easier to escape the modicum of scrutiny that is currently focused on battleground states.

financial advantage gained through the US Supreme Court's 5-to-4 *Citizens United*[53] and *McCutcheon* decisions and the torrents of corporate campaign cash to which they opened the floodgates; and of course the "Vote Wednesday" flyers and robocalls and related disinformation campaigns.

Such tactics have served their purpose if they can bring contests within smell-test distance (in tracking and exit polls), where a computerized mistabulation can be outcome-altering without being shocking, and thus suspicion-arousing, in its magnitude.[54] Restoration of the democracy Americans have been led to believe is their birthright will require addressing and reforming in turn each of these thumbs on the scale. If we agree that the most insidious thumb is the most covert, we will begin with the rescue of the votecount itself out of the darkness of cyberspace and into the light of public observation.[55]

Q: If the evidence pointed to a pervasive "blue shift," advantaging the Democrats or progressive candidates, instead of the pervasive "red shift" that you have found, do you think you would still be engaged in this work to the same degree?

A: Very frankly—human nature, or at least my nature, being what it is—I don't think so. This is frustrating, depressing, demoralizing, and

---

[53] *Citizens United v. FEC*, 558 US 310 (2010), effectively defined corporate campaign contributions as protected "free speech," gutting much of the framework for regulating or limiting it. *McCutcheon v. FEC*, 572 US __ (2014), then compounded the damage by striking down aggregate limits to corporate contributions.

[54] Harvey Wasserman and Bob Fitrakis have coined the term "strip and flip" to describe this two-pronged strategy, with the "strip" referring to the various overt schemes and the "flip" to the covert electronic manipulation, both of which appear to be on display in the 2016 Democratic presidential primaries (see Fitrakis B & Wasserman H: *The Strip and Flip Selection of 2016: Five Jim Crows & Electronic Election Theft* at https://www.amazon.com/dp/B01GSJLW0I).

[55] Harvard Law professor Lawrence Lessig, whose 2015 single-issue campaign for the presidency rested entirely on a "clean elections" platform, apparently did not agree, omitting the counting process itself entirely from the set of issues he was willing to address, despite repeated appeals for its inclusion. It just didn't seem "as important" to him. As I wrote to a colleague, "When the fringe treats you like fringe you know you're the fringe."

potentially dangerous work, and there's every incentive to stop banging your head against the spiked wall after years and years of it. It is common to view vote counting as an abstract, rather academic matter, but it all-too-obviously can be one with very real, concrete, far-reaching, practical and historical consequences. That is what makes it compelling for me and drives my continuing efforts.

I've always believed that Cassandra's fate—to see the truth and the hidden danger and never to be believed—was the worst of all the terrible punishments meted out by the jealous Greek gods. I little thought it would be my lot in life and I don't care for it one bit. If I had uncovered evidence of electronic fraud and it were both sides doing it such that it was a wash, or the Left doing it so that it was pushing America to the more progressive pole, it would still be a blot on democracy, and I would still have attempted to bring it to the attention of officials, the media, and the public. Unobservable vote counting is, whomever it benefits, inherently insane. But, after being ignored or patronized for 15 long years of these efforts, I'm pretty sure I would have been willing to mutter "*c'est la guerre*" and move on to other things. Living in the world of *CODE RED,* and immersing myself in this Alice-In-Wonderland nightmare of the Big Lie, is oppressive. Just not as oppressive as the fascism to which computerized election theft might well deliver the democracy I was fortunate enough to be born into but have stopped taking so for granted.

But the "pervasive blue shift" is a rather ridiculous hypothetical because, if it were the *Left* in control of the voting apparatus and the "shocking" results were favoring their cause, it is impossible to imagine that the political strategists and media of the Right would *not* be all over it, demanding investigations and even "observable counting." An odd asymmetry I know, but just look at all the Voter ID legislation the Right has rammed through in response to a nonexistent epidemic of "voter fraud" with no impact on electoral outcomes.[56] So it's a lead-pipe cinch that they would hardly be supine and acquiescent in the face of evidence of targeted computerized vote counting fraud that was altering the outcome of hundreds of key elections and threatening *them* with permanent minority status. I doubt *my* perseverance would be needed.

I have often been asked how my personal political views impact my capacity to function as a fair and impartial analyst of election forensics. It is, of course, a fair question and one very much worth asking. My answer is that I—and Election Defense Alliance (EDA), the organization for which I serve as Executive Director—share the nonpartisan goal of election integrity manifest in transparency, accountability, and, above all, observable vote counting. After all the deceptions and outright lies along the campaign trail, after all the infusion of now obscene and undisclosed corporate funding perverting electoral politics, even after all the "Vote Wednesday" robocalls and all the other dirty tricks to which the desperate make resort, if nothing more than the *counting of the votes* could be trusted, our particular and rather narrow mission would be fulfilled.

In our quest to restore observable vote counting—which should be a no-brainer on its face but instead seems a quaint and faintly ludicrous notion in the wake of the *fait accompli* blitzkrieg of post-HAVA computerization—we are called upon to document and analyze the red-flag patterns that result from *non-observable* vote counting. After all, if it ain't broke why fix it? And in this work, it must be said, there is *nothing random or nonpartisan* about the patterns that keep turning up wherever contests are competitive and carry either direct or indirect national significance. There is hardly ever a "blue shift"

[56] See Minnite L: *The Myth of Voter Fraud,* Cornell University Press 2010, http://www.amazon.com/Myth-Voter-Fraud-Lorraine-Minnite/dp/0801448484; see also Mayer J: "The Voter-Fraud Myth," *The New Yorker* (10/29/2012) at http://www.newyorker.com/reporting/2012/10/29/121029fa_fa_fact_mayer?printable=true.

anywhere, just a pervasive "red shift" election after election[57]—even in the elections where 11th-hour seismic political shifts overcame it and led to (diminished) Democratic victories—and a consequent inexorable veering of American politics to the right. This is the *reality*, call it partisan or call it nonpartisan as you choose.

Q: But what if I don't buy that "reality?" What would you say to someone on the other side of the great political divide who believes you've cherry-picked your evidence or that the red shift stems from faulty polls, or who believes that *Obama* stole the White House and it's the *Left* that has found a way to rig American elections?

A: OK, I'm a leftie and you're a rightie. Each of us believes the other side has been rigging elections or would be if given the opportunity. With computerized counting neither of us has any reason to trust the other side—particularly in the present political environment, so rich in anger and poor in trust. Electoral legitimacy is now being called furiously into question from all sides. *Under these conditions especially, aren't we BOTH entitled to an observable counting of the votes?*

We are seeing it now: *whether an unobservable computer count leads to actual rigging or not*, it has now begun to invite serious, dangerous suspicion, distrust, and unrest. Isn't an observable count, going forward, likely to be the *only* way to restore trust in an electoral system that is breaking down before our very eyes, right and left?

Q: The blogosphere is awash in "conspiracy theories," ranging from the highly plausible to the truly outlandish. Where would you place computerized election theft on that spectrum and how do you deal

---

[57] The shifts that so distort the translation of the public will are by no means restricted to general (i.e., inter-party) elections. As will be detailed in Chapter V, the 2016 Democratic *primaries* exhibited what appears to be among the most egregious red shifts of the computerized era. Narrowing the candidate options available to voters in November has as powerful an impact in altering political direction and thwarting public sovereignty as does rigging November itself.

with the reflexive dismissal inherent in the "conspiracy theory" label?

A: It should be obvious that not every conspiracy is a theory. *History* is awash with undisclosed agreements and arrangements to work toward the achievement of some end that would generate opposition and resistance were it openly declared. That is all a conspiracy is.

The real problem with conspiracy theories is separating the wheat from the chaff. It is possible to imagine and allege virtually *anything* when it comes to nefarious or threatening human behavior. I met a man a few years ago who claimed that the US government had, in the course of one or another of his stays at a Veterans Hospital, surgically implanted "chips" in his brain that were being used to wirelessly torment him and send "information" to his consciousness, and moreover that many others had been subject to this same secret manipulation. "Mr. Chips" maintained a calm and rational affect and he discussed other aspects of politics and economics with admirable acumen. He carried with him a thick folder of MRI films purporting to show the location of the implanted chips.

While politely repressing a reflexive snicker, I found it very disquietingly occurring to me that my own earnest presentation of the red shift and stolen elections would elicit precisely the same reaction from many auditors. "Mr. Chips" and I were both "conspiracy theorists," each readily dismissed with that damning and clever label. Was there in fact a distinction and, if so, how might it be apprehended? How does one know, without a painstaking review of all the evidence (his MRIs, my tables and graphs), what to take seriously and what does not warrant further investigation?

What "Mr. Chips" and election integrity activists *do* have in common is that the events we are alleging to have taken place are deeply disturbing to the point where the human psyche recoils against acknowledgement.[58] Concealed behavior is concealed precisely because it would meet with a negative response, ranging from opposition to outrage, were it brought into the open. If Jose Canseco could be dismissed (and ridiculed) for daring to allege that *baseball* was not what it seemed and that those majestic 500-foot home runs were the derivative of pharmaceutical enhancements rather than wholesome heroics, how much stronger the impulse to dismiss (and ridicule) allegations and evidence that not the national *pastime* but the national *future* is being systematically subverted—that America is, in effect, a sham democracy?[59]

If we sweep away all alleged conspiracies and all covert activities with a big broom, we get to live in a world of presentable surfaces that seems and feels a lot more hospitable and comfortable. I certainly did not want to "waste my time" exploring the possibility that people are walking around with government-implanted microchips in their brains, and it is exactly such aversion that gives the term "conspiracy theory" such pejorative power and such protective effect for those engaging in covert activities.

So it is really up to the auditor to use his or her best judgment, life experience, knowledge of history, and understanding of human nature in evaluating the evidence presented. That means eschewing the convenience of easy labels like "conspiracy theory" and conclusory, quasi-religious presumptions like "America is the Beacon of

---

[58] Indeed, recent research has established that both individuals and groups can be so maximally averse to the *knowledge* that they have been duped that they often choose to *continue* being duped rather than to be confronted with the evidence that they *have been* duped (see Abby Ellin: "The Drama of Deception," *Psychology Today*, July 2015, at https://www.psychologytoday.com/magazine/archive/2015/07).

[59] It is worth noting that the *vulnerability* of computerized vote counting to fraud—the *risk* of continuing to use it for our elections—can in no sense be considered a conspiracy theory, any more than can the state of disrepair of America's roads and bridges. It is the attempt to present evidence of *actual* fraud and theft that triggers the dismissive "conspiracy theory" label. Yet only suspect elections and suspicions of actual rigging seem to bring major public attention to the otherwise abstract and decidedly unsexy topic of vote counting. This is most unfortunate.

Democracy and therefore such undemocratic things could never happen here."

Q: How do we know for certain, independent of election results, what kind of country America is—how red, how blue?

A: We don't. Even in a very small polity, say a town with 5,000 residents, you can't tell much about a polarizing contest or issue without an actual vote. You may know more people who say they intend to support X, but that says more about the company you keep than about how the rest of the town, let alone the state or the country, plans to vote. One side may have the preponderance of yard signs or radio spots, but that tells us little beyond the relative size of the campaign budgets.[60] Polls might be—and obviously, in the case of major elections, are—taken *ad nauseam*. But polls are highly sensitive to the particular sampling methodology used and usually wind up dancing a fluctuating and conflicting waltz when elections are close.[61]

This is what makes voting itself so powerful and, you would think, sacrosanct. *There is really no other way to know.* As columnist James Graff, having first noted the vagaries of polling, put it most succinctly, "The truth won't come until Election Day."[62] What comes on Election Day is a *reality* of elected officials who will govern us, but can anyone say with genuine assurance that they know that this reality reflects the actual *truth* of collective voter intent?[63]

---

[60] In today's post-*Citizens/McCutcheon* "dark money" era, the size of respective campaign war chests is a far better indicator of private than of public favor.

[61] See also Chapter VII, Study V for the distorting effect of the votecount-poll feedback loop.

[62] See *The Week*, 10/19/2012, p.3.

[63] Another, rather more personal, way of framing this question: "How much would you be willing to wager on the accuracy of a given votecount and electoral outcome—say one such as Ohio 2004 draped in a forensic red flag—ten bucks, the farm, your life?" If not prepared to bet your life that the official computer count and a full, observable human canvass will produce the same result, can you say you "*know*"?

And the "truth" of which Graff speaks is more expansive than the election of Candidate X or Candidate Y. Our biennial elections, far more than the endless parade of opinion polls, *define* America—both in terms of who occupies its seats of power and as the single snapshot that becomes the enduring national self-portrait that Americans of all stripes carry in our mental wallets for at least the biennium and more often for an era. It is also, needless to say, the portrait we send abroad. False elections bequeath to all Americans—right, left, and center—nothing less sinister than an illusory collective identity and the living of a national lie. Think of our altered electoral choices as a soul-baring letter that goes out, *over our forged signature*, to the world, to the future, to our children.

Q: What link, if any, do you see between the opportunity to steal elections and the current hyperpolarization of American politics? Why do you think the GOP itself has veered and continues to veer further and further right? Do you think they all somehow *know* that elections are rigged and that they can win no matter how extreme they get?

A: Logically, a player who knows the fix is in and victory assured will "bet the house." Why not get as much bang as possible for your buck? Translated into contemporary politics, if you believe you can win an election no matter what, there is no incentive to play to the middle. You can ignore how successful "triangulation" was for Bill Clinton and indeed ignore all conventional political wisdom that says that you have to dilute your radical agenda, your "true belief," in a bid to capture the moderates and independents in the center of the political spectrum needed to win competitive general elections.

According to the "classical physics" of politics, the extremist behavior of the GOP makes very little political sense and indeed it keeps surprising pundits all along the political spectrum, who keep scratching their heads as such behavior continues to be rewarded rather than punished electorally.[64]   Such would of course be the behavior of politicians who knew the fix was in and it may be driven by chief strategists who are either involved in the rigging of elections or who have deduced that it is going on and adjusted their strategies accordingly.

But it is also possible to understand the Right's new extremism from a behaviorist standpoint as the consequence of electoral experience operating on political strategy.   That is, without inferring any *knowledge* of a rigged game, when forays in political extremism are rewarded rather than punished electorally, the conventional wisdom that says you have to play to the center is soon enough discarded in favor of a new wisdom that says "Go ahead, shoot the moon." Each successive "win" further reinforces this new wisdom.

As countless behaviorist experiments have shown, it doesn't take much such conditioning to mold new behaviors. And this is true as well of the Democrats, who conversely have been punished rather than rewarded electorally over the past decade, at *every* political level other than the White House, as they ricochet from one "losing" strategy to the next. The new hyperpolarized and right-veering American politics certainly coincides with the advent and proliferation of computerized counting, but it does not require widespread *knowledge* of systemic electoral manipulation to account for this correlation.

Q: What in your view is the significance of the year 2010?

---

[64] Of course, since the electoral results are unquestioned *fact*, reasons *must* be found for the strange voter behavior. There is a cottage industry in "explaining" the electoral results of the computerized era, from Thomas Frank's 2004 bestseller, *What's The Matter with Kansas?* (voters 'distracted' by social issues like guns and abortion) to last year's NY *Times*/ProPublica piece by Alec MacGillis, "Who Turned My Blue State Red?" Referring to Maine's far-right governor, Paul R. LePage, MacGillis writes, "His [safety-net slashing] crusade has resonated with many in the state, who re-elected him last year." That is, we know and can write that LePage's crusade "resonated" *because* he was re-elected. And we believe that re-election was an accurate gauge of public "resonance" *because* we trust a vulnerable, unobservable, partisan-programmed, computerized vote-counting system.

A: If I had been sitting in a war room with a map and a timeline and a blueprint for long-term political dominion, I'd have kept zeroing in on 2010 as the year to make it all happen. There is of course much to be gained by capturing the White House but, if one's goal is *enduring political control,* the US House of Representatives and key swing-state legislatures and administrative posts become the natural strategic targets—especially in years ending with a "zero," in which the crucial decennial (i.e., census-based) redistricting power is up for grabs.[65]

Taking over the US House and key statehouses in 2010 offered the alluring prospect—via the tactical powers of gerrymandering and administrative control of elections, as well as the enormous advantages of incumbency for both US House members and state legislators—of locking in GOP House and statehouse control for a minimum of a decade, virtually irrespective of any adverse trends in either demographics or public opinion. Maintaining House control (and a minimum of 41 Senators needed to sustain a filibuster) in turn would confront any Democratic President with political gridlock, while control of purple (i.e., swing-state) statehouses would permit

---

[65] Because US House seats must, by constitutional mandate, be proportioned to population, the decennial US Census generally results in a reapportionment of House seats allocated to different states and provides an opportunity for state legislatures to redraw congressional district boundaries—a process known, when undertaken for partisan political advantage, as gerrymandering. There are only very loose restrictions on congressional district geometry and, with the aid of "big data," including house-by-house voter profiles, it has become possible to gerrymander ever more precisely and ruthlessly, to great overall advantage.

The perfect gerrymander would create, from the same population pool, a few districts in which the opposing party would receive 100% of the votes and many districts in which your party would win each election by a small margin. The redistricting undertaken by the GOP after E2010 does not miss that ideal by much. Redistricting also affects state legislative districts, and proposals have been floated by the GOP to apportion *presidential* electoral votes by congressional district, effectively subjecting presidential politics to the gerrymander.

David Daley's 2016 book *RATF**KED: The True Story Behind the Plan to Steal America's Democracy* (https://www.amazon.com/dp/1631491628) examines E2010 as the critical election in a scheme known as REDMAP. Typically, even Daley, who delves deep into the cynicism behind REDMAP, cannot bring himself to question any of the shocking E2010 electoral results essential to its spectacular success.

systematic structural changes (passing restrictive Voter-ID and voter-qualification laws, breaking union power, exercising control of election administration and oversight) with profound impact on the electorate's composition and the electoral process itself.[66] All this was on the platter in 2010.

Recall as well that US House and state legislative elections are not individually exit-polled and that even pre-election polling for these contests is relatively sparse, so there are virtually no race-by-race baselines for forensic analysts to work from. There are a couple hundred key but essentially invisible contests scattered across the country that add up to the *aggregate* partisan victory responsible for cementing the overall political infrastructure of America in place. The *individual components* of the grand outcome receive virtually no media attention (even political junkies would have a hard time keeping in focus what is happening in Ohio-5th, Oregon-4th, Florida-13th, etc., let alone Wisconsin *State Senate*-9th!)[67] and the only forensic red flag is to be found in an anomalous *overall* statistical pattern, which likewise receives no media attention.

With the afterglow of Obama's 2008 triumph further reducing the scope and intensity of election protection efforts, the risk level associated with grand theft of E2010 was negligible, the reward was profound, the reward/risk ratio accordingly off the charts. And indeed E2010 was the election that ensured that Americans would have a choice between gridlock and right wing hegemony for years, if not decades, to come.

From the very beginning Election Year 2010 waved a succession of red flags that offered an indication of what was in store for November.

---

[66] See, e.g., Steven Yaccino and Lizette Alvarez, "New G.O.P. Bid to Limit Voting in Swing States," New York *Times*, 3/29/2014, http://www.nytimes.com/2014/03/30/us/new-gop-bid-to-limit-voting-in-swing-states.html.

[67] For readers interested in *trying*, I strongly recommend the excellent and fairly comprehensive www.ballotpedia.com website.

The January special election to fill the Senate seat of the late Ted Kennedy in Massachusetts was the first of them. The upset victory of Republican Scott Brown over Democrat Martha Coakley served to put the Tea Party on the map, eliminate the Democrats' 60-vote filibuster-proof Senate majority, and kindle expectations for a big move to the right in November.

Why was this key election suspect? For starters, there was every incentive in the world to rig Coakley-Brown and every opportunity in the world to get away with it. There were no exit polls (itself very strange for a statewide contest with such important implications), no equipment spot checks, no audits, not a single officially-sanctioned handcount to verify any optical scanner tabulation, and not a single optical scanner memory card examined for malicious code (e.g., the +X/-X zero-counter scheme introduced earlier). If in fact the vendor corporations, or any insiders or hackers with access to the programming or distribution processes, had chosen to serve a private political agenda rather than the public trust, there would be nothing in the official processes of voting, vote counting, and election certification to indicate that such a breach had occurred. Thus it was an election that could have been stolen with virtually zero risk to yield an enormous reward.

But was it? We will never *know* because the actual ballots were never excavated (from the bins at the bottom of the optical scanners) to be counted and compared with the machine counts,[68] and all have long since been destroyed.

---

[68] An attempt was made at such an excavation, when the organization MassVOTE, using Massachusetts Public Records Law, persuaded a town clerk from the Worcester suburb of Shrewsbury to allow a hand recount of the ballots from a single precinct to take place. The (Democratic) Secretary of State, rather than supporting an extension of the investigation, immediately sent letters to all city and town elections officials strictly forbidding them to follow suit. See http://massvote.org/2010/09/massvote-conducts-first-ever-independent-audit-of-massachusetts-voting-machines/.

We were presented with a seismic result with no observable evidence to support it. It could have been legitimate and it could equally well have been a cheap trick conjured in the darkness of cyberspace. So forensic analysts looked at the only evidence that *was* available—the votes of the 71 jurisdictions that counted their ballots in public by hand.[69] They found that Coakley *won* in these jurisdictions by a margin of 3%, while Brown won by 5% where the optical scanners did the counting in secret. The chance of this 8% total disparity occurring if the handcounts had been distributed randomly around the state was infinitesimal, one in hundreds of billions. But analysts recognized that the handcounts were not randomly distributed and that handcount and optical scanner jurisdictions represented discrete constituencies. Perhaps the handcount communities where Coakley won were more Democratic or had a more Democratic voting history, or perhaps they were clustered in a part of the state where Coakley was more popular.

Analysts looked at each of these "benign" explanations in turn, along with others involving such factors as advertising expenditures broken down by media market, and found that none of them held water. The handcount jurisdictions were more *Republican* by voter registration; they had voted in exact congruence with the optical scanner jurisdictions in the previous *two* US Senate races, which were noncompetitive and thus not targets for rigging; and they had given Coakley a *lower* percentage than the optical scanner jurisdictions in her only previous statewide race. Granted Coakley, thinking she was a shoo-in, ran a very lackluster campaign; granted there was a surge of enthusiasm and a big influx of money from the right, making a tight (and therefore riggable) race out of a blowout. But those factors— which would have had the same impact on voters *regardless of how their votes were tabulated*—do not explain why some 65,000 handcount voters, shown to be to the *right of a random sample*, voted so differently from (i.e., to the *left* of) the voters who voted on optical scanners. That remains entirely without explanation, unless one is

---

[69] See http://electiondefensealliance.org/files/BelieveIt_OrNot_100904.pdf, included as Study IV in Chapter VII below.

willing to consider electronic vote manipulation. Indeed, with every other explanation examined and ruled out by analysts, *only the method of vote tabulation appeared to explain what happened in Massachusetts.*

Another red flag waved a few months later over South Carolina. In the Democratic primary for the nomination to oppose incumbent Tea Party favorite Jim DeMint for re-election to the United States Senate, a bona fide candidate (State Circuit Judge Vic Rawl) was the prohibitive favorite (so much so that no one even bothered polling) against a cipher (Alvin Greene) who made no campaign appearances, had no headquarters or website, was facing the prospect of indictment on pornography-related charges, and didn't appear to possess the personal funds needed for the election filing fee, which was paid anonymously on his behalf. The Rawl challenge to DeMint had gathered a good deal of steam, the Democrat's statewide popularity such that he had already closed to a threatening 7% in tracking polls against the powerful GOP incumbent in a very red state.

The primary was held in June and the votes were tallied on paperless touchscreen (aka "DRE") computers—the darkest of voting cyberspace. Amazingly, Greene won—*with 59% of the vote.* In spite of being known to almost literally no one, he officially received *100,362 votes.* In an eyebrow-raising footnote, after losing that November to DeMint by a margin of 34%, Greene, apparently encouraged by his performance against Rawl, entered another Democratic primary, this time for a seat in the South Carolina House of Representatives. He received 36 votes.[70]

In response to his baffling defeat, Rawl brought a challenge before the Democratic State Committee, which had original jurisdiction over the conduct of the primary election. Several election integrity experts testified in Rawl's favor, citing, among other glaring anomalies, huge

---

[70] For his part, the ultraconservative DeMint abruptly left the Senate in 2013, resigning to head The Heritage Foundation, a right-wing think tank.

disparities between early/absentee votes counted by optical scanner (where the voter-marked ballots would at least theoretically be available for human recount) and the at-poll paperless touchscreen tallies. The Committee responded favorably to Rawl's case throughout the hearing, then went into closed session and voted by a margin of 55 to 10 to reject the challenge and close the case without further investigation.[71]

After such appetizers it was not surprising to find a ptomaine-laced main course served up in November 2010. With exit polls thoroughly "discredited"—unless conducted anywhere else on the planet other than in the United States—it did not seem to matter that 16 out of 18 competitive US Senate elections were red-shifted, 11 out of 13 governorship elections were red-shifted, and in the US House elections the total red shift translated to 1.9 million votes, enough to reverse the outcome of dozens of targeted House races. The "Great Tea Party Sweep" was duly reported at face value.

Beyond the dramatic red shifts, though, was an extraordinary vote distribution pattern in the E2010 Republican takeover of the US House. The GOP took comfortable—and, as we shall see, enduring—control of the House by virtue of a massive net gain of 128 seats (or 29.4% of the 435-seat chamber), the greatest such pick-up in any midterm election going back to 1970, during which period the average pick-up was a mere 42 seats (9.7%). What was even more remarkable was that the GOP achieved this extraordinary national blowout without any remotely proportional sweep of the total vote. Its aggregate popular vote victory margin for House elections nationwide (as tabulated) was a very pedestrian 6.9%, yielding an off-the-charts

---

[71] The election and challenge form the core of the 2016 documentary feature film *I Voted?* directed by Jason Grant Smith and co-produced by Katie Couric. See also http://www.bradblog.com/?p=7902. For an eerily parallel shutdown of US House candidate Clint Curtis's 2006 electoral challenge, a refusal by the (Democratic-led) House Administration Committee to admit or consider evidence in the form of signed voter affidavits indicating that enough Curtis votes had been mistabulated (uncounted or shifted) to alter the election's outcome in his opponent's favor, see http://www.bradblog.com/?p=3947.

ratio of seat gain to vote margin.[72] By contrast, the *larger* Democratic popular vote margin of 8.2% in E2006 yielded a pickup of only 61 seats, less than half of the GOP's E2010 haul.[73] At some point this "result efficiency" stops being a matter of dumb luck: the minimization of losses (E2006) and maximization of victories (E2010) *relative to votes received* is exactly what would happen in election years where close races were being targeted for manipulation so that the well-targeted shift of a small percentage of the nation's votes produced a major shift in the overall pattern of wins and losses.

In order to achieve the particular coup that was E2010, the GOP had to confound well-set pre-election expectations governing the swath of 111 House elections considered competitive. Specifically, the pre-election consensus identified 40 contests in which Democrats were "expected to win narrowly," 42 contests which were projected as "tossups," and 29 contests in which Republicans were "expected to win narrowly," yielding 11 (40 minus 29) more contests in the Democratic column. What happened was this: the GOP won this overall Democratic-leaning "competitive" swath *by 25 seats*, 68 to 43. They took nine of the 40 contests where the Democrats had the edge, lost *none* of the 29 in their own column, and they took the "tossups" *30 to 12!*

---

[72] Note that this disproportionate ratio of electoral wins to aggregate vote margin could not be attributed to the vagaries of gerrymandering, as E2010 *preceded* the decennial redistricting and the majority of in-play districts were still, at the time of the election, gerrymandered to favor *Democrats*.

[73] The numbers look even stranger when one considers the information that Election Defense Alliance received, just prior to Election Day 2010 from a source with ties to the Rove operation, that California, because of the relatively stringent election protection protocols in place, would be "left alone." Sure enough, the E2010 GOP avalanche excluded California entirely: there was *zero* change in the distribution of the state's huge, 53-seat US House delegation. Which of course means that the 128-seat net gain was from an effective pool of only 382 seats (33.5%) rather than 435, fully a third of a chamber in which the vast majority of seats are recognized as "safe."

Those are some very uncanny numbers,[74] and they are quite the companion piece to the "Landslide Denied" weirdness we saw in E2006, the previous midterm election, with a far more unpopular sitting President, from which the Democrats managed to glean so much *less* than expected in the way of representation and governing power. Both E2006 and E2010 were also red-shifted relative to the national (i.e., aggregate) House exit polls, though House races, as we've seen, are not exit polled on an individual basis, making race-by-race statistical forensics all but impossible and thus keeping the level of scrutiny invitingly low. Indeed, aside from what journalist Bob Koehler once referred to as "the silent scream of numbers,"[75] these 120 or so competitive and critical US House races scattered across the national map were effectively *beyond scrutiny*—ultra-low-risk targets all, but delivering a trove of enduring political reward. Further still off the radar were the hundreds of *state* legislative races that collectively conferred game-changing decennial redistricting and election administration powers.

Republicans—mostly the far-right Republicans who emerged from the even-further-below-the-radar primaries—pretty much ran the table and are effectively lodged in place with, at minimum, the enduring power to obstruct at will nationally and legislate at will in a swath of suddenly "red" states. This is a baseline power that can only be augmented by any subsequent manipulations. And of course E2010 (along with E2002 and E2006 before it and E2014 after it) should inform our awareness and concern about *all* "off-year" and down-ballot elections. They are prime targets and, as E2010 teaches us, the gifts that keep on giving.

---

[74] The "N" is large enough to make these outcomes highly improbable as a matter of chance: the GOP had a 1% chance of winning 68 or more of the 111 competitive contests and less than one half of one percent (0.004) chance of winning 30 or more of the tossups.

[75] Koehler B: "The Silent Scream of Numbers" (4/14/2005), at http://commonwonders.com/society/the-silent-scream-of-numbers/.

Q: Haven't pre-election polls been generally accurate over the past couple of elections? If widespread election rigging on behalf of conservative candidates were happening, wouldn't there be a chronic disparity between the polls and the election results?

A: Yes, there *would* be such a disparity—a "red shift" from the pre-election polls to the election results—*if* the pollsters were continuing to employ the sampling methodology they used before the computerized voting era. And in fact pollsters were repeatedly embarrassed during the first few years of post-HAVA computerized voting when their polls kept getting elections *wrong*, consistently predicting outcomes to the left of the official results. Enter the Likely Voter Cutoff Model (LVCM), a sampling methodology introduced by the prestigious Gallup Polling operation. One by one the other pollsters, facing the imperative to get elections *right* or go out of business, followed suit and adopted the LVCM.

The LVCM comes in various tweakings but the classic model employed by Gallup uses a series of seven "screening" questions to determine which randomly-selected respondents will be included in, and which excluded from, the sample. The questions—which include such factors as stability of residence, political awareness, and prior electoral participation—operate disproportionately to screen out students, transients, renters, and the impoverished—in other words, more of the Democratic and left-leaning constituencies.[76]

It is true, or at least an article of faith, that these constituencies generally have lower rates of voting than do wealthier, whiter, home-owning constituencies, but their rates of voting *are not zero; in fact, they are a long way from zero.* Assigning such respondents a 0%

---

[76] See Simon J: *The Likely Voter Cutoff Model: What Is So Wrong with Getting It Right?* http://electiondefensealliance.org/files/TheLVCM_0.pdf; see also, with props for being transparent, http://www.gallup.com/poll/143372/Understanding-Gallup-Likely-Voter-Models.aspx for Gallup's explanation of its model, and http://www.huffingtonpost.com/2012/10/09/gallup-poll-likely-voters_n_1950951.html for its potent effect.

chance of voting by eliminating them from the otherwise random sample, when a significant percentage of these respondents will in fact wind up casting votes, has the effect of skewing the sample sharply to the right. And, because the pollster can choose how many "incorrect" answers to the screening questions will disqualify the respondent from inclusion in the poll's sample, *the LVCM operates effectively as a tunable, right-skewing fudge factor*—a mathematically unjustifiable sampling model that mysteriously keeps getting highly competitive and significant elections (which of course are the logical targets for both polling *and* rigging) "right," thereby keeping individual pollsters and the polling industry as a whole in business.

The pollster's job, as they see it, is to do whatever is necessary to generate accurate predictions of election outcomes (fair or foul), not to *question* those outcomes. Thus pre-election polling can, without a trace of malice on the part of the pollsters, become part of a corrupted feedback loop beginning with rigged votecounts, and so become progressively more corroded and less useful as a baseline for verifying electoral outcomes.

The LVCM often "kicks in" a month or two prior to elections (as the likelihood of voting is thought to become more measurable and pollsters alter their methodologies accordingly), at which time Republican and/or mainstream candidates get a "bump" in the polls often mistaken for true momentum. This artificial bump is often seen to alter race dynamics and outcomes as voters respond positively to the perceived momentum shift. Conversely, some pollsters now use one or another version of the LVCM year-round. The effect of this full-time right-skewed polling via the LVCM has been to paint a false and distorted portrait of the American electorate, such that right-wing electoral triumphs like E2010, rather than being seen as shocking and suspect, seem instead to corroborate the poll-established "conservative" mood of the country.[77]

---

[77] Ironically, when in the run-up to E2012 certain pollsters moved *away* from the conventional seven-question LVCM screening approach (not in an effort to restore

Q: What about the exit polls as a baseline?

A: Exit polls avoid entirely the vexing question of whether the respondents included in the poll results actually wound up casting a vote. We know they voted (though whether that vote was honestly counted is another matter) because they are questioned, for the most part, immediately upon exiting their polling place.[78] The accuracy of exit polls is such that they are relied upon around the world, often with the sanction of the United States government, as one of the principal validators of elections.[79] Exit poll-votecount disparities have, in elections from the Ukraine to Peru, spurred official investigations of electoral fraud and indeed several electoral "re-dos."

Not so in America. In America, final exit polls *always* match the votecounts with what appears to be uncanny precision. They do so

---

methodological purity but simply because voters would too often hang up on telephone robo-polls that included too many preliminary questions), causing their polls to edge Democratic, there was an outcry from the pundit chorus on the right about the rash of "left-skewed" polls. Gallup, known along with Rasmussen for their consistent lean to the right, set things straight with an LVCM poll that appeared to show, for those unaware of the methodological prestidigitation, a sudden Romney surge of nearly 10% in early October.

Poll-bashing is a favorite pre-election sport of both the Right and the Left (see, e.g., Giokaris J: "Presidential Polls 2012: Skewed Polling and Biased Media Coverage . . ." at http://www.policymic.com/articles/15219/presidential-polls-2012-skewed-polling-and-biased-media-coverage-give-obama-false-advantage-over-romney). The roiling arguments about methodology leave many—right, left, and center—dismissing the polls altogether as chimerical and, again ironically, awaiting the actual election results—unobservable, unverifiable, *more faith-based than the polls*—for the "truth."

[78] With the expansion of early and absentee voting, some "exit" polling must now be done via telephone, with the screening question being some variation of "Did you in fact cast a vote other than at your polling place in today's election?"

[79] In the US, prior to the advent of computerized voting, the problem with the exit polls was that they were accurate enough that networks took to calling even close elections well prior to poll closing times, which of course had a negative impact upon turnout. A deal was struck to withhold exit poll results until after the polls had closed in the state in question. There was neither legislation nor regulation involved, merely a 'gentleman's agreement" on the part of the networks, one which appears to be slipping, as pre-poll closing exit poll results have begun to be posted on media websites; see, e.g., https://twitter.com/nytgraphics/status/697246344038256642 for 6:30 pm posting of NH exit poll crosstabs by NYT[imes] Graphics on Feb. 9, 2016.

because they are *forced* to match the votecounts, "adjusted" (this is the term of art) to virtual congruence with the votecounts on the theory that any disparity between the exit polls and the votecounts *must* stem from the inaccuracy of the exit polls, and "correcting" that "inaccuracy" will make the exit polls more useful for the kind of post-mortem academic analysis that keeps our pundits in such high demand (e.g., "How important was the economy to 35-to-49 year-old males who voted Republican?").[80]

But adjusting the exit polls toward congruence with the votecounts requires (in theory at least) some votecounts to work with. So immediately after the polls close, when there are as yet only a smattering of votecounts available, the first posted exit polls reflect (again in theory) primarily the actual responses of those polled, weighted to the pollsters' best estimate of the demographic composition of the electorate.[81] It is those exit polls—which we refer to as "unadjusted," though there is growing reason to believe that partial votecounts made available before poll closing are being used to begin the "adjustment" process *prior* to first public posting, thus

---

[80] Lurking behind this explanation for the exit poll adjustment process is a more unsettling concern. In the words of the late Warren Mitofsky, known as the "father" of exit polling: "In a democracy, it's the orderly transfer of power that keeps the democracy accepting the results of elections. If it drags on too long, there's always a suspicion of fraud." (personal email correspondence).

[81] Weighting is necessary because, although we could wish for the mathematical precision of a perfectly random sample, the reality is that there are several non-random factors affecting the exit poll sample: so-called "clustering," which refers to sending interviewers to representative precincts rather than randomly throughout the state; selection bias, the possibility that interviewers will favor certain potential respondents over others; and response bias, the greater or lesser proclivity of certain sets of selected respondents to refuse participation in the poll.

Exit pollsters measure each of these metrics carefully and factor this data into their weighting of responses. If, for example, the response rate of an identifiable group (e.g., a certain race, age group, or gender) is below or above average, the responses from that group will be upweighted or downweighted accordingly.

A great deal of historical data and pattern analysis is brought to bear upon this process. It is not perfect but it has led, in the case of contests where there are *not* grounds for suspecting manipulation (e.g., noncompetitive or unusually well-protected races), to consistently good agreement (i.e., within the stated margin of error) between exit poll results and votecounts.

narrowing any disparities—that give us what is usually our first glimpse of the "red shift," the exit poll-votecount disparity that would be so damning were it to appear anywhere else on Earth other than in our country.[82]

When the votecounts for competitive and significant elections come out to the right of the exit polls, as they so often do, an explanation of some sort has to be provided. Mere exit poll "inaccuracy" will not suffice, as that would lead to misses in *both* directions, not the unilateral pattern that continues to emerge. And since, because this is America, *the votecounts cannot be questioned*, the "explanation" that has had to be ginned up is that the exit polls chronically and consistently oversample Democrats. This would be comforting—if only it were true. Putting aside for a minute that it would be passing strange for a group of polling experts at the height of their profession—fanatical about pattern analysis and error correction, trying their damnedest to get it right and with a batch of corrective tools at their disposal—to keep making *the same error* in state after state and year after year, the fact is that we have examined exit poll samples from the six biennial elections 2004-2014 (the E2002 exit polls were so far "off" that they were withheld from the public entirely; E2012 will be examined in the next chapter) and found *zero evidence* of such a left skew.[83]   In comparing the first-posted, ostensibly unadjusted exit poll samples to *every other measure of the electorate*,

_____

[82] Because these "unadjusted" exit poll numbers disappear *forever*, often within *minutes* of appearing on network Election Night websites, analysts must preserve them for forensic use in the form of screenshots. In E2004, when an apparent server glitch allowed the unadjusted numbers to remain up for hours rather than minutes (until after midnight EST), I was able to print out (I didn't yet know how to screen-capture) a great deal of unadjusted data (most states and the national exit poll with full crosstabs). I naively and erroneously assumed that thousands of similar data captures were being made around the country and the globe but, with election integrity activism still in its infancy and as yet no general understanding of the importance of unadjusted exit poll data, I discovered by the early morning hours that I was in sole possession of this data, which, once released and analyzed, became the initial basis for the questioning and challenging of the E2004 presidential votecount.

[83] See, e.g., Simon J, O'Dell B: *Landslide Denied: Exit Polls vs. Vote Count 2006, Demographic Validity of the National Exit Poll and the Corruption of the Official Vote Count* (2007), http://electiondefensealliance.org/files/LandslideDenied_v.9_071507.pdf.

including census and registration data as well as multiple academic surveys,[84] we have found neutral or, more frequently, right-skewed exit poll samples in every case.

We believe a major reason for this is that those valuable first-posted, ostensibly unadjusted exit polls are weighted in large part to demographics drawn from the *adjusted* exit polls of prior elections— because it is the adjusted polls that are deemed "accurate." How were those prior polls adjusted? Inevitably to the right to match red-shifted votecounts, and when you adjust the exit poll *results* to the right, the exit poll's *demographics* (what the electorate looked like) are carried along for the ride.[85] So a sample that was initially 39% Democratic to 35% Republican, when "adjusted" (i.e., reweighted) to make the "who did you vote for?" numbers match the votecounts, might now become 37% Democratic, 37% Republican.[86] And that then

---

[84] See, e.g., American National Election Studies (ANES), affiliated with the University of Michigan, at http://electionstudies.org/index.htm.

[85] The adjustment, or "forced weighting," process involves the imposition of a final weighting factor, keyed to the candidate-preference results, on the existing weighted data.

If, for example, a state's final percentage for candidate Bush were 55% but his weighted exit poll percentage were 50%, the adjustment would upweight Bush's exit poll results by 10% (1.10 x .50 = .55). This upweighting factor would be applied not just to the "who did you vote for?" question but to every question on the questionnaire of every respondent who indicated he/she voted for Bush, including of course all the demographic questions. Thus, if there were 1000 respondents who indicated they had voted for Bush, and 700 of these indicated that they were "Republican" voters, following the adjustment process, that number would become 770 (700 x 1.10), and the percentage of "Republican" voters among the exit poll respondents (and, if we trust the votecount and therefore the adjustment process, among the voters) would increase accordingly.

This reweighting would also affect such measures as gender, age, race, income, etc.; the strength of the effect would depend on the degree to which the particular measure was correlated with candidate preference (e.g., gender would likely be less correlated than party-ID). Respondents whose candidates' votecounts came in below their exit poll percentages would of course be downweighted, along with all the demographic measures of their questionnaires.

[86] This is in fact what occurred in the 2004 Presidential election nationwide (and also in Ohio). A 4% demographic red shift may not look like much but it was enough to provide the "winning" margin for Bush and to give the GOP what amounted to a 4% exit poll handicap in the *next* election, which of course serves from a forensics

becomes, in effect, the "truth" about the electorate and the new standard for weighting future exit polls (which are then further "adjusted" if even that right-skewed weighting fails to match the votecounts).

Taking this all into account, when, as is generally the case, the exit polls are "off" such that the votecounts come out to their right, while it is clear that the exit poll sample is at worst neutral (or, more likely, right-skewed), it provides strong evidence of *vote mistabulation.*

That evidence becomes even stronger when we have the data available to perform *second-order comparisons.* A first-order comparison would consist of measuring the disparity between exit polls (or any other baseline) and votecounts in either a single election or a series of elections. When the disparities are large (near or beyond the margin of error) and in the same direction in a significant proportion of the contests examined, it is possible to calculate some very large numbers representing the odds of the set of such disparities occurring—say "one in 4.24 billion." This certainly *looks* impressive, and the mathematics are correct, but the counter-argument would be that there are difficult-to-quantify factors not impounded in the mathematical margin of error—with exit polls, such factors would be clustering and selection and response bias—that account for much of the disparity pattern. In meeting such arguments, even a very impressive probability number like one in some-odd billion can have limited value. Perhaps the exit pollsters simply screwed up.

A second-order analysis finds a related series of contests with which to compare the red-flag series. In a sense we are looking at the disparity of disparities. A classic example has presented itself in the presidential primaries of 2016. It will be analyzed in greater detail in Chapter V, but the essence of it is that the Democratic primaries exhibited large exit poll-votecount disparities in state after state, while in the

standpoint to fully negate a would-be 4% red shift and thereby *fully cover* any future manipulation of that magnitude.

Republican primaries the exit polls were essentially spot-on. It becomes much harder to simply dismiss the exit pollsters as incompetent or their methodology as flawed when it performed brilliantly through a whole series of elections in one party's nomination battle but kept over-representing the vote of the same candidate in state after state in the other party's nomination battle. Another example is the comparison of disparities between votecounts and polls interviewing the same set of respondents regarding competitive and noncompetitive contests.   The noncompetitive contests, unlikely targets for manipulation, serve as a control.[87] When we find radically different patterns of disparities in a series of competitive versus noncompetitive contests, that is a glaring red flag that can't be explained away by exit poll skeptics.

All that being said, the debate over exit polls as absolute *proof* of votecount fraud is likely to remain inconclusive.   Neither side is permitted access to the raw data (held to be the property of the pollster and its major network clients) that might be helpful in resolving the dispute.[88] Nor, in the final analysis, are exit polls, or any other form of indirect measurement, the *best evidence* of voter intent and public will. But can we say that votecounts emerging from the

---

[87] See, e.g., Simon J, et al: *Fingerprints of Election Theft: Were Competitive Contests Targeted?* (2007), presented as Study III in Chapter VII and at http://electiondefensealliance.org/files/FingerprintsOfElectionTheft_2011rev_.pdf.

[88] Two reasons have been given for withholding this data: reluctance to identify exit-polled precincts out of concern that might give rise to an effort to influence voters at those sites; and protection of the confidentiality of respondents which, it is claimed, could be compromised by a release of the raw data.

Neither reason holds any water. Regarding the first, if the pollsters return to the same set of precincts in successive elections, then any potential "influencers" will know what precincts to target whether precinct-identifying raw data is released or not. If they change locations from one election to the next, then the post-election release of raw data will not tip anyone off for that or subsequent elections.

Regarding the second, forensic analysts have requested a *very limited* set of raw data: candidate preference responses and the most basic demographics (age, race, gender). There is *zero* risk that from such a data set, any of the respondents (who fill out exit poll questionnaires anonymously) could be individually identified.

When such specious reasons are given for the withholding of data, it should raise our level of suspicion about the actual reason.

fraud-inviting darkness of cyberspace are *better* evidence? The best evidence, *indeed the only truly reliable evidence,* resides on the voter-marked paper ballots (where such exist), and it is only from an examination of that evidence—i.e., a public and observable count of those ballots—that a reliable conclusion can be drawn about what, collectively, the voting public intended.

Q: What about *Citizens United* and the influence of Big Money? Wouldn't that explain the recent and future electoral success of the Right?

A: If, having set a goal of "perpetual rule," you are going to rig a lot of elections over a long period of time, at some point it will become noticeable that the pendulum isn't swinging freely, that not only are *individual* election results "surprising" but far too many of these surprises are in the same direction and the overall *pattern* defies explanation. The pendulum is seen to swing, but oddly and off-center, as if there were a magnet hidden in the wings stage-right. We have at least flirted with that point in our politics: witness a parade of articles in the media straining to explain why, as one put it, "conservatives always win."[89]

This is of course the hustler's challenge: *figuring out the maximum that can be taken while still keeping the mark in the game.* The smartest rigger would of course let the pendulum swing just enough to keep the game going. But the game becomes a whole lot easier if some blanket explanation can be found such that both individual election results and the whole pervasive pattern no longer seem so bizarre. This is where *Citizens United* and the Big Money factor come in: if it can be established as conventional wisdom that Big Money decides elections, the rigger's tracks are effectively covered with the readily available glut of corporate cash that *Citizens United* has swept into the electoral game. It matters not that there is likely a powerful

---

[89] Brewer J: "The REAL Reason Conservatives Always Win," Common Dreams (6/22/2012), at https://www.commondreams.org/view/2012/06/22-12.

law of diminishing returns such that Big Money ultimately runs out of steam when it comes to buying/influencing voters. All that matters is the established *perception* that Big Money wins elections.

Thus, in the critical Wisconsin Governor's recall election early in 2012—where exit polls revealed a dead heat and also established that *virtually all voters had made their minds up well before the late surge of Big Money into the state*—the Republican Walker's "easy" 7% victory was nonetheless credited by the vast majority of pundits (David Brooks being a notable exception) to the 8-to-1 ratio of expenditure on Walker's behalf relative to his Democratic opponent. Certainly *Citizens United* and the Big Money advantage of the Right will, *even where ineffective in fact*, provide ample *cover* for rigged elections going forward.

Q: Almost all airtime for hand-wringing has been devoted to the *overt* schemes to win elections—Big Money, voter suppression, "Vote Wednesday" robocalls, etc. In discussing *Citizens United* just now, you seem to be suggesting that these are just red herrings. Could you clarify?

A: If the minority is going to gain power in a democracy, and then *retain* power in spite of rabidly pursuing policies that operate to the clear detriment of the majority, that minority is going to have to pull out all the stops.[90] Rove's sought-after "permanent majority" (or even permanent gridlock—holding just enough power to permanently block the other side's agenda and vision) requires an *array* of tactical gambits ranging from deceptive messaging to corporate Super-PAC money inundation, to voter suppression (through a sub-array of tactics ranging from discriminatory Voter ID laws, to selectively scrubbing

---

[90] Of course the smaller and more extreme the minority, the more suspect its electoral seizure and maintenance of political power. But a nation that counts its votes unobservably, and entrusts that counting process to radically partisan corporations, should not be surprised to discover that its obituaries for a radical and grossly unpopular splinter such as the Tea Party and a "washed-up" strategist like Karl Rove were premature.

voter rolls, to caging[91] and other forms of voter intimidation, to targeted misinformation, such as making "Vote Wednesday" robocalls and sending "Vote Wednesday" flyers to likely supporters of the candidate marked for defeat).

Each of these tactics takes a certain toll on what we would recognize as a fair and ethical electoral process and, to the extent that they are practiced primarily by the forces of the minority, each serves to reduce the electoral margin that the majority would otherwise enjoy. I agree that they are all pernicious and they are all ugly. But they are all *overt* and they are all also *limited* in their bottom-line effect. When we examine what this new century's election outcomes would have been in the *absence* of the pervasive "red shift" (which, when exit poll-based, is independent of these overt tactics), it tells us that all these overt tactics combined are insufficient to produce the magnetic-pendulum gridlock we have been experiencing, let alone Rove's "permanent Republican majority." But what these ugly overt tactics *do* achieve is to narrow the prevailing majority-minority political gap sufficiently that the *covert* tactic of computerized rigging can deliver the electoral *coup de grace* while managing to pass the smell test. So it is almost certainly a case not of either-or but of both-and.[92]

The overt tactics also serve as a kind of misdirection, distracting would-be election integrity guardians from the decisive covert game. As a voter and election integrity advocate I have been bombarded with literally hundreds of institutional emails and letters presenting

---

[91] Caging involves turning up at the polls with long lists of likely opposing voters and using them to challenge each individual's right to vote. Generally, the result of such challenges, undertaken almost exclusively by right-wing operatives, is to force the voter to submit a "provisional" ballot, and the reality is that many, if not most, provisional ballots go uncounted. See generally, Palast G: *Billionaires & Ballot Bandits; How to Steal an Election in 9 Easy Steps.* New York: Seven Stories Press, 2012; http://www.amazon.com/Billionaires-Ballot-Bandits-Steal-Election/dp/1609804783.

[92] The history and working of these combined "strip and flip" tactics are well-presented in Bob Fitrakis's and Harvey Wasserman's *The Strip and Flip Selection of 2016: The Five Jim Crows & Electronic Election Theft*, CICJ Books, 2016 (https://www.amazon.com/dp/B01GSJLW0I).

frenzied alarums about *Citizens United*, voter ID, voter intimidation, false-info robocalls and flyers, etc. Not a single one of these alerts and calls to remedial action is willing to contemplate a still darker possibility. None seems to have asked the obvious question: Is there really a bright ethical line between making "Vote Wednesday" robocalls to the supporters of the candidate targeted for defeat and simply taking the far more efficient approach of setting the zero-counters on, say, 50 memory cards to +100/-100, thereby undetectably shifting 10,000 net votes and stealing yet another seat in the United States House of Representatives or a key state legislature? Once the tactical means are embraced, the sky really is the limit—anything that can pass the stuffed-nose smell test.

And yet the ACLU, People For the American Way, and of course the Democratic Party (to pick on just a few of the many), recognize and decry the robocall exploits, while the yet more sinister prospect of computerized rigging is beyond the pale and hence entirely ignored. Since there is no contesting the manifest vulnerability, as established by experts in study after study, it must be the bright ethical line that so reassures these guardians of democracy—that is, *It Could Never Happen Here.*

Q: What does it take to know that an election has been honest, that the votes have been counted reasonably accurately given the large numbers involved?

A: It takes an open, transparent, and observable process. There can't be any point in the counting process where the magician disappears behind the curtain, even for a few seconds, because a few seconds is all it takes to change the outcome of an election inside a computer.

Apologists for the current computerized counting system will point to all the aspects of "openness:" how observers can be present at the polls, how the machines are "certified" and put through a sample ballot test at some point before the election, how when opscans are used all the actual ballots can be counted if there is any question, how with VVPAT (i.e., "paper-trail") DREs the voter gets to see *a receipt*!

What they will conveniently leave out of that reassuring presentation are the crucial concealed passages along the pipeline, and the fact that *a system is only as transparent as its most concealed point.* A computer can without difficulty be programmed to pass any pre-election test with flying colors and still shift votes at the time of the actual election. You can deploy an army of observers at the polling places and central tabulation locations and none of them will be able to see the actual count (or miscount) inside the computers. Where opscans are used, the reality is that the actual ballots are virtually *never* examined: mere citizens have no right to do so and candidates, where they might have such a right (and noting that it is generally made prohibitively expensive at precisely the stage at which candidates have emptied their campaign chests), are under enormous pressure not to exercise it, lest they be labeled "sore losers" and so torpedo their future political careers. Certain states, following Florida's lead, have gone even further and outright banned hand counting to verify the machine counts. Finally, touchscreen computers with so-called "paper trails" can easily be programmed to print a vote for "A" on the "receipt" while recording a vote for "B" in the official count, and these receipts for digitally cast votes are even less likely than actual voter-marked ballots to ever see the light of day.

An open and observable process would entail visible counting that could be witnessed by representatives of all candidates and the public at every stage. There would be, *as there once was,*[93] a "tabulation tree," with the precinct counts observed directly and publicly posted, and the subsequent aggregations at the town, county, and state levels capable of being reconciled (the process is simple addition) from the

---

[93] It is all too easy to forget that, as a nation, *we have done this before*—indeed, throughout most of our history. The fact that we have grown more populous does not much alter the equation, as the need for and supply of vote counters expand correlatively and remain proportional.

lowest level to the highest. No observation or vigilance will ever insure a "perfect" count, but the minor inaccuracies, the "noise," in the system will break evenly, only extremely rarely affecting electoral outcomes, and those so close that full recounts would be undertaken as a matter of course. Under an observable counting process there would be no opportunity to, in effect, perpetrate a rolling coup and steal a nation.

Q: What about audits?

A: Post-election audits, for the most part, constitute a well-intentioned effort to make vote counting pseudo-observable by requiring a second count of a select portion of the computer-counted ballots for verification of the initial count. If it is well-designed, scrupulously executed, and mandates a hand count rather than simply running ballots through the computer a second time, an audit can expose a computerized fraud and thus can also operate as a powerful fraud deterrent.

The question naturally arises what level of risk a prospective election rigger will tolerate before deciding that stolen electoral victories are not worth the risk of exposure (leaving aside the matter of punishment, exposure would presumably result in reform to a much more secure system). Of course we know of no election riggers who have come forward to discuss their thought processes and calculations, but it is hard to imagine that an enterprise of such pith and moment is undertaken without a rather fine-tuned rational calculation of risk and reward. Karl Rove has spoken of "perpetual rule" and it would seem that a reward of that magnitude would be worth a great expenditure of effort and resource as well as a fair amount of risk.

National-grade election riggers, however well-compensated financially or radical in their belief system, are nonetheless rational actors who can be deterred by high-risk threat of exposure but who also almost certainly have the resources and determination to find and exploit any path left deliberately or inadvertently open. For an audit protocol to be effective as a deterrent, it must set up high-risk roadblocks on all such paths.

Specifically, it must count enough ballots to have a decent mathematical chance of detecting any outcome-altering manipulation; the selection of such ballots must be random and not telegraphed in advance; the secure chain of custody of the ballots must be strictly maintained (i.e., they can't be left, as they so often are, stacked up in some unlocked storeroom, warehouse, or garage); the audit design must be sensitive enough to pick up deliberate manipulations and at the same time selective enough not to throw red flags at incidental "noise" in the system; and failed audits must lead, in a prescribed sequence, to effective remedial action.

All of these requirements are necessary and none of them is trivial. Consider for instance the logistical challenge of selecting the counts to be audited and then immediately proceeding with the audit without allowing any opportunity for the swapping out of ballots in locations now revealed to the riggers to be "hot." In *practice* most of the audits we have thus far seen undertaken have failed on one or more of these counts.[94]

---

[94] Perhaps most egregious was Ohio 2004, where precincts were cherry-picked with the guidance of the equipment vendors, who also provided "cheat sheets" to election administrators to help ensure that the audit counts would square with the official computer counts (see http://www.thelandesreport.com/ConyersReport.htm at p. 81). Recounts have also been plagued with such irregularities and are rife with opportunities to alter or swap ballots to erase evidence of computer mistabulation.

When ballots are counted in a recount, a days-later audit, or even on Election Night at central counting stations that require the ballots to be transported, continual public observation is lost and there is no way to be certain that the ballots being counted are the same ones as were cast. Counting outside the precinct (i.e., central tabulation), delayed audits, and recounts would all require a radical (and expensive) tightening of chain-of-custody protections to qualify as observable counts.

It remains an open question within the ranks of election integrity advocates to what extent a fully paper-based system with a mandated and robust audit protocol would provide sufficient public "observation" (albeit indirect) to meet the standard of observable counting. While robust audits, especially Risk-Limitation Audits

About half the states have adopted audit schemes of widely varying strength and efficacy.[95] Proposed federal audit legislation, most notably a bill introduced in 2007 by Rep. Rush Holt of New Jersey, has been assailed for its weakness and has in fact bitterly divided election integrity advocates between those who believe "half-a-loaf" incremental progress is the best to be hoped for and those who see such "progress" as ineffective to stop rigging and falsely reassuring to boot. New legislation, incorporating several improvements over Holt's bill, is currently in the drafting stage as part of the proposed VOTE Act.

My own position relative to audits has evolved over the years and is now one of support for well-designed audit protocols, particularly for the Risk-Limiting Audit (RLA), put forward by several statisticians,[96] in which the extent or magnitude of the audit essentially varies in inverse proportion to the size of the first-count margin of an election: closer finishes draw bigger audits.

---

conscientiously executed, could indeed serve as an effective deterrent to the rigging enterprise, we have seen in practice that audits themselves often have been ineffectual or corrupted. That laxity would have to change dramatically.

It is vital to recognize that if the incentive to manipulate a votecount in order to capture or hold office is X, the incentive to *conceal* that manipulation in the very rare cases where a red flag has been raised and some sort of investigation has been undertaken is 1000X, orders of magnitude greater. At stake at that point is not merely the office in question but the threat of exposure of the entire fraudulent enterprise and the potential "death penalty" remedy of serious reform of the vote counting system to effectively end the man-behind-the-curtain, faith-based process that currently holds sway.

[95] See Verified Voting Foundation, Rutgers Law School Newark Constitutional Litigation Clinic, Common Cause: "Counting Votes 2012: A State by State Look at Voting Technology Preparedness," at http://countingvotes.org/sites/default/files/CountingVotes2012_Final_August2012.pdf (pp. 14 - 16 and *passim*).

[96] I give particular credit here to Howard Stanislevic, Kathy Dopp, and Philip Stark, though many others have been involved in the application of risk-limitation principles to the votecount process. In 2006 my colleague Bruce O'Dell and I proposed an alternative approach, known as Universal Ballot Sampling, which entailed an observable human count of one of every ten ballots, wherever and however cast, making for a very simple and easily executed protocol and offering a very high level of precision for verifying machine counts (see http://electiondefensealliance.org/files/New_UBS_811Update_061707.pdf).

The RLA has much to commend it and, if faithfully executed, is not by any means easy to thwart or evade. The essence of the RLA's rationale is that it is harder to find and catch a tiny fish than a big one *and we don't really care about dead fish of any size.* A "dead fish" is any mistabulation that does *not* alter the outcome of an election. With all respect to the oft-repeated mantra "count every vote as cast," that is not a realistic standard for major elections. Vote counting, like any other operation dealing with large numbers and multiple sub-operations, is *not a perfect process and 99.99% of the time does not have to be.* We can and are obliged to tolerate a mistabulated (or misinterpreted) vote here or there; machines and humans will not always see eye to eye on every single ballot. *That is not, however, how elections are stolen.* We can't afford to get bogged down in disparities of one or two votes per thousand, unless the election outcome is exceedingly close and those disparities—assuming they were deliberate, cumulative, and unidirectional and so did *not* cancel each other out—could make the difference.

This is the "mindset" of the RLA. It grows more teeth, or drops more hooks, when the fish is both alive and small because those fish are harder to catch. If, for example, the official margin of a race is 40%, for any rig to have been *outcome altering* it would have had to shift a net of 20% of the votes, or at least one vote out of every five, from the loser to the winner; in other words, a *lot* of votes, a big fish. That magnitude of disparity (between opscan readouts and the voter-marked ballots contained within) is quite a sore thumb and easy to catch with even a tiny (say 0.5%) audit, assuming the precincts to be audited are not telegraphed in advance so that a clean-up team can get in there and substitute ballots.[97] Only if the margin is *close* could the theft of relatively *few* votes have altered the *outcome*: and that is when the RLA drops lots of hooks, so that even a small (but successful) rig is likely to be caught. You don't *need* a big, labor- and capital-

---

[97] RLAs are not statewide or jurisdiction-wide random samples; they are full counts of randomly sampled *precincts*, which work just fine as long as the selection process is real-time and not telegraphed in advance.

intensive audit for the vast majority of election contests; you don't need to waste resources in the name of elevating form over function.

One can imagine how huge a selling point that last sentence is to every rational and budget-constrained election administrator out there. And isn't that where we're at now: trying to get effective protocols adopted soon or sooner, before it all becomes academic?

I was initially an RLA skeptic but, upon examining its workings critically and carefully, I have come to recognize both the soundness of its theory and the practicality of its execution. It focuses specifically on what matters about elections: outcomes that reflect the collective majority/plurality intent of the electorate.[98] And it applies basic logic and very simple statistics (it's reducible to a single page with two columns: first-count margin and %-to-be-audited) to protect those outcomes. It also has a fighting chance of broad, even universal, adoption if election integrity advocates can get behind it and work *with* election administrators to make sure the protocols are sound in design and execution.

Q: I take it that you see Internet Voting as a step in the wrong direction?

A: It should come as no surprise that the vast majority of election integrity advocates view Internet Voting ("I.V.") as an anathema, not merely a step but a giant leap in the wrong direction. It also should come as no surprise that, despite a few notable successes in beating it

---

[98] For better or worse, the vast majority of US elections remain winner-take-all contests. There are, however, a few critical elections that are proportional in nature, a very recent example being the 2016 presidential primaries where, even in a noncompetitive state, the difference between a margin of, say, 35% and 40% might translate to a difference in delegates awarded to each candidate. The RLA would be inappropriate to such elections and a flat percentage audit recommended instead.

back, I.V. is spreading, having been adopted in one form or another in a growing number of states.[99]

I.V.'s seductions are the usual ones of convenience, speed, budgetary savings, and increased turnout (though obviously voters lacking internet access will be put at a serious disadvantage)—all taken one step further. We have already seen how hard it is to say no to that package of goodies and, viewed through the same rose-colored glasses that gave us HAVA and computerized voting in the first place, I.V. presents itself as something of a no-brainer: a logical extension of our technological capacity, making the chores of voting and vote counting still easier and cheaper. Given that the vast majority of us do everything *else* online, you can just about *taste* the inevitability of I.V.

So why fight it?   Because I.V. takes the fundamental hazard of *all* computerized voting—that we as citizens and voters haven't a clue about what the programmer is doing with our votes—and adds to it a gilded invitation to *outside* interference, as it is by now a given that virtually *nothing* that runs on the internet is immune to hacking, manipulation, and surveillance.[100]   I.V. drew a major security-based thumbs-down from the National Institute of Standards and Technology (NIST) in 2011[101] and white-hat hackers have had a field day demonstrating the flimsiness and easy penetrability of the security protocols of I.V. systems thought to be ready to roll.[102]

---

[99] Internet voting had been adopted for at least some class of voters (e.g., absentee, military) in over 30 U.S. states or territories as of May 2014.
See http://online.wsj.com/articles/pamela-smith-and-bruce-mcconnell-hack-the-vote-the-perils-of-the-online-ballot-box-1401317230?KEYWORDS=Hack+The+Vote.

[100] It would be hard to dispute that whatever protection there *is* on the internet these days derives less from impenetrable firewalls and encryptions than from simple "safety-in-numbers." There is so much data to steal and use, only so many sophisticated hackers, and only so much time, so that the odds that *your* scrap of data will wind up in their clutches are tolerably small. But of course this Russian-roulette mode of "protection" does not apply to intrinsically high-value targets such as election results. The hue and cry in 2016 is "The Russians are coming!" but it really could be anyone.

[101] See http://www.nist.gov/itl/vote/upload/NISTIR-7700-feb2011.pdf.

[102] See, e.g., the work of Harri Hursti and Alex Halderman, detailed at fns 2 and 3 to this chapter.

Nonetheless I believe that the fight against I.V. is less straightforward than some of my EI colleagues would have it. For one thing it is a delicate matter to oppose I.V. without seeming by inference to defend, or at least be resigned to, the woeful status quo (i.e., the opscans and DREs) that I.V. would be replacing. Drawn between I.V. and existing computerized voting, the line of battle slides still further away from our goal of an observable count.

It is also worth thinking about how the ridiculously insecure process of internet voting stacks up against the ridiculously insecure process of good old computerized voting. Two differences jump out at me. The first is that I.V. is a lot like what gangsters refer to as an "open city;" that is, given the ultimate vulnerability of all things internet, I.V. is something of a come-one-come-all cyber-arena, as opposed to the monopolistic fiefdom of a few partisan corporations dealing out discrete memory cards, to the programming of which they alone have access. The second is that, even to the unwashed, I.V. (unlike opscans and even DREs) is obviously and unmistakably *computerized* voting. The public will *get* what it is being asked to trust and every bigtime online hack headline, every CHANGE YOUR PASSWORD!!! alert, every chilling tale of identity theft, and every new revelation of surveillance-state snooping will chip away at that trust.[103] Embraced at first virtually without reservation, the internet environment and our safety in cyberspace are now objects of a growing queasiness, and there is no sign that full trust is likely to be restored any time soon.

The end result if I.V. is widely adopted? Who knows. But one can easily enough imagine a variety of I.V. meltdowns and disasters—

---

[103] As an example, I very recently had an experience that has become all too common: having placed an online order for a subscription to the *New York Times* at $286.00 for a year, I received a receipt notifying me that I would be billed for $286 + tax every *week*, or $16,098.94 for the year. As of this writing, I am still wrestling with customer service trying to figure out how to undo this computer "glitch." Of course, had 286 *votes* been magically transformed into 16,099 *votes* (or vice versa), there would have been no collective receipt to put anyone on notice to challenge or question the results. Not confidence inspiring.

ranging from intrinsic systemic glitches to white-hat hacks ("Mickey Mouse gets 4 billion votes!") to foreign interference—that would sharply focus attention on the vulnerabilities not just of I.V. but of *all* computerized vote counting. I'm thinking here of the principles of judo, where the momentum of an opponent's over-reach is used against him. One can imagine a backlash to the disasters of I.V. carrying us all the way back to an observable counting process. Meanwhile I.V. elections would likely be cyber free-for-alls, more or less equal-opportunity rigging, and to my eyes even *that* absurdity would be something of an improvement over the current state of affairs which, as we have seen, has been effectively one-sided.

I don't support internet voting. In fact, given the current and projected state of cyber-security, I am with my EI colleagues in thinking it is insane. But I also think that unless arguments made against I.V. nimbly pivot on public recognition of internet-related dangers to call *all* unobservable vote counting equally into question, we will, even if successful in blocking I.V., have done little more than to perpetuate an *equally insane* status quo.

Q: Given the recent revelations about NSA surveillance, along with other signs that American democracy is deteriorating irrespective of which party governs, would an honest vote counting system even matter anymore?

A: There was a brief glimpse during the Occupy movement of what public anger at American Systemic Injustice might come to if it found a way to assemble, to come out of its isolated private homes and apartments and shelters and cubicles into the public squares of the nation. It was a powerful image, and one that so shook America's rulers in their corporate and governmental corridors of power that they soon resorted to a federally-coordinated blitzkrieg to empty those squares and kill Occupy before it multiplied any further and before the Bastille was in any real danger.

One of the most important takeaways from the Occupy experience is the recognition of a previously hidden divide in the American body politic: that of the "99%" and the "1%." Throughout American history our enduring system of representative democracy has thrived on the two-party dialectic. Certainly for living generations, the vision we have of politics is that of the Democratic and Republican parties carrying the ark into battle for their relatively evenly matched constituencies, taking turns holding sway and advancing an agenda as the political pendulum swung.

That is still the image of American politics you'll see in the *New York Times* or on CNN: another sporting event really, presenting two venerable teams perennially butting heads somewhere around the 50-yard line, a never-ending political Super Bowl. It is easy enough, if you listen to the play-by-play announcers, not to notice a very important change in the game, a tectonic realignment of which Occupy began to give us a hint and which subsequent developments have confirmed. The battle that is coming to characterize The New American Century is that between the *Elites* (called "the 1%" by Occupy, but more accurately the corporate class that would replace democracy with its trappings, masking dominion) and *Everyone Else*. And this battle, as the 'treasonous' Edward Snowden brought so dramatically to our attention, is largely about *information*.

Knowledge is indeed power: in the case of the surveillance state, the power to intimidate, the power indeed to blackmail, the power to infiltrate and sabotage any perceived threat, stifle any organized or ultimately individual dissent. And the battle lines are indeed simple: a ruling elite, corporate and governmental, that is attempting to know as much as possible about you and me while seeing to it that we know as little as possible about them. Of course this is not unprecedented; history offers up its share of J. Edgar Hoovers. But The Information Age has turned a limited and rather selective battle into what amounts to *total war*, whether or not it is yet universally recognized as such. In a very real sense, in this war not over land or even treasure but over knowledge, *The Public* has become *The Enemy*.

The weapon that has been handing the ruling elites one victory after another in this war is *fear*, specifically fear of "terrorism" (though as an American you were several thousand times as likely to be killed by an American with a gun last year as by a terrorist[104]). With the ghastly and iconic images of planes puncturing towers and bodies leaping from fiery windows—precisely the "new Pearl Harbor" imagined in 1997 by right-wing think tank PNAC[105]—seared into every American's brain, and with Operation Iraqi Freedom-incubated ISIS reanimating those memories on what seems a weekly basis,[106] the surrender of privacy on every front becomes an easy sale. *Whatever it takes* to keep us mythically "safe" in a "war" rather brilliantly conjured to be without end.

Naturally the National Security Agency was not about to let *us* in on its various "legal"[107] spying schemes[108] and, when finally exposed by the

---

[104] A statistic which the Guardians of Our Safety have been quick to attribute to the effectiveness of their spying activities in keeping terrorism at bay. At first a dozen, then 20, then over 50 "terrorist plots" were foiled in 2014 alone, to hear them tell it on successive days after the Snowden bombshell hit, as a result of phone and email snooping by the NSA. Of course that is easy enough to say, and rather conveniently impossible to verify or challenge since all details are naturally "classified" and secret in the name of *security*.

[105] The Project for the New American Century (PNAC), a non-profit organization founded in 1997 by prominent Republican leaders, called for a transformation of America to exercise military total-spectrum dominance and unchallenged worldwide hegemony. The PNAC program in a nutshell: America's military must rule out even the possibility of a serious global or regional challenger anywhere in the world. PNAC's most important study noted that selling this plan to the American people would likely take *a long time*, "absent some catastrophic catalyzing event like a new Pearl Harbor," (PNAC, *Rebuilding America's Defenses*, 1997, p.51); see also https://en.wikipedia.org/wiki/Project_for_the_New_American_Century.

[106] "Operation Iraqi Freedom" was chosen to replace the awkward initial designation, "Operation Iraqi Liberation" ("O.I.L."), as the official code name of the Second Gulf War.

[107] Apologists from both parties have been quick to point out that a special (secret) court, the FISA Court, must approve NSA applications to tap your phone or email. In 2012 there were 1896 such applications, of which the FISA Court approved 1896. And they said DiMaggio's hit streak would never be broken!

treasonous Snowden, took great pains to reassure us that it's "only gathering data" and won't actually read our emails and listen in on our phone calls *unless it really feels it needs to*. For example if you were trying to organize the next Occupy movement, or threatening the "eco-terrorism" of opposing Monsanto, getting serious about a third-party or independent challenge to the D-R power duopoly, or perhaps organizing to "liberate" our ballots from their opscans so that they could be counted observably in public.

This is the *bone structure* of The New American Century, whatever its face and skin may look like. Corporate America has a stranglehold on *both* major parties; the corporate-owned MSM is cheerfully along for the ride; threatening opposition movements like Occupy are infiltrated and, where necessary, obliterated. Where does that leave The People? Where does that leave the 99% on the day it figures out it *is* the 99%?

It leaves us with the electoral process. With the chance—in a fair, observably counted election—to elect to office candidates outside the power duopoly, who have refused to feed at the corporate trough, and who are pledged to bringing genuine change to the system and seriously addressing American Systemic Injustice.[109]

Of course there are other obstacles beside rigged votecounts: money, media, lies, infiltration, assassination. But at least there would be a fighter's chance! Money faces a law of diminishing returns when it is spent in obscene amounts to buy votes and elections; there are means of communicating messages outside the mainstream media; lies can be exposed, infiltration, threats, and even assassination overcome—as

---

[108] President Obama proudly dubbed the NSA activities "transparent." While Glen Greenwald's publication in *The Guardian* of Edward Snowden's leaked NSA documents was certainly a step in that direction, it is hardly one for which the President, who has attempted to prosecute Snowden on charges of espionage or treason, can gracefully take credit.

[109] To see what lies in wait for such a candidate in our current electoral circus, look no farther than Chapter V and the forensic story of the 2016 Democratic primaries.

we have seen elsewhere around the world and throughout history—when a cause is just and vital and when the forces of greed, repression and control have overplayed their hand. In primaries and in independent challenges, candidates with the courage to oppose the forces of wealth and injustice smothering our democracy could stand for election before an electorate that the ruling elite had finally pushed too far.

At that point we had better be counting the votes *in public view.*[110] It is absurdly naive to believe that the corporate totalitarians, who hardly blanch at subverting every *other* mechanism of democracy, would, with their own computers counting the votes in secret, go gentle into the good electoral night.

We are suffering from a virulent disease and will need strong medicine. *But let us not say it's all so rotten that elections no longer matter.* Because after elections all that is left is revolution and, even if we could imagine one here in the Land of Genetically Modified Milk and Honey, such events are not ordinarily festive but chaotic and traumatic. Indeed, it was memories of such traumas that likely gave birth to history's *first* elections. So let us neither mistake the lines of battle nor fail to recognize the crucial part electoral integrity—*beginning with the observable counting of votes*—is destined to play in an age in which the critical lines of battle are all about what can be seen and what cannot.

Q: What can be done? Is there any real prospect of observable and honest elections in the United States?

A: Democracy, contrary to the facile assumptions of those born into it and apt to take both its blessings and its workings for granted, is no sure thing. While political evolution in the modern era has seemed to be inexorably bringing democracy of one sort or another to more and

---

[110] It goes without saying that in 2016 we were *not* counting the votes in public view.

more of the world, the countercurrents—both historical (Hitler, Stalin, Franco, Pinochet, *et al*) and contemporary (Russia, China, Egypt, etc.)—are very strong and have certainly not ceded the field.

Power, always seeking consolidation and control, has a way of finding the chinks, slipping in the explosives and blowing democracies and genuinely representative governance up. Or, more subtly and patiently, slow-dripping its acid onto the scaffolding that holds democracy upright. We've seen in America the metastasis of the security state, the infiltration of big money into politics, and the consolidation of the mainstream media under control of a handful of corporations. All of these developments make America *look* less democratic. The process may not be explosive, like a coup, but it is visibly erosive.

Election theft is different in that it allows its perpetrators to keep "democracy" perfectly intact and *looking* like a democracy even after it's been effectively gutted. It is also something that very few Americans of our time ever thought they'd have to worry about, and something that they'd still very much rather not worry about (as it goes against every premise of positive national identity and esteem), especially if they have a seat at or anywhere near the power table. So we are in a very dark and dangerous place and facing an historical tragedy in the making.

It is not unrealistic to imagine systemic election rigging giving rise to a politics so one-sided or so out of sync with the public will that eventually the inkling that something is very wrong with the whole picture becomes irrepressible.

It is also possible to imagine something ultimately more damning: a carefully titrated rigging strategy that would preserve, perhaps indefinitely, the *illusions* of a freely swinging pendulum and of public sovereignty.

And finally it is not wholly inconceivable that a hidden game of rigging, thwarting, and counter-rigging—a kind of domestic electoral equivalent of the spy-thriller antics of the Cold War—will come to characterize our best-in-class, made-in-the-USA model of democracy.

It is not yet entirely clear which it will be, though it is becoming clearer. As we will now proceed to examine, the elections of 2010, 2012, 2014, and 2016, taken together, shed a good deal of light on how the electoral computer game is likely to be played as we move further into the New American Century.

III. E2010 and E2012: A PATTERN EMERGES

The truth will set you free, but first it will piss you off.

— Gloria Steinem

Obama won. Again. It's safe to go back in the water. The outcome of E2012 proves that votes are counted honestly and accurately in the United States. Even if electronic rigging is theoretically possible, E2012 provides blanket assurance that it is just not something that anyone—no matter how bent on winning, no matter how in thrall to some agenda, ideology, or worldview—would *do*. Thank God we don't have to worry about this anymore or deal with the massive burdens of observable counting or even serious audits! It's all good.

Or is it?

Recall E2008: Change you could believe in; safe to go back in the water; concerns about election theft greatly overblown. It seemed that all but the most cynical among us took time out to watch the Obama victory celebration in Grant Square, many to join in. But a few of us stayed at our computers, doggedly screenshotting, downloading, and spreadsheeting—focused on the process rather than the outcome. Having seen all the indicators in 2004, 2006, and 2008, we were then not at all surprised by E2010, when the Tea Party swept in, Democrats and Republican moderates were sent packing, and what promises to be a very long-term occupation of both federal and key state governments was installed by those same red-shifted votecounts that had somehow escaped general notice two years earlier in 2008 when they weren't red-shifted *enough* to keep Obama out of the White House. Who else, in December 2008, saw E2010 coming? Who, in December 2012, was thinking E2014? Who is paying attention to the emerging pattern, watching the pendulum's weirdly distorted, precessional swing? Who understands that a corrupted voting system does not equate with every election being successfully rigged?

Obviously, not every election contest is targeted for manipulation: some are relatively unimportant, without any national significance; some are too one-sided to reverse without provoking undue suspicion; some rigs may be under-calibrated in light of subsequent political developments; and still others may be deterred or thwarted in the darkness of cyberspace. There is strong reason to believe that it is this last fate that befell the attempted manipulation of the 2012 presidential race.

Looking at E2012 overall, while the Democrats took what were regarded as the major in-play prizes of the White House and Senate (adding to their narrow majority in the latter), the Republicans maintained a solid grip on the US House (despite Congressional approval ratings hovering in the single digits and despite an overall Democratic victory in the national popular vote for the House[1]), as well as on a sizeable majority of statehouses. In effect, though the election was initially depicted as a pendulum-swinging repudiation of both extreme right-wing politics and the impact of vast corporate and Super-PAC expenditures on voter choice, *little if anything changed in the actual political infrastructure as a result of E2012.*

It is also worth noting that, much as in E2008, it required a dismal campaign run by a feckless, tone-deaf, and lackluster candidate trying desperately and all-too-transparently to "Etch-A-Sketch" away an

---

[1] It was only the fourth occurrence of this win-the-vote-lose-the-House phenomenon in over 100 years, the others involving outsized Democratic margins in what was then the "solid South."

indelible impression of extremism left over from his self-styled "severely conservative" primary season—not to mention a series of gaffes by GOP Senate candidates ranging from the seriously injurious to the instantly fatal—to bring about even this tepid electoral result that did little more than maintain the status quo, leaving a leadership class still jarringly out of tune with an American electorate that had *just voted*.

So What Happened?

It does sound like the stuff of spy novels,[2] but there is every reason to believe that a planned manipulation of the presidential vote was blocked in cyberspace on Election Night 2012. As for the down-ballot contests, while there was not the familiar red shift relative to exit polls in most contests of national significance, as there had been in every biennial election since 2004,[3] it is difficult to determine whether that was because the votecounts were accurate or because the exit polls were in one way or another pre-adjusted to accommodate the anticipated red shift of the votecounts.[4] The would-be rig that

---

[2] Indeed, there is a good one, of recent vintage: *The Lafayette Campaign: A Tale of Deception and Elections*, by Andrew Updegrove, an attorney with thirty years' experience servicing hi-tech clients, at www.amazon.com/dp/0996491910/.

[3] In E2002 the exit polls were withheld entirely from public disclosure, seen as both worthless and embarrassing because of the extreme red-shift disparities between them and the votecounts.

[4] It must be noted here that exit polling and pre-election polling, are, each in its own way, responsive to official electoral results and hence become part of a feedback loop contaminated when those results are distorted.

In the case of exit polls, the raw response data must be stratified according to the pollster's best estimates of electoral composition (which is to say, oversimplifying a bit, that there should be x% Democrats, y% Republicans, p% whites, q% nonwhites, etc., in a given sample). This stratification of course affects the poll's outcome and it is in turn influenced strongly by the demographic percentages drawn from *previous* elections' exit polls.

But the exit polls from the prior election(s) used for this purpose are exit polls that have been *adjusted to congruence with the votecounts in those prior elections* (this is standard practice, on the theory that the votecounts are unquestionably accurate and therefore any exit poll that is not congruent with those votecounts must be inaccurate, not only as to its "who did you vote for?" results but as to its demographics).

appeared to have been thwarted on Election Night was of the "real-time" variety (i.e., a "man-in-the-middle" attack[5]), but it remains unclear whether and to what extent a pre-set rig (i.e., one programmed into memory cards installed prior to Election Day) may have affected the outcomes of down-ballot (e.g., US House and state-level) elections, critical to the overall political power balance but not exit-polled.

Not Over Till Karl Rove Sings?

One of the weirdest indications of submerged 2012 Election Night drama was the infamous public "meltdown" of Karl Rove, star of the FOX News Election Night coverage team, as he stubbornly persisted in challenging *his own network's* call of Ohio and the presidency for Obama, citing a rapidly closing gap between the candidates that did not jibe with *any* publicly reported returns.[6] Of course millions of votes *were* being tabulated on remote networked servers, including many from key swing states such as Ohio. This method of vote "processing" permits votecount manipulation in "real time" calibrated to suit, and a shift of fewer than 170,000 *total* votes among the states of Ohio, Florida, Virginia, and New Hampshire would have reversed the Electoral College outcome and put Romney in the White House. In

---

Thus (and, again, to oversimplify a bit), if a previous election required a 5% rightward exit poll adjustment in order to match the official votecount, that shift will be reflected in correspondingly shifted exit poll demographics (e.g., %R/%D), and it is those demographics that will find their way into the stratification of the current exit poll, pushing the current sample to the right and therefore the exit poll results to the right.

So a red shift of x% in the previous election will effectively *cover* a rig of x% in the current election by erasing the votecount vs. exit poll disparity that would otherwise have accrued. Which is to say that if the current election is no more rigged than the previous one it will appear, using the exit polls as baseline, *not to have been rigged at all.*

[5] A man-in-the-middle attack involves the interception and alteration of digitized data in the process of storage or transmission; see, e.g., http://electiondefensealliance.org/man_in_the_middle.

[6] See, e.g., https://www.youtube.com/watch?v=rKqQBvWeO6E; see also Pema Levy, "The Real Reason Why Rove Went Into Denial On Election Night," *Newsweek*, 1/21/14, at http://www.newsweek.com/real-reason-why-rove-went-denial-election-night-226695.

disputing his fellow right-wingers on the FOX broadcast, Rove made reference to *server issues*, eerily reminiscent of the parallel scenario in E2004, in which Mike Connell's SmarTech operation took over the official Ohio elections website at about the same late hour of the evening and Bush suddenly surged ahead as the "late" votes came in.[7] So, as long as one assumes he had reason to believe that a repeat performance was on the program and those necessary votes could be ginned up in cyberspace, Rove's insistence was not quite as absurd as it seemed.

Rove—a brilliant, disciplined, and careful calculator never heretofore prone to such humiliations—so clearly and publicly expected a different result, and seemed so clearly and publicly to be counting on something happening that did not happen, that it begs the questions "What?" and "Why didn't it?"

And indeed, the group Anonymous took credit, days after the election, for having disabled Rove's vaunted ORCA operation.[8] Billed as a sophisticated GOTV network, ORCA was in fact designed to be capable of accessing votecounts as well as databases. And, sure enough, the servers in Ohio went down on Election Night 2012 exactly one minute earlier than they had gone down on Election Night 2004, when the votes were shunted to Mike Connell's SmarTech servers in Chattanooga for "processing." But, alas, after the untimely 2008 death of Connell, his chief of technical operations, Rove was obliged to rebuild his IT department and all did not go well in that endeavor. Specifically, as a result of infiltration of Rove's IT team, Anonymous reported that ORCA's technicians were locked out from their own servers by what amounted to a counter-hack. While they feverishly and unsuccessfully keyed in dozens of superseded passwords, Rove

---

[7] In E2012, in addition to SmarTech and its servers operating out of Chattanooga, several other outfits with partisan ties, such as Command Central and Scytl, were also contracted to "process" votes sent through cyberspace to remote servers.

[8] A founding member of the group confirmed to me in May 2016 that Anonymous had succeeded in blocking Rove on Election Night 2012 through changing the ORCA passwords and locking out its resident users.

continued to wait (and wait . . . and wait) for Romney to surge as Bush had in 2004.[9]

As wild as that scenario might seem, it does make sense that, after a decade-long parade of malodorous computerized elections, some countermeasures, some back-channel "immune response," would finally be triggered. It is evident that the crazy-quilt pattern of partial safeguards *intrinsic* to the vote counting process would not have stood in the way of the alternative outcome that seemed plausible only to Rove. Deterrence—a sufficient upping of the risk factor in the reward/risk ratio—or outright rig-thwarting would have had to come from some type of *outside* intervention, whether in the form of electronic counter-manipulation, infiltration, or quiet threat of exposure or prosecution. This is a sobering thought and we must ask ourselves as Americans whether we are willing to accept a kind of electoral "Wild West" where elections are won and lost and our future determined by "white hats" and "black hats" hacking it out in electoral cyberspace.

Strange Numbers in The House

Looking beyond the presidency, in E2012 America re-elected a Congress of which it overwhelmingly disapproved and we must ask whether the advantages of incumbency, gerrymandering, discriminatory Voter-ID laws, corporate cash, and political dirty tricks are enough to explain this jarring incongruence between voter sentiment and electoral result.

Nationally, while the Democrats won the aggregate *vote* for the US House, the Republicans won a comfortable majority of the *seats* (234 – 201), a rare event that echoed the strange outcome in E2010, in

---

[9] For an illuminating take on the events of Election Night 2012, see Thom Hartmann's "The Big Picture 11/19/2012," viewable at
http://www.thomhartmann.com/bigpicture/full-show-111912-did-anonymous-save-election (at 47'23" – 57'56").

which the Republicans achieved a spectacular net gain of 128 seats by virtue of a very pedestrian (apparent) 6.8% aggregate popular vote margin, a seats-to-votes ratio unprecedented in US history. In Pennsylvania, for example, the Democrats *won* the aggregate House vote but the GOP came away with a *13 to 5* margin of the state's 18 seats. Gerrymandering is reflexively given credit for this disproportionate coup, and its impact was certainly felt, but what then accounts for the equally bizarre results of *E2010,* when a majority of the districts were still drawn to favor *Democratic* candidates?

There was little dispute that a *single-digit* Congressional approval rating, 35 to 40 percentage points below that of the President, reflected primarily voter anger over the behavior of Republicans in Congress,[10] who consistently used the filibuster to block both legislation and appointments in the Senate and wielded House majority control inflexibly (to put it mildly) against any initiatives that might threaten corporate hegemony, address the gaping New Gilded Age income and wealth inequalities, or attempt to ward off looming environmental catastrophe.[11] It would be difficult indeed, even after giving gerrymandering and incumbency their due, to explain to a visitor from a far-off land why this political intransigence and obstructionism were electorally rewarded rather than punished when voters nationwide finally had the opportunity to weigh in.

How, *in a democracy*, can popularity and power so radically diverge? And how can that radical divergence persist, remain so uncorrectable? What thumbs, visible and invisible, must be on the scale for this to happen? Is there another mechanism, more pernicious still than

---

[10] The abysmal ratings have been consistent following a sharp downward plunge dating from the spring of 2011, a few months after the Republicans took control of the US House in the E2010 rout.

[11] The Republican House instead devoted a good part of its energy to the serial passage of bills to repeal all or part of the Affordable Care Act (ironically "Obamacare" was the spawn of the Republican "Romneycare" plan, which had its beta test in Massachusetts under Romney's governorship), reaching an impressive score of 63 such empty gestures by the start of 2016.

gerrymandering, to be investigated for its contribution to the egregiously undemocratic results in Pennsylvania and elsewhere across America?

Pre-set and Real-time Rigging

Based on the body of evidence from the past decade, it is virtually certain that attempted electronic election theft on a national level has not confined itself to reliance on a single logistical tactic. Forensic analysis strongly suggests that election rigging has evolved into what might best be described as a two-tiered strategy, consisting of pre-set and real-time manipulations.

Of these, pre-set rigging is by far the more facile. For example, it is quite simple, as we have shown, to set the zero-counters on the memory card deployed in a precinct tabulator to +X for the supported candidate and −X for the candidate whose defeat is desired. At the end of the day an election administrator will perceive a "clean" election in which the total ballot count matches the poll-book (i.e., sign-in) total of voters, unaware that a net of 2X votes has been successfully shifted per tabulator so tainted. Similar exploits can also be used to rig central tabulators. All that is required is the insertion of a few lines of malicious code among the hundreds of thousands of lines on a given card, and it is trivial to replicate this alteration on hundreds or thousands of such cards. Given the current level and practice of election security, such a rig is virtually undetectable and needs only to pass the numerical smell test.[12]

---

[12] Although there is no real technical limit to the magnitude of such a rig, the smell test comes into play at some point because the likelihood of suspicion, investigation, and ultimate exposure of the rigging enterprise increases with the magnitude of the rig. Although there have been a few egregious "outliers," red-shift evidence over the years suggests that the outer limit of electronic rigging is generally in the 7% - 10% range.

The recent forensic contributions of Francois Choquette and James Johnson have strong relevance here. They have shown, through a precinct-level forensic technique known as Cumulative Vote Share (CVS) Analysis, that suspect elections present what could be characterized as a "signature" pattern in which the allegedly benefited candidate's vote share increases with increasing precinct size. Having controlled for "benign" factors

The difficulty with pre-set rigs programmed into memory cards deployed weeks or months before the election, however, is that of accurate calibration, guessing well in advance the minimum number of votes needed to be stolen to reverse the outcome of a given contest. This is far from a trivial problem: in both E2006 and E2008 late-breaking political developments so changed electoral dynamics that what appeared (from the red-shift numbers) to be robust pre-set rigs were overwhelmed and rendered far less effective, in terms of altering outcomes, than would have been anticipated at time of deployment.[13]

Real-time rigging, executed as the votes are tabulated on Election Day (or more often late on Election Night), avoids this problem. The manipulation can be precisely calibrated to overcome what would be the losing margin and so reverse the outcome. It requires, however, the deployment of infrastructure to intercept and alter votecounts, and thus is bulkier and riskier than the simple pre-set, memory card-based rig. The operation that permitted interference with the Ohio presidential vote in E2004—the SmarTech servers set up under the late Mike Connell's direction in Chattanooga, Tennessee—was eventually detected, through its IP footprint, and privately investigated, coming very close to fatal exposure of the entire rigging

---

(e.g., urban/rural differences), it appears that the most likely explanation for this recurrent pattern is that larger numbers of votes can be safely shifted in larger precincts without failing the smell test and raising a red flag (compare, for example, 100 votes shifted from a total of 200 votes = 50%, vs. the same 100 votes shifted from a total of 1000 votes = 10%). Larger precincts offer a better reward/risk ratio and are therefore preferred targets for rigging. See Choquette F & Johnson J: *Republican Primary Election 2012 Results: Amazing Statistical Anomalies* (2012), reprinted at http://electiondefensealliance.org/files/PrimaryElectionResultsAmazingStatisticalAnomalies_V2.1.pdf. See also the CVS forensic analyses of Elizabeth Clarkson, Chief Statistician at the National Institute for Aviation Research, at www.bethclarkson.com.

[13] In each of these elections, unanticipated events—in 2006 the Foley scandal and in 2008 the collapse of Lehman Brothers and the kickoff of the Great Recession—occurred in mid-September, turning close elections into routs. Recalibration and redeployment of the pre-set rigs would not only be impractical at that juncture from a technical and logistical standpoint, but would also, in order to be successful in achieving overall Republican victories, have likely had to be of too great a magnitude to pass the smell test.

enterprise.[14] So there is a tradeoff between the upside of real-time control and the downside of risk of detection (or, as we saw in E2012, operational interference).

It is evident that each species of manipulation, pre-set or real-time, is best suited to a specific type of electoral contest. Where the volatility is low and the ultimate outcome can be roughly predicted well in advance, *or where one needs outcome-altering success in only some fraction of a large set of contests* (e.g., to take majority control of the US House or a state legislature), the pre-set rig is likely to be effective enough.[15] Where the volatility is high, however, and the contest(s) subject to unpredictable shifts in the political wind, or *where the target is a single contest* (e.g., presidency, US Senate seat) rather than a subset of a large group, pre-set rigs are more likely, as in E2006 and E2008, to undershoot (or overshoot) the mark and come up short (or suspiciously "long").

Of course there is essentially no *technical* limit on how large a pre-set, memory card-based rig can be deployed, but obviously to take all the votes is neither necessary nor desirable. Indeed, the *cardinal algorithm* of election rigging is *take no more than you need*: since the risks of suspicion, investigation, and detection increase with the magnitude of the rig, it is advisable if not imperative to shift no more votes than are needed to bring about the desired electoral outcome (and, where necessary, avoid either a mandatory or an elective margin-based recount). Rigs of too great magnitude, such that they do not or might not pass the smell test, are dangerous and inadvisable.

---

[14] Had star witness Connell not been the victim of the plane crash that ended his life just prior to the completion of his testimony in the *King Lincoln-Bronzeville v. Blackwell* case, such fatal exposure of the rigging enterprise might well have become a reality.

[15] "Effective enough" because, in such a situation, undercalibrating a few contests—letting a few fish off the hook—would not adversely impact the overall goal of attaining an aggregate majority; a decent batting average will suffice.

In examining E2012 it is clear enough that the presidential race and the critical US Senate races were of the high-volatility genus. Not only were pre-election polls in fluctuating disagreement about the prospects of these highly competitive contests, but outcomes were further subject to the vagaries of current events such as the recording of Romney's "47%" gaffe and the political hay-making opportunities presented by Hurricane Sandy. It would have been extremely difficult to predict with the necessary accuracy even a month in advance what magnitude of vote shift would be necessary to guarantee victories in these top-of-the-ballot battles. Lower profile down-ballot races for the US House and state legislatures would, on the other hand, be much lower in volatility and far easier to gauge. And while it would of course be possible for a given race to turn sharply on a gaffe or a brilliant attack ad, the much greater number of these races would, *in the all-important aggregate*, smooth out such one-off bumps. And while it would also in theory be possible to see a repeat of something like the Foley scandal of 2006, which managed to sink a slew of down-ballot Republican boats, the likelihood of such a "perfect storm" event reoccurring and having a comparable impact was exceedingly small.

It is therefore plausible to posit a two-tiered rigging strategy in which a pre-set rig covering competitive US House and statehouse races would be complemented, where feasible, by a real-time rig targeting the more volatile top-ballot races for President and US Senate.[16] Such critical top-ballot races might also be set up for manipulation via both pre-set and real-time methods.[17]

Older readers who recall playing the popular board game "CLUE," may hear echoes here of "Professor Plum, in the Kitchen, with the

---

[16] Recalling that reversing the outcome of the presidential election would have come down to a shift of fewer than 170,000 total votes (about 0.13% of votes cast nationally) in only four states.

[17] In this scheme, a limited (i.e., safe) pre-set rig could then be "topped off" where necessary by a precisely calibrated real-time rig of the type that Rove gave appearance of counting on in very publicly protesting the "premature" call by his employer Fox News.

Wrench." Given the concealment of the key data (voter-marked ballots, memory cards, code, raw exit poll numbers), neither the weapon of choice, nor the site of attack, nor indeed the perp is our case to make. Perhaps it was Colonel Mustard, in the Conservatory, with the Candlestick. The evidence that *is* available is more than sufficient to establish a *corpus delicti*—a body with enough wounds to spur us to look beyond natural causes. It is not unreasonable to call for an inquest. It goes also without saying that the whole house is *unsafe*, a deadly set-up for our unsuspecting elections. *Our case is that we need as a nation seriously to investigate whether a crime has been or is likely to be committed, and rectify a situation that invites it to be committed over and over again.*

E2012, like E2008 before it, set back that cause significantly. But E2012, like E2008 before it and contrary to popular perception, offered no genuine cause for relief or celebration. Part of the rigging enterprise may have been disarmed by what amounted to cyber-vigilantism, but the vote counting system remained concealed, privatized, profoundly insecure, and an open invitation to future manipulation, especially in "off-year" elections like E2014 and below-the-radar primaries.[18]

---

[18] The apparent defeat of Congressman Eric Cantor, Majority Leader of the US House of Representatives, in the June 10, 2014 Republican primary election in Virginia's 7th CD set a chilling tone. It was an election counted on a combination of DREs (paperless and thus unauditable and unrecountable) and opscans (which, by Virginia law, are recountable only by running the ballots a second time through the same opscans; human inspection is barred). Thus there was literally no way for an electronic rig to be discovered and exposed, and consequently zero risk for any rigging enterprise.

The far-right (though occasionally uncooperative) Cantor—consistently ahead by more than 30 points in both internal and public polls and having outspent his far-far-right Tea Party opponent, David Brat, 20-to-1—lost the election by 12 points, the first Majority Leader *in history* to suffer this fate. The *Times* echoed virtually every observer of the shocking outcome by terming Brat's feat "unimaginable" ("In G.O.P., Far Right Is Too Moderate;" Times Editorial Board, June 11, 2014; at http://www.nytimes.com/2014/06/12/opinion/in-gop-far-right-is-too-moderate.html).

The entire media and political class, including to my knowledge every *progressive* commentator of note, then proceeded to offer up a smorgasbord of contorted explanations for the "unimaginable," without once entertaining so much as a hint of a question about whether the vote totals—unverified and unverifiable—could possibly be erroneous, whether the secret vote counting process could just possibly have been

Misdirection

American politics shuffles on in a perennial two-step of presidential and midterm election cycles. If we look at it, as riggers almost certainly do, from a risk/reward standpoint, the risk factors in the non-exit polled, below-the-radar elections for the US House and state legislative control are very low indeed, and that applies even more strongly to the primary contests for these offices. The risk factors are certainly far lower than for the high-visibility and relatively high-scrutiny, *on*-the-radar Presidential and US Senate elections.[19] But what about the reward? What do you get, how much political bang for the buck, by stealing off-year and down-ballot elections?

You get what it should be obvious that the radicalized GOP has gotten and should be able to keep for the foreseeable future: a guaranteed *minimum* power level of gridlock, an effective and enduring blockade of the opposing agenda. For all practical purposes the Right's indomitable beachhead requires majority control of the House and 41 Senators, an entrenchment that the Democratic "victory" in E2012 could not disturb. But what was achieved in E2010 had especial strategic value because, along with the shocking US House massacre, the GOP took control of critical statehouses in "purple" swing states

---

subject to some species of manipulation or interference. Not one clearing of a throat, not one raising of an eyebrow.

Then all alike moved in quick lock-step into deep and fascinating discussions of the *implications* of this "seismic" political development that none (with the exception of a few of our hallucinating Cassandras) had seen as remotely possible. The implications according to the punditry? No Republican can henceforth dare to ignore or even attempt to finesse the far-far right "base;" the Tea Party, which was barely on life support, is back in control with a vengeance; hyperpolarization shall give way to hyper-hyperpolarization; far-right is the new center.

Unimaginable result, seismic impact, secret and unverifiable count, childsplay rigging options, zero risk, zero investigation, zero questions asked. Welcome to The New American Century.

[19] Apart from a much lower risk of detection, because these down-ballot contests are well-suited to pre-set, as opposed to real-time, manipulations, real-time counter-hacking *interventions*, such as essayed by Anonymous in 2012, are not a concern.

throughout America, giving itself command of the decennial redistricting process and immediately using that gerrymandering power to lock in its US House and state legislative majorities through at least 2020.[20] Add in restrictive and discriminatory Voter-ID laws—rammed through by these same legislatures in purported response to a nonexistent "epidemic" of voter-impersonation fraud, but operating in effect as a modern-era poll tax[21]—and a host of other provisions all designed to make the casting of a vote more difficult.[22] Fill in the picture with the now nearly complete displacement of GOP moderates by radicals via primary victories—virtually all of them low-profile, low-scrutiny; many of them, like the Cantor shocker, suspect—and one can begin to see how it is possible to quietly, massively, and enduringly shift the governmental balance of power in America. E2010 provided the infrastructure for nothing less than political hegemony—perpetual rule. In retrospect we can now recognize this jack-in-the-box election as a kind of self-sustaining coup, the gift that keeps on giving—achieved, as are most magician's tricks, with the help of misdirection as audience attention was riveted elsewhere on the "major" battles of presidential years.

With the demographics all trending Democratic and with the Republicans more and more nakedly the party of the wealthy elites, promoting many unpopular causes and virulently obstructing a host of popular ones, they will nevertheless, if form holds, remain stuck like a bone in America's throat, courtesy of "magical" elections like E2010, where truly no one was looking at the Man Behind The Curtain.

---

[20] In the US House, for example, the fiasco of Donald Trump's lead-balloon campaign notwithstanding, a mere 37 (out of 435) seats are expected to be competitive in E2016. Majorities impervious to such gale-force headwinds may safely be characterized as locked-in or, in Rove's own language, "permanent."

[21] See Minnite L: *The Myth of Voter Fraud.* Cornell University Press, 2010. http://www.amazon.com/Myth-Voter-Fraud-Lorraine-Minnite/dp/0801448484/ See also Mayer J: "The Voter-Fraud Myth," *The New Yorker* (10/29/2012) at http://www.newyorker.com/reporting/2012/10/29/121029fa_fa_fact_mayer?printable=true.

[22] See, e.g., Yaccino S, Alvarez, L: "New G.O.P. Bid to Limit Voting in Swing States", *NY Times*, 3/29/2014, http://www.nytimes.com/2014/03/30/us/new-gop-bid-to-limit-voting-in-swing-states.html.

IV. E2014: WHAT DEMOCRACY DOESN'T LOOK LIKE

If voting changed anything, they'd make it illegal.

-- Emma Goldman

Nothing Succeeds Like Failure

It is one thing to gain power, another thing entirely, having exercised that power badly, to retain it. Representative democracies operate, in effect, by right of review, and the hallmark of a functioning representative democracy is that unpopular representatives and parties must stand for re-election and can be given the boot. "Throw the bums out!" is really what stands between public discontent and revolution. Considered in this light, E2014 was nothing less than a failure of democracy. Public discontent, indeed outrage, found no expression, no outlet, in the electoral process.

The latest and most ominous completed chapter in the story of computerized vote counting in America, E2014 was a Republican rout with a mighty strange asterisk. As progressive pundit John Nichols put it, in a column for *The Nation* that was typical of post-mortem analysis, "[V]oters who came to the polls on November 4 were sufficiently progressive and populist to support minimum-wage hikes, paid sick leave, crackdowns on corporate abuses of the environment, expansion of healthcare and radical reform of a money-drenched campaign-finance system. *They just didn't elect Democrats.*"

Nichols' explanation for this weird electoral schizophrenia? "[P]ersonalities, dark-money interventions *and plenty of other factors* were at play. But the *consistent pattern of progressive policy votes* in combination with Republican [candidate] wins provides the starkest evidence of the extent to which the Democratic Party was an incoherent force in 2014."[1]

And so a Republican party whose rule of Congress had earned *single-digit approval ratings*[2] found itself rewarded for its good work with its strongest grip on combined federal and state political power since the days of Herbert Hoover,[3] while the Democrats and progressives could be heard in wailing chorus blaming themselves and their campaigns, asking (of course) for more money, and pitching around desperately for yet more new strategies to replace the ones that had apparently

---

[1] Nichols J, "Democrats: The Party of Pablum," *The Nation*, Dec. 1 – 8, 2014 (emphases added). A familiar tautology is evident: the Democratic Party *must have been* "an incoherent force" *because they lost.* Or their candidates lost while their ideas were winning. Needless to say, the possibility of computerized election theft was not among the "plenty of other factors" Nichols chose to explore.

[2] Source: Rasmussen Reports at http://www.rasmussenreports.com/public_content/politics/mood_of_america/congressi onal_performance. Rasmussen's measure of congressional approval hovered consistently between 6% and 8% during the months preceding E2014. During pre-election week just 29% of likely voters Rasmussen surveyed thought their *own* representative was "the best person for the job." This was the first time in polling *history* that at least a plurality failed to approve of their own representatives.

[3] Most notably, in the most "throw the bums out" political climate yet measured, exactly *two* out of 222 incumbent members of the US House Republican majority lost their seats, *a re-election rate of over 99%.*

Republicans, at this writing, hold a 54 – 44 advantage in the US Senate, a 60-seat margin (247 – 187) in the US House, nearly a two-to-one (31 – 18) proportion of governorships, a better than two-to-one (68 - 30) grip on state legislative chambers, and full control (governorship and both branches of the state legislature) of 23 states to the Democrats' seven (20 remain divided). This power ratio has not been equaled in nearly a century and seems, to say the least, a strange distortion of contemporary America as measured by any yardstick other than that of its computers tallying elections for public office.

As described by the analysts at Ballotpedia, "Democrats have lost a total of 913 [state legislative] seats since [Obama] took office in January 2009, . . . an historical number of legislative seats lost by a two-term president's party during his term. . . [T]he average number of seats lost has been 450 since World War II." Obama's approval rating— which currently stands at 56% favorable, never dipped below 40% during his tenure, and hovered around 50% in the run-up to E2014—can hardly be invoked as the probable cause of this more than double the average down-ballot carnage in the least scrutinized of all contests with national significance. See http://ballotpedia.org/Links_to_all_election_results,_2014.

just failed so miserably. It is difficult to avoid *looking like,* and believing yourself to be, "an incoherent force" when you've just had your electoral clock cleaned. Certainly everyone was shocked at the sheer magnitude of the beat-down—everyone, that is, except those of us who take seriously the corporate control of America's electoral apparatus and the perils of unobservable vote counting. To us E2014 fit rather neatly and symptomatically into the pattern we have seen emerging over the past several election cycles and was, it must be said, eminently predictable.

The Usual Suspects

Let's set aside for the time being any thought that the votecounts behind those DECISION 2014 blinking states and pie charts could possibly have been manipulated, in order to examine the various PG-rated explanations that have been put forward for the confounding results of E2014: low turnout, voter suppression, dark money, gerrymandering, and skewed polls.

> **Low Turnout:** Low turnout provides a very convenient and rather reflexive explanation for Democratic losses, the assumption being that the core of the electorate is made up disproportionately of Republican voters while the Democratic constituencies are more likely to include "fringe" voters. Thus when turnout is low it's a good bet that the Republican voters showed up (because they always do) while the Democratic voters stayed home.
>
> The problem with this analysis is that there is no reliable direct measurement of which party's voters did in fact show up in greater numbers. The reasoning is instead strictly tautological: the Democrats lost (we know this because the trusty votecounts tell us they did); therefore *their* voters must not have shown up.[4] But we

---

[4] Low Democratic turnout was also one of the explanations given for Bush's 2004 victory in Ohio, patently absurd in the face of videographic evidence showing lines, frequently several blocks and hours long, at typically Democratic precincts throughout

would have no way of knowing if they *did* show up and an outcome-altering share of their votes were "mistabulated" and shifted to their opponents. How do we know, except via our faith in the computers and their programmers, that it wasn't *Republican* voters who expressed their disgust with a Republican-controlled Congress by staying home?

So, while *overall* turnout is measurable and was just marginally lower than in the previous several off-year elections, we really don't know *who* stayed home. What we do know, from the results of the unadjusted exit polls,[5] is that the voters who *did* turn out— i.e., the actual electorate—said that they voted well to the left of how their votes were tabulated. The "low turnout" explanation cannot make this red flag go away. We also know that the actual electorate passed, often by wide margins and often not in blue states, all sorts of progressive ballot measures,[6] and that too does not square with the low (Democratic) turnout theory.

Voter Suppression: Voter suppression encompasses a variety of schemes and tactics cynically aimed at insuring low turnout specifically among the voters likely to support one's political opponents. As practiced by the Republican strategists who in E2010 took control of the legislatures and/or governorships of a swath of key "purple" swing states,[7] voter suppression schemes

---

the state, while voters in Republican precincts could walk in, vote, and head home virtually without breaking stride (see, *No Umbrella*, a documentary by Laura Paglin, at http://www.noumbrella.org/index.htm).

[5] "Red shift" refers to a poll vs. votecount disparity in which the votecounts are to the right of the poll results. "Unadjusted" exit polls refer to the initial public posting of the poll's results, before those results are "adjusted" to congruence with the emerging votecounts. As these unadjusted exit polls are ephemeral and disappear forever shortly after posting, they must be preserved and documented by one form or another of screen capture.

[6] See Study VII in Chapter VII for specific ballot measures in E2014. See also http://ballotpedia.org/List_of_ballot_measures_by_state.

[7] Vital as well was the E2010 Republican sweep of Secretaries of State (17 of 26 states where elections were held for that key position in statewide election administration); see https://ballotpedia.org/Statewide_elections,_2010.

openly targeted millions of "fringe" voters in the Democratic ranks.[8]

Voter-ID laws, passed on the transparent pretext of countering a factually nonexistent epidemic of voter-impersonation fraud,[9] operated like a modern-era poll tax by imposing costs and barriers that disproportionately impacted the poor and transient. Ditto the shortening of both poll hours (a serious impediment for working-class voters) and early-voting periods, and the consolidation of precincts to make it more difficult to reach one's polling place without vehicular ownership. Purging of voter lists to remove not just ex-felons but a broad penumbra of non-felons whose names *resembled* those of ex-felons, as well as voters who had changed addresses (renters, transients, college and graduate students, the elderly), stripped even more among the Democratic constituencies of their voting rights. And "caging," or sending operatives to the polls to challenge the rights of targeted voters and thereby relegate them to the casting of (frequently uncounted) "provisional ballots," whittled down the electorate still further. Taken together these ugly schemes were aimed at disenfranchising over three million would-be voters,[10] or about 4% of the total electorate, the

---

[8] The gates were opened in 2013 to a flood of templated voter-suppression laws and regulations by the 5-to-4 party-line Supreme Court decision in *Shelby County v. Holder*, gutting a key section of the Voting Rights Act of 1965 and turning states loose to revive Jim Crow free of federal oversight.

[9] See http://www.washingtonpost.com/politics/election-day-impersonation-an-impetus-for-voter-id-laws-a-rarity-data-show/2012/08/11/7002911e-df20-11e1-a19c-fcfa365396c8_story.html. See also Chapter II, fns. 56 and 66. According to the *Washington Post*, 37 states have either enacted or considered tougher Voter ID laws, including many with stringent photo-ID requirements. All told, an exhaustive Carnegie-Knight investigation into voter fraud found exactly *ten* instances of voter impersonation, the species of fraud that photo-ID would combat, since the year 2000, during which period just short of a *billion* ballots have been cast at the polls of America. Specious? Cynical? Intentionally discriminatory? Yes to all, according to a spate of recent federal court decisions striking down such laws.

[10] See http://www.gregpalast.com/gop-led-purge-threat-to-3-5-million-voters/; and, generally, Palast G, *Billionaires & Ballot Bandits; How to Steal an Election in 9 Easy Steps*. New York: Seven Stories Press, 2012. The coordinated purging program, dubbed Interstate Crosscheck, was the work of Chris Kobach, Republican Secretary of State of Kansas. The program, purporting to catch voters who voted under the same name in

vast majority of whom were demographically part of the Democratic constituency.

But *none* of these tactics, no form of voter suppression, can account for the red shift. Exit polls included only those voters who could respond that they had actually cast their ballots, and so *excluded* would-be voters who had been purged, were unable to obtain qualifying ID, discouraged or precluded by shrinking of access (hours and/or location), or successfully caged.[11] The effects of the voter suppression schemes and the tabulation errors reflected in the red shift are *additive*—in the phrase coined by Fitrakis and Wasserman, "strip and flip."[12]

Dark Money: If, in the language of the corporate protectorate that was the Roberts Court circa 2014, "money" is translated as "speech," then "dark money" would be the speech of anonymous bag-over-the-head hecklers who wish their words to be heard loud and clear without taking on the risk of being identified as the speaker.[13] After the *Citizens United* decision opened the floodgates to unregulated corporate cash in 2010, the damage was compounded when Congress failed to enact the source disclosure

---

different states (a lot of trouble to go to, if you think about it for a moment), contained literally millions of names and was, in Palast's words, "rife with literally millions of obvious mismatches." All of these would-be voters, most of them among the Democratic constituencies, were purged and found themselves disenfranchised. This sort of naked scheme for suppressing the (Democratic) vote is what passes, with a chuckle, in GOP brainstorming sessions, for "election integrity." Evidence from the 2016 primaries suggests it has now metastasized to *Democratic* brainstorming sessions.

[11] Provisional ballots do present a challenge to the exit pollster. While identifying provisional voters is easy enough, estimating the proportion of provisionals cast that may not be counted, in order to downweight such respondents accordingly, is trickier, though much historical data is now available to inform this estimation.

[12] Fitrakis B, Wasserman H: *The Strip and Flip Selection of 2016: Five Jim Crows & Electronic Election Theft,* at https://www.amazon.com/dp/B01GSJLW0I.

[13] The fear is primarily of consumer boycotts and other forms of populist punishment for perceived corporate attempts to "buy" elections. To return to an earlier observation (p. 85): "[T]he battle lines are indeed simple: a ruling elite, corporate and governmental, that is attempting to know as much as possible about you and me while seeing to it that we know as little as possible about them."

requirements that even the Court seemed to expect would bring a necessary element of public accountability to all the "speaking" it had just enabled.[14]

It is not disputed that E2014, like its two post-*Citizens* predecessors, was awash in dark money along with plain old traceable corporate cash. With the corporate point of view so loudly and expensively presented, many have argued that *Citizens United* was at the root of the rightward electoral veer. Apart from the fact that, like the turnout numbers and voter suppression, it leaves the red shift unaccounted for, this money-based explanation does not appear to fit the facts we find on even the shallowest of drilldowns. Looking at the aggregate spending for E2014, The Center for Responsive Politics found that the totals for the two sides were all-but-equal, a $1.75 billion to $1.64 billion edge for the Republicans, or all of 3.2%[15]—hardly the kind of differential to fuel a rout. More significantly still, major spending advantages were *not* associated with victory in many of the key races.

Clearly money is needed to mount nearly all successful campaigns, whether it goes to establish name recognition, drum in a rudimentary message, or mercilessly pillory one's opponent. Not clear, however, are the levels at which additional spending becomes progressively less effective, ineffective, or even counter-productive. There comes a saturation point, after all, at which beleaguered voters have heard it all and heard enough, such that yet more messaging is as apt to annoy them and turn them off as change their minds or motivate them. There is evidence that money-bath campaigns often cross this line and fail to buy more

---

[14] Far from applying a corrective, however, the Roberts Court most recently, in yet another 5 – 4 party-line decision (*McCutcheon v. Federal Election Commission*, 572 U.S. __ (2014)), went further and removed all aggregate limits on contributions to national parties and candidate committees, effectively setting out the Billionaire Welcome Mat in front of the door it had blown open with *Citizens United*.

[15] See http://www.opensecrets.org/news/2014/11/money-won-on-tuesday-but-rules-of-the-game-changed/.

votes at *any* price.[16] As ugly and inimical to the spirit of democracy as big-donor funded campaigns (and particularly those funded anonymously) seem to be, neither dark money nor the fund-fests enabled by *Citizens United* and *McCutcheon* pass muster as valid explanations for the electoral patterns that have come to characterize the computerized voting age.

Gerrymandering: Gerrymandering, or political redistricting for partisan advantage, can work one of two ways: if you command an aggregate popular majority, you can divide it up among the districts[17] in such a way that your party maintains a slim margin in every one of them, shutting the opposing party out; or, more commonly, you can minimize the opposing party's electoral victories by drawing districts in such a way as to concentrate as many of its voters as possible into as few districts as possible. If this is done with sufficient ruthlessness and artistry it generally results in a significant incongruity between electoral support (i.e., votes) and candidates elected to office. In fact, it is often possible for a party with minority status among the electorate to nonetheless hold a majority of the seats within a state.[18]

---

[16] In the 2011 Walker recall election in Wisconsin, for example, it was found that most of the lavish spending (eight to one in Walker's favor) occurred after all but a tiny percentage of the voters had made up their minds (see p. 75).

[17] Gerrymandering works for both US House and state legislative districts and might be applied as well to the selection of presidential electors. The US Senate, statewide and thus not subject to gerrymandering, is nonetheless grossly disproportionate as a representative body, with half the US population being represented by just 18 out of 100 senators. Given this large state-small state imbalance, which correlates fairly strongly with America's blue state-red state division, it is a telling measure of the major parties' respective popularity (at least as measured by the results of top-of-the-ballot, high-profile, exit-polled and high-scrutiny contests) that the Democrats have been more than able to hold their own in Senate representation even after the collapse of the Solid (Democratic) South.

[18] For example, in 2012 the 18-member US House delegation from Pennsylvania sported 13 Republicans to five Democrats, in spite of the fact that the Democratic House candidates had, statewide, received an aggregate *majority* of the vote. The GOP maintained that margin in E2014, also increasing their State Senate margin from five to 10 seats and State House margin from 20 to 35 seats, while the Democratic gubernatorial candidate won handily by a 55% - 45% margin.

Gerrymandering takes its name from the Revolutionary Era's Elbridge Gerry, so we can be assured that it has held a place in the arsenal of American political tactics for a very long time. What has changed dramatically, with the advent of the computer age and "big data," is the remarkable, practically house-by-house, precision with which districts can be carved up to include and exclude voters based on their known or suspected partisanship.[19] With nearly all of the guesswork and blurriness removed, gerrymandering has become an extremely potent political weapon and tool of partisanship.[20,21]

---

[19] See "Redistricting, A Devil's Dictionary" at http://www.propublica.org/article/redistricting-a-devils-dictionary/single. Although gerrymandering for partisan advantage is nominally unconstitutional, the standards actually applied by the courts have become so lax that essentially *any* contiguous shape, however jagged and meandering, will pass muster, allowing ample latitude to divvy up voters for maximum political gain. Justice Stevens, while on the Court, waged devoted battle against this most cynical (in design and effect) distortion of the electoral process, but lost to the bloc led by the late Justice Scalia.

[20] Gerrymandering has an understandable appeal to seated members of *both* parties, since it tends to produce "safe" seats and often reinforces the already formidable advantages of incumbency. It is worth noting, however, that Democratic voters, who are more likely to be clustered in dense and easily enclaved urban communities, present significantly more vulnerable targets for the gerrymanderer's Sharpie. It is a lot easier geometrically and geographically to draw the gerrymanderer's holy-grail 90%+ district of Democratic voters than of their Republican counterparts. California is notable among states for having bestowed the redistricting power on an independent board, the California Citizens Redistricting Commission, ostensibly free of partisan control, though in practice that standard is virtually impossible to achieve.

[21] Although the presidency has thus far been immune to the warpings of the gerrymander, a scheme has been floated to change that.

The American Legislative Exchange Council (ALEC), is a nominally nonpartisan but radically right-wing nonprofit founded in 1973 but relatively quiescent prior to the dawn of the New American Century. Almost entirely corporate funded, most notably by the billionaire Koch brothers, ALEC templates right-wing legislation, very often procedural in nature (as in Photo-ID bills), for rubber stamping by GOP-controlled state legislatures, its theatre of operations of course greatly expanded by E2010 and E2014 (see generally http://en.wikipedia.org/wiki/American_Legislative_Exchange_Council).

Among ALEC's most recent brainstorms is a plan to "gerrymander the presidency" by apportioning presidential electors by congressional district in key swing states like Michigan, Ohio, and Wisconsin where Republicans hold trifecta control. This would be a perfectly legal and constitutional, if hyper-cynical, tweak of the presidential election game. States are free to depart from the winner-take-all presidential model (which itself is subject to a pointed fairness-based critique) and replace it with what seems abstractly on the surface to be a fairer and more reasonable one. The consequence, however, is anything but abstract: by shifting at least half the electoral

The decennial US Census records population changes and serves as the basis for the major gerrymandering opportunities that present themselves at the beginning of each decade. Under-the-radar state legislative victories in E2010, to which I have previously referred as "the gift that keeps on giving," set the GOP up to seize these opportunities and, predictably, they did so with both fists and all the big data they could feed into their supercomputers.[22] The result was a steep and artificial tilt of the political table which many have cited as yet another major cause of the E2014 rout.

It would be silly to deny the impact of gerrymandering on the outcome of E2014 and the current political balance of power. The impact is formidable, as the architects of the E2010 rout grasped well before the media, let alone the general public, caught on. It would take a massive GOP political implosion, coupled with an observably counted election, to overcome the advantages that gerrymandering has conferred upon GOP candidates for the US House and a broad swath of state legislatures. Nonetheless gerrymandering cannot be invoked to account for the rout that was E2014. Gerrymandering has no impact on US Senate and gubernatorial contests, of which dozens were red-shifted, and it has no impact on the red shift in *any* contests, including the aggregate red shift of the US House. It is a heavy thumb on the scale for the US House and state legislatures, but it takes *several* heavy thumbs to produce the kinds of incongruities that now characterize American politics. Gerrymandering, potent as it may be, is only the set-up for the haymaker.

---

votes of these large and presidentially blue states to the Republican column (*recall that the congressional districts of these states have already been gerrymandered to the GOP's overwhelming advantage*), it becomes, in the words of one bootless Democratic plea for intervention, "virtually impossible for a Democratic [presidential] candidate to win, even if they win the national popular vote overwhelmingly" (see https://www.dailykos.com/campaigns/1011). It remains to be seen whether, or at what juncture, ALEC and its backers will push the button on this politically nuclear weapon.

[22] See, Daley D, *RATF**KED: The True Story Behind the Plan to Steal America's Democracy*, 2016, at https://www.amazon.com/dp/1631491628.

Skewed Polls: As we have seen, none of the phenomena we have examined—low turnout, voter suppression, dark money, or gerrymandering—has any significant bearing on the red shift, the rightward disparity between exit polls and the votecounts, which we have become accustomed to finding in American elections in the age of computer counting. Since the possibility of votecount manipulation cannot be admitted, it has become axiomatic among the punditry to account for the red shift with a standard line or two about the polls being "off again" because they "oversampled Democrats." According to this narrative, the Democratic voters then pulled a fast one on the pollsters by not turning out to vote, and we're told to believe this because the Democratic candidates (but strangely not a hefty stack of progressive ballot propositions) *lost* (or did worse than expected), having received a smaller percentage of the vote than the polls indicated. You can see the circularity of this reasoning: the "oversampled Democrats" conclusion rests on a turnout assumption which in turn rests on the presumed accuracy of the votecounts. Everything falls neatly into place *as long as we don't question the presumption of an accurate count.*[23]

The red shift in E2014 was egregious. In the elections for US Senate for which exit poll data was available, the red shift averaged an impressive 4.1%, with a half dozen races seeing red shifts of over 7%. Out of the 21 Senate elections that were exit polled, 19 were red-shifted. In the exit-polled gubernatorial elections, the average

---

[23] See, e.g., Nate Cohn's 6/27/16 NY *Times* article, "Exit Polls, and Why the Primary Was Not Stolen From Bernie Sanders," at
http://www.nytimes.com/2016/06/28/upshot/exit-polls-and-why-the-primary-was-not-stolen-from-bernie-sanders.html?_r=0. Cohn's analysis is impeccable and his deductions about exit polls, in 2016 and historically, follow with *perfect* logic from his starting *premise*, not qualified as such, that all the votecounts tabulated in the computer era have been accurate. It brings to mind the scene from the Harrison Ford movie, *The Fugitive*, in which a reporter raises the question of Dr. Kimble's possible "innocence" to the blowhard spokesman of the Chicago PD, who interrupts to respond, tartly and with great impatience, "He's not innocent. He's guilty. He was convicted in a court of law!" As indeed he was.

red shift was an even greater 5.0% and 20 out of the 21 races were red-shifted. In US House elections, which are exit polled with an aggregate national sample,[24] the red shift was 3.7%. This is the equivalent of approximately 2.9 million votes which, if taken away from the GOP winners of the closest elections, would have been sufficient to reverse the outcomes of 89 House races such that the Democrats would now hold a 120-seat (277 – 157) House majority.[25] Although the thousands of state legislative contests are not exit-polled, it is reasonable to assume that the consistent red-shift numbers that we found in the Senate, House, and gubernatorial contests would map onto these critical (as we have seen) down-ballot elections as well.

So the polls (both exit and pre-election) got it very wrong yet again. But were all these polls "off?" The answer to that question is almost certainly "Yes." But not in the direction commonly supposed.

Approaching E2014, in fact on the day preceding the election, I published an article, entitled "Vote Counts and Polls: An Insidious Feedback Loop,"[26] detailing the corruption of our forensic baselines as pollsters systematically amended their polling methodologies to remedy the string of embarrassing misses (marked by persistent red shifts) with which they began the computerized voting era. In the article I addressed two specific methodological changes that together have a potent effect on poll outcomes: the first is the use of the Likely Voter Cutoff Model for selecting the sample,

---

[24] The sample size of the House poll exceeded 17,000 respondents, yielding a Margin of Error (MOE) of less than 1% and a Total Survey Error (TSE) of less than 2%. The odds of a 3.7% red shift occurring by chance were less than one in a billion.

[25] Of course I am not suggesting that vote theft can be targeted with such exquisite and infallible precision. But it would make no sense at all *not* to target vote theft to the closer races and shift enough votes to ensure narrow victories. When one couples the evidence of a nearly 3 million vote disparity with even a modestly successful targeting protocol, the result is easily enough to flip the balance of power in the US House.

[26] http://www.truth-out.org/news/item/27203-vote-counts-and-polls-an-insidious-feedback-loop.

disproportionately eliminating respondents belonging to Democratic constituencies; and the second is the use of demographics (including partisanship) from the *adjusted* exit polls of prior elections to weight the current sample.

Each of these adaptations is discussed in detail in the aforementioned article and in Study V of Chapter VII of this book, but the overall effect is to *undersample* Democratic constituencies in both exit and pre-election polling such that, with these methodologies employed, an honestly counted election should produce consistent *blue* shifts (votecounts more Democratic than the polls),[27] or exactly the opposite of what E2014 presented.

I concluded my article with the observation that "on Election Day, *accurate* polls should be seen as a red flag," because a methodological contortion like the Likely Voter Cutoff Model should get election results *right* if and only if those election results are *wrong*. Instead we had wildly *inaccurate* polls, a massive red shift *beyond* that which was, via such contortions, already anticipated by and built into the polls. These "double red flag" results are extremely hard to reconcile with any scenario in which votes were tabulated as cast in thousands of elections across America in E2014.

The Consequences: A Nation Lost in Translation

America prides itself on being the first and best representative democracy, and representative democracies are about the translation—via elections, the casting and counting of votes—of the public will into a representative government, a team of officeholders empowered to set policies and chart direction. A quick review of the scorecard shows the GOP, now purged of essentially all of its

---

[27] This appears to be precisely what transpired, in an intra-party context, in the 2016 Democratic primary in Oklahoma, a red flag detailed in the next chapter.

moderate elements,[28] holding a 10-seat majority (54 – 44) in the US Senate, a 60-seat majority (247 – 187) in the US House, nearly a two-to-one gubernatorial advantage (31 – 18), a better than two-to-one grip on state legislative chambers (68 – 30), and full control (governorship and both branches of the state legislature, now termed the "trifecta") of 23 states to the Democrats' seven. Judging by its array of officeholders, America in the wake of E2014 can only be seen as a very red country.

But a major component of that red-paint reality, a kind of secondary effect of all the shocking and fundamentally inexplicable defeats, goes beyond the array of actual officeholders. Outcomes—winning or losing—are part of an educational feedback loop and when outcomes are grossly distorted it is the political equivalent of receiving a bad education, of being taught that 2 plus 2 equals 5. Nor is the routed party the only student in the class. The nation itself, in believing its officeholders to be duly elected and thereby representative, develops, through looking into that distorted mirror, a distorted self-portrait: "America *is* a red country"—it's right there on the blinking Election Night map and winds its way through every item of political news until it becomes a truth embedded in all of our brains, and until in such a country, more such outcomes cease to be shocking at all. It takes a long time, many election cycles, however, for another, more ominous recognition to dawn: that *no matter how we all vote, we keep getting a government that most of us don't want*, a government that, divided as we may be on many fronts, we begin to recognize does not represent any of us, respond to any of us, or translate our collective will into laws, policy, and national direction.

----

[28] It is worth reiterating here that primary elections, and particularly down-ballot primary elections, are the lowest hanging fruit an election rigger can pick. There are almost never any baselines (exit polls or pre-election polls) for forensic analysis and media/public scrutiny is generally nonexistent. In the very rare cases where the level of scrutiny spikes and rudimentary baselines *are* available, as in the "unimaginable" (according to the *Times*) primary defeat that unseated House Majority Leader Eric Cantor earlier in 2014, the usual suspects, however ridiculous, are trotted out and no investigation of the votecount process even considered.

Karl Rove's long-sought *perpetual rule* and *permanent majority* have come to near-full fruition. That this doesn't come close to being an accurate translation of the public will and the "soul" of America could not matter less to the likes of Rove and his clients: the permanent majority he has engineered is a permanent majority of rulers, not subjects. But, as the next chapter will explore, it *does* matter to the public itself. Our finally perceived loss of sovereignty—verging now on government without the consent of the governed—has begun to have a profound impact on the American psyche, and we are watching it start to play out in American politics. This is what the era of computerized vote counting has wrought and, with no pleasure in being such a downer, I suggest that any possible way out begins with facing the full reality of this achievement in all its formidable dimensions.

V. E2016: THE CHICKENS COME HOME

'What is a Caucus-race?' said Alice, not that she much wanted to know.

— *Lewis Carroll,* **Alice's Adventures in Wonderland**

Tip of the Hat?

Chess, at its highest levels, is a game of patient and far-seeing strategies, foundation building, and inspired positioning. In observing a grandmaster's chess match and seeing a far-sighted strategy coming to fruition, one is inclined to tip one's hat to the skill and brilliance of the player who brought it off. That inclination would be tempered though if one had also observed the master, when his opponent momentarily arose from the board to get some air, stealthily moving twice. Chess, like politics, is a finely balanced game, one that becomes a lot easier to win with just one extra move and no contest at all if you can pull off that little stunt several times in the course of a match.

Working from the bottom up, taking advantage of American media and public obsession with presidential politics to quietly take control of the power structure whose foundations are dug further down the ballot, is a very smart and patient plan, one worthy of a master strategist. As we have seen, state-by-state control of that political infrastructure spawns massive positional advantages and the capacity to lock in political domination impervious to adverse developments in popularity (e.g., single-digit approval ratings) or glaring incongruence with the public will. All of that has been planned and executed brilliantly and would be worthy of at least a tip of the hat, were it not for those "extra moves" that we have seen but the opponent, who was out getting some air, apparently missed.

Yet the master plan, even though we suspect computerized election theft has been a critical component of it, still presents an element of brilliance. The *decision* to cheat is unremarkable—it fits the times. The *capacity* to cheat, to take full advantage of an insanely vulnerable system, is clear enough. What *is* remarkable is the ability to read the psyches of the players and guardians of the game, so as to determine rather precisely how flagrantly one can cheat, how dramatically alter the course of events without getting caught, without even getting investigated. It is in this all-too-accurate reading of *us* that the true sinister genius of a master player lies.

But the rigged election game gets more difficult as the disconnect between the voters and their supposed representatives widens. E2014, with approval ratings in the single-digits, was the quintessential throw-the-bums-out election that wasn't, leaving in its wake large swaths of the public, left and right, clenched in political outrage or mired in political despair. That's a lot—indeed, according to every poll, a super-majority—of frustrated, angry, and disgusted voters ready to go "in a different direction"—populist and, from the corporate point of view, dangerous.

2016: The Politics of Disgust

And so we arrived at the year 2016—presidential and thus-far unfathomable. Barring some extra-curricular hi-jinx, the American electorate will be offered a choice between the most despised, distrusted, indeed hated brace of major-party presidential nominees in living memory, if not in history: Hillary Clinton and Donald Trump carry the highest unfavorability ratings ever recorded.[1] This *prix fixe*

---

[1] For a snapshot of the numbers, which of course fluctuate but have consistently tunneled through the subterranean strata, see, e.g.,

menu is the product of a primary season featuring a series of elections as suspect as any we have yet observed in the New American Century.

Before turning to the evidence gathered in support of that assertion, let's begin by taking note of what the American people came into this election year seeming to *want*. It is hard to miss the energy that swirled around two candidates, Trump and Bernie Sanders, who, from the right and left respectively, were screaming "ENOUGH ALREADY!!" and promising to shake up the status quo in dramatic fashion. This angry, sometimes bordering on nihilistic, energy dwarfed whatever scant enthusiasm greeted the other major candidates—from Clinton down the gamut of current and erstwhile Republican office-holders (Marco Rubio, Chris Christie, Jeb Bush, Ted Cruz, John Kasich, et al)— who were all perceived, wherever they attempted to position themselves on the political spectrum, as card-carrying members of the establishment. Let us also notice that, of the two candidates who excited the voting public, the one on the right became the presumptive Republican nominee while the one on the left was stopped cold, just short of his party's nomination. And the one on the right was bathed in a constant media spotlight while the one on the left was effectively ignored until it was no longer remotely possible to do so. It does not take an advanced degree in political science to recognize that in the parade of presidential aspirants Sanders was the only one who, from the standpoint of the power elites, was both electable and dangerous enough that he had to be stopped.

The R-Word Comes into Common Usage

By the time of the Democratic Convention, there were millions of hopping mad Sanders supporters, convinced not only that their hero was robbed but also that Hillary Clinton herself was the thief or at

---

http://www.gallup.com/poll/193376/trump-leads-clinton-historically-bad-image-ratings.aspx.

least was aware of the heist.[2] What these voters saw had the look of a thoroughly "rigged" game, though it was Trump, not Sanders, who kept resorting to the R-word in reference to the nomination process.[3]

To begin with, there was the spectre of their candidate drawing first large, then huge and wildly enthusiastic crowds—far outstripping those of Clinton—and yet being all-but-ignored by mainstream media. They saw a candidate raise an enormous war chest from millions of individual contributions and entirely without drinking alongside Clinton (and other candidates) at the corporate trough—a feat with the potential to revolutionize American politics that nevertheless somehow failed to impress the press. Then they saw, often up close and personal, in state after state, obstacles thrown in the path of would-be Sanders voters, sometimes as the result of legitimate, if cynical, regulations governing registration deadlines and qualifications, but often a function of what seemed to be targeted purges of voter databases and deliberately erroneous instructions given to election administrators and to voters. Millions of voters were relegated to the dread "provisional" ballot, with a fair proportion of those votes going uncounted. And the impact of all of these schemes was all too obviously and disproportionately to Sanders' electoral detriment.

---

[2] While it is natural enough to assume that the *beneficiary* of a covert manipulation was in fact its *perpetrator*, there are certainly non-candidate bad actors—foreign and of course, though the media seems hell-bent on denying it, domestic—with strong motivation to influence and alter electoral outcomes, such that the beneficiary of such activities may not only not be their perpetrator but also may be entirely unaware of their existence. We are witnessing an unobservable vote counting process giving predictable rise to chronic suspicion of fraud, knee-jerk assignment of blame, and a general breakdown in the trust necessary for a legitimate and peaceful electoral and political process.

[3] Trump has already begun applying the R-word prospectively to the *general* election contest, giving rise to a growing concern that results adverse to him may not be accepted as legitimate. It is ironic that the ark of election integrity may be carried into battle by such a champion. Ironic and distressing as well the sudden alarm that our electoral system may be vulnerable to *outsider hacking*—which of course it is—as if the possibility of *insider rigging* had never occurred to anyone.

It didn't help when a hacker's and/or insider's leak of emails seemed to confirm that the Democratic National Committee, supposedly an unaligned umpire and facilitator of nomination battles, was surreptitiously promoting Clinton's cause in a variety of ways, and that elements of the mainstream media were also in on the game.[4] And of course there was the thick padding—the hundreds of "superdelegates" chosen not by the voters but by the Democratic Party establishment, 90% of whom would vote at the convention for the anointed candidate, Clinton—amounting to a nearly *20% handicap* operating against the delegate count of Sanders (or any other "outside" candidate who might have had the temerity to mount an intra-party challenge).

Those were thumbs on the scale that voters *could see*. And because, unlike in a suspect one-day November election such as E2004, the primary season extended for months, the hits kept coming and the distress and eventual outrage kept building, along with ever increasing levels of vigilance and distrust. Questions (and lawsuits) hung over the electoral procedures of many primary (and caucus) states, with egregiously visible fiascoes coming to light in, among others, Arizona, Kentucky, Ohio, New York, and California. This three-ring electoral circus was what the voters *saw*.

What the voters *couldn't see* was what was happening to the votes that had been cast. But the question naturally framed itself that, if Clinton was, as it appeared, the beneficiary of all these *discoverable* thumbs on the electoral scale, how could a vote counting process that was unobservable and so highly vulnerable be blithely presumed to be immune to an *undiscoverable* thumb? And the obvious follow-up: how bright is the ethical line between mass-purging voters to suppress their votes and simply mistabulating their votes? To a multitude of Sanders supporters, at least, not very bright.

---

[4] See https://en.wikipedia.org/wiki/2016_Democratic_National_Committee_email_leak.

Primaries and Caucuses

Although the vote counting process was of course not directly observable, as each state weighed in numerical evidence began to emerge and pause-giving patterns become established. It was hard not to notice, as the Sanders candidacy established itself and the nomination battle heated up, a glaring divergence between the election results in primary versus caucus states. In 14 states, pledged convention delegates were chosen in caucus meetings where the principal method of counting votes was observable and where state totals could be reconciled via a traditional tabulation tree to the counts at each individual caucus. The first caucus, in Iowa, led off the nomination battle and resulted in a razor-thin Clinton victory (49.9% to 49.6%) amidst various allegations of procedural mismanagement.[5] The second caucus, in Nevada, brought forth another narrow Clinton victory (52.6% to 47.3%) and more allegations.[6]

Following the Nevada caucus and heading into March, it became apparent that the nomination would be a battle and not a coronation. The table below presents the results of the 12 remaining state caucuses:

2016 Democratic Party Caucuses (3/1 - 6/7)			
State (Date)	Sanders %	Clinton %	Sanders Margin
Colorado (3/1)	59.0%	40.3%	18.7%
Minnesota (3/1)	61.6%	38.4%	23.2%
Kansas (3/5)	67.7%	32.3%	35.4%
Nebraska (3/5)	57.1%	42.9%	14.2%
Maine (3/6)	64.3%	35.5%	28.8%

---

[5] Concerns "ranged from the potential for incorrect vote counts due to crowding to confusion over the role of coin tosses to settle some tie results." See http://www.desmoinesregister.com/story/news/politics/2016/07/26/87576058/.

[6] This time the main problem was that many Clinton staffers and supporters were not required to register in order to vote. See http://www.dailykos.com/story/2016/2/26/1491957/-Nevada-and-Iowa-DNC-run-caucuses-full-of-fraud-lies-vote-irregularities-wrong-winner-announced.

Idaho (3/22)	78.0%	21.2%	56.8%
Utah (3/22)	79.3%	20.3%	59.0%
Alaska (3/26)	86.1%	18.4%	67.7%
Hawaii (3/26)	69.8%	30.0%	39.8%
Washington (3/26)	72.7%	27.1%	45.6%
Wyoming (4/5)	55.7%	44.3%	11.4%
North Dakota (6/7)	64.2%	25.6%	38.6%
Average	**68.0%**	**31.4%**	**36.6%**

As can be seen, *every* caucus was won by Sanders, all by wide margins, ranging from a low of 11.4% to a high of 67.7%. *Sanders' average margin of victory was 36.6%, a better than two to one ratio of caucus voters.*

Were the caucus states a discrete and homogeneous swath of America, an identifiable bastion of Sanders support? An argument could be made that, with the exception of Maine, which could be considered penumbral to Sanders' Vermont, each of these states is located west of the Mississippi; in most of them, voters were more likely to be white (though not young) than in the primary states where Clinton built her narrow margin of pledged delegates. There is, however, substantial political and cultural diversity within the caucus set (Minnesota, Colorado, Washington, and Hawaii hardly mirror Utah, Idaho, Kansas, and Nebraska).

Then there is the divergence of the Dakotas, North and South. In South Dakota, a primary state, Clinton edged Sanders 51.0% to 49.0%; in North Dakota, a caucus state, Sanders blew out Clinton 64.2% to 25.6%. The black population of each state is 1%. The North Dakota caucus and the South Dakota primary were held on the same date, June 7. Is it unreasonable to wonder what, other than the method of counting votes, might account for such a dramatic difference in outcomes, greater than 40%, in these neighboring and demographically similar states? And more generally, *what would account for the entire run of Sanders caucus blowouts?* For there is nothing subtle here in these numbers, nothing that can be reassuringly written off as a figment of race, age, gender, or any other all-encompassing demographic or political explanation.[7]

2016 Exit Polls: A Tale of Two Parties

If there was any remaining doubt that doubt was in order, it was removed by the exit polls. We have been treated to yet another, and perhaps the most heated, revival of the Great Exit Poll Debate, which had its first primetime run in the wake of E2004. In this snarkfest, those questioning the fidelity of the votecounts cite exit poll-votecount (EP/VC) disparities as evidence indicative of votecount mistabulation, while defenders of the faith in turn attack the reliability of exit polls (at least in the US) and often can't resist weaving in an obbligato line of mockery directed at the "conspiracy theorists" who can't seem to understand why we should doubt the exit polls while trusting the votecounts.

The problem with the Great Exit Poll Debate is that it is fated to be inconclusive because *neither* side has access to the evidence that could resolve it: neither raw exit poll data (individual responses to the exit poll questionnaires) nor voter-marked ballots are publicly accessible; both are held to be proprietary and off-limits. So what we have is in essence a concealed counting system alongside a concealed polling system, *neither of which is self-evidently accurate.* It would be something of a credibility draw, except for the fact that the exit pollsters' business model rests rather heavily on the perceived accuracy of their polls, which translates to publishing polls (and it is now recognized that any iteration of an exit poll prior to final

---

[7] One explanation worthy of further investigation attributes much of Sanders' caucus-state strength to the personal and public nature of caucus proceedings and the aggressive, at times intimidating, behavior of Sanders partisans at these events. If the thuggery was indeed so widespread and pronounced as to have resulted in this multi-state run of Sanders routs, so out of step with the primaries, it is testament to the alteration in political attitudes and behavior consequent upon the breakdown in basic trust in the electoral process. *Perception* of a fraudulent process undermines the behavioral norms and standards upon which a healthy political system must be based.

adjustment to virtual congruence with the votecounts will likely be preserved via screen-capture, thus immortalizing any disparities) that are at least within spitting distance of the electoral results. Major and particularly *serial* departures from those electoral results—no matter what is said by way of disclaimer that exit polls in the US are not "designed" to approximate votecounts—are a serious embarrassment, bad for business. Hence the exit pollsters are fanatical about pattern analysis and error correction—they try hard to "get it right." It is in that context that we must try to comprehend the performance of the exit polls in the E2016 primaries.

In examining the performance of the E2016 primary season exit polls it would be natural to conclude that each party's primaries had been handled by a separate polling outfit, or at least that different methodologies and protocols were employed for the Democratic versus the Republican polls. Of course neither of these things was true: all voters, Democratic and Republican, were polled by the same firm, Edison Research, using the same methodological approach, on the same days, at the same precincts, in the same weather, with the same strict protocols. How then to explain the resulting pattern? Why did the polls perform superbly throughout the run of Republican primaries,[8] while they were such a fiasco in the Democratic primaries that exit polling was *abruptly and quietly canceled* with the elections in New Jersey, New Mexico, and (critically) California remaining on the schedule?[9]

How stark was the contrast? The mean "error" or EP/VC disparity for the 23 Republican primaries for which data was available was 0.6%.[10]

---

[8] Time-stamped screen-capture data, necessary for EP/VC comparison, was available for 23 out of the 25 Republican primaries that were exit polled.

[9] Other primaries not exit polled took place in Delaware, Kentucky, Montana, North Dakota, South Dakota, Oregon, and Puerto Rico. Although cancellation of the exit polls in 19 states in E2012 was noted by the MSM at the time, a search of *NY Times* and *Washington Post* websites revealed not a single article of any genre regarding the sudden cancellation of the 2016 exit polls.

[10] We treated the Republican primaries as a contest of Trump against "the field" of his opponents. We took this approach both because, while Trump was a constant in all of

In only two of the 23 elections were EP/VC disparities outside the Total Survey Error (TSE),[11] about what we would expect from the rules of probability. Of the individual election disparities greater than one percent, 11 favored Donald Trump while nine favored his opponents, again the kind of balance indicative of both accurate polling and accurate vote tabulation. This level of performance over a long string of elections confirms the competence of the pollsters and the soundness of their protocols and methodology.[12]

It is a competence and a soundness that seem to have vanished when polling Democratic voters. In the 25 Democratic primaries the mean error or EP/VC disparity was 6.0%, *or ten times that in the Republican primaries*. In *10* of the 25 elections the EP/VC disparities exceeded the Total Survey Error; we would normally expect to see *one* such failure. And of the individual election disparities greater than one percent, *three* favored Bernie Sanders while *21* favored Hillary Clinton.[13] You can see why Sanders voters began to wonder what might be happening to their votes, questioning the counting process along with the registration process and the various thumb-on-the-scale party rules.

The Great Exit Poll Debate Redux has of course focused on this run of disparities and whether it is in any way probative of systemic problems with the vote counting process. On the one side are those who see in the exit polls *proof* that the Democratic primaries have

---

the primaries, the rest of the field varied as candidates dropped out; and because it facilitated an apples-to-apples comparison with the Clinton/Sanders contest. Analysis of the performance of the exit polls in the Republican primaries, although somewhat more complex, did not change significantly when EP/VC disparities were viewed candidate by candidate.

[11] Total Survey Error, while built on the mathematical Margin of Error (MOE) for a purely random sample, is generally somewhat larger than the MOE because it takes into account certain non-random factors in the administration of an exit poll. We employed TSE for both Republican and Democratic primaries.

[12] The exit polls for the hotly-contested 2008 Democratic primaries also exhibited an expected level of accuracy.

[13] For the complete tables, compiled by statistician Theodore Soares, see www.tdmsresearch.com.

been rigged. They look at the math, much as we did in E2004 and other red-shifted elections of the computer-count era, and see a pattern of disparities that, from a statistical standpoint, is all but impossible. On the other side are those who see the exit polls as essentially worthless, crude instruments with no probative value at all when it comes to assessing the accuracy of a given votecount or of the entire vote counting process. As in many such polarized disputes, the truth most likely falls somewhere in between.

A key point of contention—given that the Republican polls were essentially spot-on, confirming the general competence of the exit polling operation and the soundness of its methodology—has been whether the Democratic exit polls were distorted by an "enthusiasm gap" between Clinton and Sanders voters. According to the "enthusiasm gap hypothesis," similar in nature to the (debunked) "reluctant Bush responder" hypothesis of E2004, younger and more enthusiastic Sanders voters were more likely to participate in the exit poll when selected than were older and presumably less enthusiastic Clinton voters. Of course there is no dispositive evidence either way, since enthusiasm, unlike gender, race, or age, is not a visible trait subject to quantification in those refusing to participate. But we do know that the exit pollsters keep careful count—by gender, race, and approximate age—of refusals to participate, and use this count in weighting their polls. Thus if, as the critics suspect, young voters were more apt to respond to the exit poll when selected, they would be down-weighted accordingly to bring their age cohort in line with its actual proportion of the voting public. And, because enthusiasm and youth were acknowledged to be strongly correlated, the age-based weighting would have neutralized most if not all of any enthusiasm gap.

It is unfortunately the nature of the Great Exit Poll Debate to come down to skirmishes like "reluctant Bush responder" and "Sanders enthusiasm gap," which most often cannot be decisively settled with the information and data made available.[14] But for those who seek to dispel concerns about the vote counting process, a "tie" is as good as a win. The political timeframe during which elections hang in the balance, such that interest and passions peak, tends to be very short (it often ends with a losing candidate's concession), while the timeframe for in-depth academic debate of the subtleties of data analysis can be measured in weeks, months, sometimes years. Once a debate becomes "academic" in nature, the political "moment" is almost guaranteed to pass and with it, regardless of whether or how the debate resolves, passes all prospect of action. In the case of the 2016 Democratic primaries, concession has taken place, the Convention following, a time for "healing" and "pulling together." The next battle awaits, the next election, the next exercise in blind faith.

Oklahoma!

Peter Falk's "Columbo" had a famous tagline. Just when the villain seemed to have wriggled out of the net of suspicion with the perfect alibi and a patronizing smirk, Columbo would cock his head slightly to the side, hesitate a beat, and say, "Ah, just one more thing." Then would come the killer question about some little-noticed detail, and the next thing you knew the bad guy was on his way to the slammer.

In that spirit, we direct our attention now to Oklahoma. This otherwise uninteresting (to Democrats at least) red state stands out as the contrarian—one of just a few states where Sanders' votecount exceeded his exit poll total and in fact the most Sanders-shifted (6.1%) of all the Democratic primaries. This in itself would be unremarkable (every long table has its "least" and "most," seemingly every graph its

---

[14] An unprecedented legal action to obtain the data that might resolve such debates is now under way. *Johnson v. Edison Media Research, Inc.* was filed in federal court in Ohio on July 11, 2016, seeking the release by the exit polling firm of the raw data from the 2016 exit polls. A companion suit is also being contemplated to obtain access to actual ballots under public records law. Each legal initiative faces significant hurdles, reflecting the thoroughly non-transparent and non-public status of the vote counting process.

outlier) except for one factoid, one "little-noticed detail:" *Oklahoma turns out to be the only state of all the states on the Democratic primary chart in which the state itself, rather than the vendors or their satellite contractors, programs the voting computers.*

These are two dots that you don't have to be Columbo to connect: Dot 1) absence of the suspected vector of access to the programming; Dot 2) reverse EP/VC disparity (i.e., a pattern-defying absence, indeed reversal, of the virtually ubiquitous Clinton-shift). This is quite a correlation.[15] Mere coincidence? Perhaps. But how many such correlations can we brush aside as mere coincidences in the interest of protecting the shield?

Can we also brush aside the stark contrast in exit poll performance for the Democratic and Republican primaries of 2016? Can we brush aside the radically different results in observably-counted caucus states? Can we brush aside the pervasive red-shifts of every midterm election since the passage of HAVA in 2002? Can we brush aside the glaring disparities between competitive and noncompetitive elections? Can we brush aside the 59% of the statewide vote won by a cipher candidate in 2010 or the key senatorial election in which the only explanation left standing for the enormous disparity between hand-counted and opscan-counted ballots was the method of counting itself? Can we brush aside the growing data set of

---

[15] We note that the shift in Oklahoma (6.1%) is significant, near the margin of error for the poll. If we conclude that the denial of the vendor-programmed access vector led to a "clean" count, then we would expect an *accurate* exit poll result, not a 6.1% shift. All the more so if there was in fact an "enthusiasm gap" in Sanders' favor, as has been suggested by critics of exit poll-based forensics.

This suggests something even more ominous. We know that exit pollsters study their own error patterns fanatically, and make whatever tweaks to sampling and weighting they believe necessary to avoid the serial embarrassment of continually getting elections "wrong" in the same direction. Does the glaring exception that is Oklahoma then suggest that *other* states, also being subject to such anticipatory tweaking (which in the case of putatively *unrigged* Oklahoma backfired), displayed mitigated exit poll-votecount disparities significantly *smaller* than they would otherwise have been? If so, then the egregious exit poll-votecount disparities throughout the Democratic primaries would be even larger and screaming even louder that electronic manipulation was endemic.

Cumulative Vote Share (CVS) graphs that show the telltale upslope of suspect candidates as precincts get larger and votes consequently get easier to shift without risk of detection? Can we brush aside a sudden presidency-determining flip in exit polls and votecounts alike when a state website "went down" in the early morning hours of November 3, 2004 and the votes were rerouted to a "backup" server set up by none other than Karl Rove's IT guru? How much can we brush aside and continue to sleep at night believing that our democracy is safe and sound?

To brush or not to brush, that is the question.

VI. THE WAY FORWARD

Those who make peaceful revolution impossible make violent revolution inevitable.

-- John F. Kennedy

You'd have to search long and hard to find a subject more important and less sexy than election forensics. Dependent as it is on charts full of numbers, indirect measurements, statistics, probabilities, baselines, margins of error, and meta-analyses, even our best work has serious eye-glazing potential. And yet the reality is that only in the immediate forensic aftermath of shocking elections does election integrity seem to *come alive*, hit home, and become a focal interest to more than a handful of full-time advocates. The rest of the time, after the shockwaves and suspicious odors have dissipated, our vital subject customarily recedes into obscurity and seeming irrelevance. Separated from the drama of suspect and bizarre electoral outcomes and the transient outrage they may engender, vote counting becomes again a "process" issue, rather abstract, something to discuss politely—or, better yet, let other people discuss politely—but hardly a top-priority, urgent, storm-the-Bastille matter.

Nonetheless it is on that seemingly unspectacular process issue—the simple question of whether votes counted unobservably can ever be the trusted basis for the electoral translation process at the core of democracy—that I believe we must ultimately make our stand. If you took all of the analyses in this book—every calculation of the red shift, every flipped vote, every suspect result, all evidence of fraud, and the whole big picture of political incongruence—and tossed them in the trashcan, if you said it was all a conspiracy theorist's mirage, *what we'd still have sitting on the table in front of us is an unobservable vote counting process.* Without an observable and publicly posted count, on Election Night at the voting sites before the ballots leave the public view, elections are fatally compromised as the legitimate foundation of democracy, *and this basic truth requires no forensics, direct or indirect, to establish.*

There is essentially no way of knowing what the collective intent of the public, as expressed in the votes cast in thousands of elections in the computerized voting era, really has been. Successfully rigged, unsuccessfully rigged, partially rigged, pristine; legitimate or illegitimate: *the count is unobservable so there is simply no way to know.* That is one hell of a stupid risk and *that is the real problem,* though it very unfortunately seems to come into focus only when specific outcomes are such that major-league fraud is suspected.

But we neither expect, nor indeed seek, to remedy that fraud, to re-do elections, to unseat even the most suspiciously elected officeholders. We can't go back to E2014, let alone E2010 or E2004; even investigation into this year's putrescent primaries is rapidly becoming academic. There *is* no going back. That is all water under the bridge and, even if we suspect it is filthy and polluted water, there is nothing in the real world to be done about it.

The only remedy we seek is prospective—that we begin, in our communities and as a nation, to count our votes once again in public and not in the dark of cyberspace. That is the very most or, to put it another way for those fearful of upheaval or instability, the very "worst" that can come of all our efforts to have the matter of vote counting in America taken seriously.

An observable count of votes will not immediately undo the anti-democratic damage that has been inflicted upon our electoral and political systems during the era of computerized voting. Districts will remain gerrymandered; voter suppression schemes will still be on the books; *Citizens United* will remain the law of the land and floods of corporate cash will not be readily diverted. It is a very, very deep hole America has dug. But without observable vote counting Americans will have not even a shovel with which to try to dig our nation out.

Rights and Duties

The great task that confronts us is that of changing a process passively accepted as a *fait accompli* and currently possessing the vast weight of legal, bureaucratic, and habitual inertias. This change, to an observable counting system, will require a reawakening in the American citizenry of a compelling sense of both its collective rights in, and concomitant duties to, our democracy. For can we not agree that the majestic *right* to honest elections and an observable votecount carries with it the near-trivial *duty* once in our lifetimes to be a participant in that counting process? If we nevertheless insist on outsourcing that collective duty to others, indeed to a few unvetted corporations operating behind a proprietary curtain of secrecy, have we not thereby acquiesced in the compromise of the treasured right? If we place convenience, expediency, or our own ease and entertainment first, ahead of this basic duty to our democracy, can we really be judged to *deserve* that democracy as our right?

So three fundamental questions must be addressed in the name of election integrity:

1) Are the citizens of America willing to stand up for the right to an observable count as intrinsic to the right to vote?

2) Are the citizens of America willing to fight secret vote counting with the same energy that they would fight mass discrimination and disenfranchisement?

3) Are the citizens of America willing to assume the modest burden of direct participation that an observable count would impose on them?

Progress on each front will require powerful initiatives of education and outreach, encompassing all age-groups[1] and political creeds, employing all available media, including a major reliance on bottom-up social media to compensate for the sluggishness, stubborn indifference, and deliberate gatekeeping and stonewalling of established top-down media. And "opinion leaders" *outside* of politics—writers, athletes, entertainers with Facebook and Twitter audiences that guarantee that your thoughts and messages will be heard collectively by millions—*please take special note*: this is, in a way, your era; your influence can be profound; you are indeed "followed."

Fortunately, the ground is fertile for this campaign: when voters were asked in a national poll taken in October 2012, "Would you be willing to work as a volunteer vote counter for 4 hours at some time during your lifetime as part of a national effort to make vote counting in our elections public and observable?" a solid majority of 57% responded "Yes" (to 23% "No").[2] That represents nearly 80 million Americans

---

[1] The power of childhood educational initiatives can be seen in the heightened awareness among America's young of the need for ecological stewardship. Observance of Earth Day and other such additions to the school curriculum have had a significant cumulative effect and one can imagine educational initiatives related to the electoral process giving rise to a generation both more aware of its rights and more devoted to its duties. Of course an unfortunate trend in the opposite direction when it comes to teaching civics in the schools would have to be overcome. And "adult education" must be part of the curriculum if there is to be much of a democracy left for the children to serve.

[2] Positive response was found among majorities of both Democratic and Republican voters, across all age groups, among both white and minority voters, and in all geographic regions. In response to a companion question, fully 60% of voters expressed some degree of "worry" that "insiders or hackers could change the results of important elections by manipulating the Electronic Vote Counting Systems that count the votes here in America," a majority again maintained across the political spectrum (poll conducted by Zogby Analytics 10/28 – 10/30/2012; Margin of Error +/- 3.4%). Polling in advance of an election provides a better picture of public concern regarding

willing to put in the hours necessary to have a fully public, unpaid vote counting "labor force" for American elections.[3]

It is now our job not only to impress this reality upon reflexively nay-saying election administrators and politicians, but to let the American people know what we may not yet know about ourselves: that we are ready and willing to work for and serve our democracy, that we are more genuinely patriotic than anyone would have guessed.

How Do We Get There From Here?

One path to this epiphany would be to organize, record, and promulgate a serious and substantial public counting and auditing of a series of mock elections. Such an effort may be within the compass and capabilities of EDA and our fellow election integrity organizations, but we would encourage established good-government and civil-liberties organizations—ACLU, Common Cause, NAACP, et al—to join us in inspiring Americans back to the ways of participatory democracy.[4]

Even more promising would be to commence a "We Count" Campaign to recruit such a public counting force nationally, collaborating with these same established organizations and using our growing understanding of social media to spread the word far more effectively. Observable counting and even public auditing have been reflexively written off not only as a Luddite retreat (who needs humans to do

---

election integrity than do post-election polls, in which doubts are expressed disproportionately by the losers.

[3] In a typical protocol that has been proposed, citizens would be vetted, as they are for jury duty, and would work in teams of three counters selected from pools representing each major party and minor party/independent voters, so both major parties and the growing remainder of the electorate would be represented in each counting team and at least three sets of eyes would be on every ballot counted.

[4] Having participated in a small-scale pilot for such an undertaking, I am happy to report that even the counting of mock ballots in what we all knew was a mock election brought out a genuine *esprit de corps* in every one of the two dozen or so counters. Two hours flew by and, although the election was "mock," the feeling of civic pride in the room was very real.

anything when you have computers booted up and ready to go?) but also as impractical and unduly burdensome to administrators and citizenry alike. "Where are we ever going to dig up folks willing to stay late and count?" is the first question election administrators generally ask.

It is up to us as a public to *show* them where, to present the Election Boards of every state and locality with teeming rosters of signees, each testifying that he or she is committed to the job and volunteering to be called upon as a counter on Election Night. "We are not demanding that our country do something for *us*," our We Count campaign, echoing JFK, would let it be known to all. "We are demanding that we be permitted to do this for our country."

And yes, it is doable. One county does it now and has been doing it for several years. In Columbia County, New York, the Elections Board opens up their opscans at the close of voting and proceeds to count the voter-marked ballots within, a full 100% canvass as a check against the computers. The two Co-Commissioners of Elections, Democrat Virginia Martin and Republican Jason Nastke, recognized the vulnerability of the computers to error and manipulation and resolved that they would not be signing their names to and certifying election results embodying that risk. They fine-tuned and streamlined their process. No one is complaining; no bad actor, of course, would think of pulling a stunt like off-setting the zero-counters; and Columbia County has become a shining example of civic engagement. Perhaps some of the other 3143 counties in our country will take notice, give Commissioners Martin and Nastke (who will be pleased to offer guidance) a call, ask them how it's done. Why not?

One can imagine an Election Night as congregational and celebratory as New Year's Eve—Americans of all stripes at work together in our democracy's service. This vision, this revival can be ours—our new reality for The New American Century. Why not, indeed?! It is, ultimately, up to us.

Linking Arms, Metaphorically and Physically

Looking forward then, our plan of action is first and foremost to raise consciousness about the critical importance of observable vote counting for the health, well-being, and ultimate survival of our democracy; about the public duties inherent in this process; and about its demonstrable practicality. We believe the American people are prepared for this revisiting of the meaning of participatory democracy and will respond with enthusiasm and determination to a well-framed, well-presented, and well-publicized call to action.

We need to understand though that scattered and inchoate demands for observable vote counting will not be enough. This is no "niche" issue. Its implications could not be broader or deeper—yet it has wandered the streets like an orphan in rags. One can only imagine where we would be today if just a few of those groups whose agendas and visions rest so heavily on the outcomes of American elections had devoted even a small part of their energies to electoral integrity and reclaiming the vote counting process from the darkness of cyberspace. Instead, here we are, our political discourse plunging lower than most of us would have ever thought possible and promising to descend lower still, our nation sinking in the quicksand of political mistrust and disgust. Now, at this late hour, I call upon *all* activists—all advocates for all the specific embodiments of peace, justice, fairness, humanity, ecological sanity, and democracy itself—to grasp the big picture and recognize that the strife of the New American Century is not simply a scattered bunch of isolated skirmishes and battles. It is, sadly, a war.

The forces of control and domination understand this and are pursuing an integrated strategy to drive us off of common ground and destroy democracy at its roots. Failure to comprehend that and respond accordingly will lead the defenders of democracy and advocates for its many blessings to a general and catastrophic defeat. As my colleagues Victoria Collier and Ben Ptashnik—in calling for all advocates of progressive, ecological, human-rights, and pro-democracy causes to recognize the critical salience of honest elections and observable vote counting to the fate of their own individual agendas—recently wrote:

> We cannot continue struggling separately for myriad causes, while social progress is reversed piecemeal and democracy itself dismantled. Unless we organize *to preserve the ability of the people to shape public policy (i.e., to have their votes counted honestly and accurately)*, it is crystal clear that there will be no justice, no peace, no ecological sustainability, no amelioration of climate change and no end to poverty and economic oppression. Now is the time to link our formidable strengths as organizers and activists.[5]

Yes, we will have to come together and work together in our demand for observable vote counting. And we will have to *focus* that demand and apply it like a welder's torch to the joints of the electoral system, beginning with the local administrators who are responsible for many of the decisions impacting the conduct of our elections. We will also have to be prepared to back up our demand for observable vote counting with civil action and, to the extent that all more cooperative tactics have been exhausted, with civil disobedience.

Why civil disobedience? Why not just start, or continue, writing letters to the editors and our representatives? Why not just keep gathering data, doing analyses, comparing exit polls and votecounts, making alarming statements about this or that aspect of a process that has been a rock of national faith, quite likely the very first thing that comes into your mind when you think of the great achievements of America?

Because the system has proven itself terminally unresponsive. And because it has been designed, or re-designed, to withhold its best

---

[5] See "A National Call to Link Arms for Democracy," *Truthout* (5/31/2014); http://www.truth-out.org/opinion/item/24033-a-national-call-to-link-arms-for-democracy.

evidence, to tease us with exit polls and baselines, anomalies and upslopes, while keeping concealed the only data that could definitively answer the critical questions of whether the vote counting was honest and accurate, and who actually won each and every election. *That data, that evidence, is the voter-marked ballot.* In most states, it exists in every election and it exists in a particular place: the catch-bins of the opscans that count the lion's share of our votes all over this land.

Opscan Parties

When the Civil Rights movement sought a breakthrough in overcoming the deeply ingrained prejudices and practices of oppression, its leaders knew that letters and speeches, and even great marches, were not enough. The torch had to be applied to the joint— the school bus, the lunch counter, the college steps—the situs for the denial of rights. When the anti-nuclear movement sought to stop the proliferation of weapons and power plants, the situs was the missile silo and the power plant gate. When the earliest, Civil War-era suffragettes sought the vote for women, the situs was the voting booth, where they went to cast a vote and be arrested for having done so.[6]

The situs for an observable vote count is where the ballots *are*. On Election Night.

Secret vs. observable vote counting comes down to the question "Whose ballots are they? To whom do they belong?" I think the answer could not be more clear: those are *our* ballots; they should belong to the voters, the people, with the state as custodian. But, right now, not only don't they belong to us, we can't even borrow them, can't even look at them, let alone count them. They've been handed over, uncounted, to the state, which has outsourced them to a few private corporations, and all powers agree that that is the last the

---

[6] See Jill Lepore, "The Woman Card," *The New Yorker* (6/27/2016), p.23.

voters will ever see of them. They are off-limits, along with the hardware and software used to turn them into binary digits and combine and process and transport those bits and bytes behind a proprietary cyber-curtain where none of us can see.

The Boston Tea Party, which took place in 1773, was an on-site protest against the "taxation without representation" to which the American colonists were subjected. It was instrumental in the process which gave birth to our nation, though it was essentially about money and involved the destruction of property, the illegitimately taxed tea dumped into Boston Harbor.

Now, more than two centuries of national history later, we find *ourselves* in the shoes of patriots aggrieved by a loss of sovereignty. We have written the letters, gathered the data, performed the analyses, offered the evidence, begged and pleaded and protested— to no avail. Elections remain outsourced, secret, suspect; our politics poisonous. Can we act? Can we gather and link arms for an Opscan Party?

Our latter-day act of nation-saving disobedience, an Opscan Party involves neither money nor the destruction of property. It is a peaceful and very simple reclamation of the right to a public and observable counting of our votes. To participate, simply form a group of about a dozen voters from your precinct; remain there at the close of voting; form a circle around the optical scanner; link arms and request that the scanner be opened, the ballots removed, a public and observable human count of at least one major contest initiated, the numbers compared with the tally from the opscan, and the ballots returned to the precinct for storage. Remain in a circle around the opscan until that request is honored or until you are removed. When asked what right you are asserting, answer, "The people's right to an observable vote count. Those are our ballots." Record the proceedings for public posting and sharing. It will surely go viral.

An Opscan Party is a powerful and appropriate action in a number of ways. It is neither labor- nor capital-intensive. It is quintessentially local yet will carry profound national impact. It is neither destructive nor dependent on force. It meets the problem exactly where the problem *is*, where and when our ballots are captured and taken away from us. And perhaps most important, it is unmistakably *just*, and can hardly be perceived or fairly portrayed as anything but.

Imagine an Election Night with a hundred (or more) Opscan Parties organized across our nation. In some localities, where poll workers are won over, opscans will be opened and public counts undertaken. Perhaps disparities will be revealed, perhaps not; the breakthrough act of public counting is enough. In other places, the request will be denied and the "partiers" removed. Perhaps among them will be a few who are widely known, opinion leaders, celebrities: their removal will, by the handbook of modern media practice, *have* to be covered. And the social media will spread the videos showing the encounters, whether cooperative or confrontational, at the place and at the time of greatest relevance and impact—*our* lunch counter, *our* school bus, *our* college gate.

Any of the above outcomes is, in its own way, a game-changer. All have in common the recognition that the public is no longer on the outside trying in vain to look in through windows that have been painted black. This is not academic. This is not statistical. This is a very simple and direct question about a very precious kind of information. Who does it belong to? "Those are our ballots and we are here to assume the duty of counting them!"

For those made queasy by the prospect of "civil disobedience," confrontation, arrest, I can only point to the fact that freedom of assembly is a crucial right with roots in the deepest strata of our political and cultural heritage, and ask that we do more than pay mere lip service to it as a useless relic. We are being told to be good little passive citizens, cast a vote (or not) then go home and sit back and enjoy the show. *We are better than that.* And we are stronger, if we only knew. If we want our democracy, if we are to deserve it, we have the right *and* the duty to do more.

I ask what has become of the courage that founded this country, that steered it through shoals of prejudice, inequity, and oppression to the America The Nearly Beautiful into which most of us were born? Have we not the energies of our forebears—the Suffragettes, the Freedom Riders, Rosa Parks, Medgar Evers, Martin Luther King, Jr., the countless protestors against injustice? We would not be what and where we are as a people and a nation without their energies, their often lonely bravery.

Can we bring a fraction of such energy and such bravery to bear on the test of our times, the reclamation of this most fundamental right of all, an honest election, the bedrock protocol of any democracy? Are we content instead to stand futilely by as the concealment of the vote counting process enables a distortion of the public will that results in, and appears to have already resulted in, a loss of public sovereignty and an all-too-visible breakdown of the political process? That loss of sovereignty and that breakdown lead ultimately either to destructive revolution or to torpid resignation—America The Ugly. There is just too much at stake to stand by.

Final Word

It all begins with communication. The most important single action you and I can take—it is my charge to all who have read this book—is to *communicate*: to write, or text, or email, or simply *talk* to others about this issue, about *CODE RED*, about what we are facing, about what we can do. Organization builds on communication. And meaningful action will spring from organization.

My goal in writing this book has been to bring the issue of vote counting, and the perils it presents in the New American Century, into the public discourse. I hope also that reading *CODE RED* will help those who have been keeping to themselves their suspicions, concerns, or outrage about our faith-based, man-behind-the-curtain electoral system to recognize that they are neither crazy nor alone.

There are genuinely difficult problems facing us as a nation and as a species in the years to come: climate change, over-population, food and resource distribution, weapons control, the security-versus-privacy dilemma, and all manner of ecological challenges, just to name a few. Religious or secular, we have long approached our planet from a standpoint of dominion and are just now learning—with great reluctance and resistance from some quarters—to assume a ministerial rather than magisterial role on Earth.

Compared to these challenges, the basic counting of votes—in an observable way that ensures the legitimacy of our elections and vouchsafes the public an undistorted voice in the making of all these hard choices—is an easy assignment. We need only to break a spell that has been cast on us—a spell of convenience, passivity, helplessness. We need only remember that democracy is not something that we watch; it is something that we do.

VII. EVIDENCE AND ANALYSIS

"The devil is in the details."

— Anonymous

STUDY I.

The 2004 Presidential Election: Who Won the Popular Vote?
An Examination of the Comparative Validity of Exit Poll and Vote Count Data

January 2, 2005

Jonathan D. Simon, J.D.

Ron P. Baiman, Ph.D.
Institute of Government and Public Affairs
University of Illinois at Chicago

Published by the Free Press (http://freepress.org)

The views expressed are the authors' own and are not necessarily representative of the views of their respective institutions. Comments or questions directed to the authors are welcome.

Executive Summary

> There is a substantial disparity—well outside the margin of error and outcome-determinative—between the national exit poll and the popular votecount.

> The possible causes of the disparity would be random error, a skewed exit poll, or breakdown in the fairness of the voting process and accuracy of the votecount.

> Analysis shows that the disparity cannot reasonably be accounted for by chance or random error.

> Evidence does not support hypotheses that the disparity was produced by problems with the exit poll.

> Widespread breakdown in the fairness of the voting process and accuracy of the votecount are the most likely explanations for the disparity.

> In an accurate count of a free and fair election, the strong likelihood is that Kerry would have been the winner of the popular vote.

The Significance of a Popular Vote Victory

Although it is the Electoral College and not the popular vote that legally elects the president, winning the popular vote does have considerable psychological and practical significance. It is fair to say, to take a recent example, that had Al Gore not enjoyed a popular vote margin in 2000, he would not have had standing in the court of public opinion to maintain his post-election challenge for more than a month up until its ultimate foreclosure by the Supreme Court.

In the 2004 election now under scrutiny, the popular vote again has played a critical role. George Bush's apparent margin of 3.3 million votes clearly influenced the timing of John Kerry's concession. Although the election was once again close enough that yet-to-be-counted votes offered at least the mathematical possibility of a Kerry electoral college victory—and although, once again, concerns about vote counting were beginning to emerge from early post-election reports and analyses—Kerry apparently believed that, unlike popular vote-winner Gore, he did not have effective standing to prolong the race.

As ongoing inquiries continue to raise serious vote counting issues, Bush's apparent popular vote margin has loomed large as a rationale for minimizing these issues, at least as far as their impact on the outcome of the race. While much concern has been expressed about "counting every vote," even the Kerry camp has issued disclaimers to the effect that their candidate does not expect that so doing will alter the outcome.

With the results in Ohio currently subject to both recount proceedings and legal contest, dramatic developments compelling a reversal of the Ohio result cannot be ruled out at this time. Yet to overturn the Ohio result, giving Kerry an electoral college victory (or even to disqualify the Ohio electors via challenge in Congress, which would deprive Bush of an electoral college majority and throw the election to the House of Representatives), would likely be regarded as unjust and insupportable by a populace convinced that Bush was, by some 3.3 million votes, the people's choice.

Thus, although the popular vote does not legally determine the presidency, its significance is such that we must give due consideration to any evidence which puts the popular vote count itself at issue.

Sources of the Exit Poll and Votecount Numbers

As the analysis we undertake below is based upon the conflict between two sets of numbers, one generated by the exit polls for the presidential race and the other generated by the vote counting equipment, it is necessary to review the nature of the two sources of results. Exit polling, since its invention several decades ago, has performed reliably in the projection of thousands of races, both here at home and, more recently, abroad.[1] The record of exit polling from the 1970s through the 1990s was essentially free of controversy, except for the complaint that publication of exit poll results prior to poll closings dampened voter turnout by discouraging late-in-day voters from bothering to vote, the race having already been "called."[2] Voters could be so influenced because they had come, indeed, to regard exit poll projections as all but infallible. Significant exit polling problems began to appear along with the development and spread of computerized vote counting equipment, since which time exit polls have had a notably poorer track record in spite of improvements in polling methodology.

Compared to standard pre-election polling, exit polling has certain advantages and disadvantages. On the plus side, exit polls sample actual rather than just "likely" voters and do not fail to include voters who are not attached to a conventional phone line or who screen their calls.[3] This results in significantly greater accuracy. On the minus side, exit polls employ a cluster sampling technique, grouping respondents by precinct, rather than a fully homogenized random sample of the

---

[1] See *Polling and Presidential Election Coverage*, Lavrakas, Paul J, and Holley, Jack K., eds., Newbury Park, CA: Sage; pp. 83-99.

[2] This problem was theoretically resolved by a gentlemen's agreement to withhold release of exit poll calls until the polls had closed.

[3] Because only actual voters are included, these might more accurately be referred to as "exit samples" rather than "exit polls."

target venue. This results in somewhat less accuracy. On the whole, the advantages in accuracy an exit poll enjoys over a pre-election poll of the same sample size tend to outweigh the disadvantages.

The exit polling in Election 2004 was performed by the combined firms of Mitofsky International and Edison Media Research, under exclusive contract as "official provider" of exit poll data to six major media organizations (CBS, NBC, ABC, CNN, Fox News Channel, and the Associated Press), which collectively formed the National Election Pool.[4] Exit polling operations were under the principal direction of Warren Mitofsky, credited as the inventor of exit polling and recognized throughout the world as the leading expert in the field. With over 35 years of exit polling experience, encompassing nearly 3,000 electoral contests in the United States and abroad, Mitofsky has achieved consistent success in the field and has continued throughout his career to refine and improve the methodologies and protocols of exit polling.[5] In 1999 Mitofsky received the Award for Lifetime Achievement from the American Association for Public Opinion Research.

Election 2004 presented a particular challenge and opportunity for Mr. Mitofsky, whose exit polling operation was hampered in 2002 by a massive computer breakdown.[6] It has been reported that preparations for Election 2004 were especially thorough, entailing increased staff

---

[4] As described in the National Election Pool Edison Media Research/Mitofsky International homepage: www.exit-poll.net/index.html.

[5] Exit polling has been relied upon as a check mechanism for the vote counting processes in numerous foreign elections. Indeed, Mitofsky himself received public commendation from Mexican President Carlos Salinas for his contribution to the credibility of that nation's 1994 election. Most recently, exit polling has been instrumental in the overturning of election results and the ordering of a new election in the Ukraine.

[6] As a result, exit polls were not employed in the projection of election outcomes in 2002.

numbers and training, upgraded computer hardware and software, expanded surveys of absentee and early voters, and dry runs beginning in July to prepare analysts for the full spectrum of possible election night scenarios.[7] It may fairly be said that the exit polling for Election 2004 was a more advanced, sophisticated, and meticulous operation than any previously undertaken.

In contrast to the uniform methodology of the exit polls, a variety of methods are employed to record votes on election day, including optical scan devices, direct electronic recording (DREs or "touchscreens"), punch cards, paper ballots, lever machines, and data-point devices, in that order of prevalence. An additional variety of methods are then employed to transmit these votes to central locations and tally them at the county and state levels. Ownership and operation of this mosaic of machinery is fully privatized and is concentrated predominantly in the hands of four corporations: Diebold, ES&S, Sequoia, and Hart Intercivic. The partisan proclivities and activities of each of these corporations are a matter of public record.[8] Because of the proprietary nature of the election system throughout the United States, these vendors of the voting equipment design, program, operate, maintain, and repair it at every level, most often without outside or public scrutiny, and with at best a minimal process of testing and

---

[7] Newark *Star-Ledger*, 10/28/2004, page 1, "Networks Will Look to Somerville on Tuesday." See also, Bauder, D., "TV Networks to Test New Exit Polling System," The Associated Press, Oct. 13, 2004, reprinted at
http://aolsvc.news.aol.com/elections/article.adp?/id=20041013122209990005&_ccc=6&cid=946. The specific methodologies and protocols employed are detailed on the websites for Mitofsky International (www.mitofskyinternational.com), Edison Media Research (www.edisonresearch.com), and the National Election Pool (www.exit-poll.net).

[8] See, e.g., Smyth, J., *Cleveland Plain Dealer*, August 28, 2003, reprinted at: http://www.commondreams.org/headlines03/0828-08.htm; see also http://blogs.salon.com/0002255/.

certification.[9]   Boards of Election and state level authorities over election protocols have often accepted financial support from the equipment vendors[10] and have also been seen at times to act under the influence of partisanship, appearing to elevate outcomes over fairness of process.[11] Such systemic conflicts of interest do little to enhance the integrity or credibility of the vote counting system.

Computer experts have documented the susceptibility of both the recording and tabulating equipment to undetected errors, hacking, and deliberate fraud.[12]   A substantial component of the system (DREs, which are responsible for recording approximately 30% of the vote) generates no paper record and is effectively immune to meaningful recount. Central tabulators responsible for compiling over 50% of the vote employ an operating system that has been demonstrated to be vulnerable to entry and manipulation through a standard laptop PC.[13] In spite of these vulnerabilities of the counting system, few if any

---

[9] See Zeller, T., "Ready or Not, Electronic Voting Goes National," *The New York Times*, Sept. 19, 2004 (reprinted at http://aolsvc.news.aol.com/elections/article.adp?id=20040918145609990001&cid=842).

[10] See "On the Voting Machine Makers' Tab," *The New York Times*, Sept. 12, 2004, Editorial Page.

[11] See, e.g., Welsh-Huggins, A. "The Next Katherine Harris?" Associated Press Report Oct. 27, 2004, reprinted at http://aolsvc.news.aol.com/news/article.adp?id=20041027161309990012 (detailing actions taken by Ohio Secretary of State J. Kenneth Blackwell).

[12] See, e.g., Rubin, A., "An Insider's View of Vote Vulnerability," *Baltimore Sun*, March 10, 2004 (reprinted at www.commondreams.org/views04/0310-02.htm); Levy, S., "Black Box Voting Blues," *Newsweek*, Nov. 3, 2004 (reprinted at http://msnbc.msn.com/id/3339650/)

[13] The GEMS system, employed by Diebold in central tabulators serving about half the venues, is particularly susceptible to entry and manipulation (hacking or preprogramming) as was dramatically demonstrated on national television (CNBC: "Topic A with Tina Brown") when critic Bev Harris led Howard Dean through the necessary steps in less than two minutes (see Hartmann, T., "Evidence Mounts That the Vote May Have Been Hacked," at http://www.commondreams.org/headlines04/1106-30.htm).

questions about the accuracy of the numbers it produced were raised on election night.[14]

Election Night 2004: The Exit Poll/Votecount Differential

On Election Night 2004, the exit polls and the vote counting equipment generated results that differed significantly. In the early morning of November 3, 2004, a CNN.com website screenshot entitled "U.S. PRESIDENT/NATIONAL/EXIT POLL" posted national exit poll results updated to 12:23 A.M., broken down by gender as well as a variety of other categories.[15] The time of the update indicates that these results comprised substantially the full set of respondents polled on Election Day, but were free from the effects of a subsequent input of tabulated data used to bring about ultimate congruence between the exit poll and votecount results.[16]

The CNN posting indicates the number of respondents (13,047), the gender breakdown of the sample (male 46%, female 54%), and the candidate preferences by gender (males: 52% Bush, 47% Kerry; females: 45% Bush, 54% Kerry). For the national exit poll taken as a

---

[14] Such unquestioning acceptance may be portrayed in a positive light. As Warren Mitofsky himself has said: "In a democracy, it's the orderly transfer of power that keeps the democracy accepting the results of elections. If it drags on too long, there's always a suspicion of fraud." The perils of unquestioning acceptance of what may, given the vulnerabilities of our vote counting system, be falsified results should, however, be self-evident.

[15] The time-stamped screenshot was printed out by Simon at 1:29 A.M. on Nov. 3, 2004, and is attached for reference as Appendix A. The posting time of 1:25 A.M. may be seen faintly on the top banner. The data derived from the CNN screenshots printed by Simon for the individual states may also be referenced at http://www.scoop.co.nz/mason/stories/HL0411/S00142.htm.

[16] This practice is referenced in "Methods Statement: National Election Pool Exit Polls Nov. 2, 2004," (.pdf) at http://www.exit-poll.net.

whole, therefore, the result was 48.2% Bush, 50.8% Kerry.[17] The vote counting equipment produced a markedly different result: 50.9% Bush, 48.1% Kerry.[18] The differential between the two counts, which were virtually mirror images of each other, was 5.4% overall (see Chart 1).

Chart 1: Exit Poll vs. Popular Vote Comparison (National)

	Bush %	Kerry %	Bush Margin%
National Exit	48.2%	50.8%	-2.6%
Popular Vote Count	50.9%	48.1%	2.8%
Difference	2.7%	-2.7%	5.4%

The reaction of Election Night analysts interpreting this differential was immediately to query what had "gone wrong" with the exit polls. This was a curious approach both in light of standard accounting practice, which compels independent examination of *both* sets of numbers that are found to be in conflict, and in light of much-voiced pre-election concerns about the accuracy and security of the computerized vote counting systems. We offer an alternate approach to the conflicting data, based on fundamental statistical and accounting principles.

---

[17] The totals for the full sample are computed by combining the candidate preferences of male and female respondents: Bush = [(males)46% x 52%] + [(females)54% x 45%] = 48.2%; Kerry = [(males)46% x 47%] + [(females)54% x 54%] = 50.8%.
Alternatively, if Kerry's exit poll share is minimized by assuming maximum female and minimal male shares subject to rounding (to zero decimals), whole integer numbers of voters, minimal Nader votes, and minimal gender vote shares subject to rounding, Kerry would get at least 50.22% of the vote. The reported actual Kerry vote of 48.1% is still far outside of the 95% confidence interval of + 1.1% and has just a one in 10,256 chance of occurrence (see analogous calculations for a Kerry exit poll result of 50.8% in text).

[18] Approximately 1% of the total vote went to minor candidates. Therefore, a vote percentage of 49.54% rather than 50.0% constitutes a winning margin for either Bush or Kerry. It is important to bear this in mind in reading the analysis below.

Statistical Analysis of Exit Poll Results

Steven F. Freeman of the University of Pennsylvania has analyzed Election 2004 exit poll results for battleground states,[19] and has drawn certain conclusions regarding the significant disparities between exit poll results and votecounts for several critical states. In particular, the odds against the disparities in Ohio, Florida, and Pennsylvania occurring together are computed at 662,000-to-one, or a virtual statistical impossibility that they could have been due to chance or random error. Receiving somewhat less emphasis is the overall pattern of disparity in the state polls—again with the votecounts turning in Bush's favor, though less dramatically in the non-battleground states, as will be discussed below. The national popular vote is not addressed in that paper, but the same statistical principles are applicable, and will be employed in this analysis.

While the individual state samples totaled 73,678 reported respondents,[20] a national sub-sampling was undertaken by Edison/Mitofsky, which comprised 13,047 reported respondents, chosen as a representative random sample of the nation as a whole. This sample was drawn from 250 targeted polling places and from 500 individual telephone interviews with absentee and early voters.[21]

What is remarkable about this national sample of 13,047 is its size. When compared with more familiar pre-election poll samples of about

---

[19] Freeman, S., "Was the 2004 Presidential Election Honest? An Examination of Uncorrected Exit Poll Data," Working Paper #04-10, rev. Nov. 23, 2004; http://www.buzzflash.com/alerts/04/11/Expldiscrpv00oPt1.pdf.

[20] For the 47 states and District of Columbia for which data was captured by Simon, see: http://www.scoop.co.nz/mason/stories/HL0411/S00142.htm.

[21] See "Methods Statement: National Election Pool Exit Polls: National/Regional Exit Poll," available from the National Election Pool in .pdf format at www.exit-poll.net/index.html

2000 - 2200 respondents, it is approximately six times as large. Such augmentation of sample size reduces a poll's margin of error (MOE) from the ±3% to which we have become accustomed, down to ±1.1%.[22]

The ±1.1% MOE tells us that, barring specific flaws in the design or administration of the poll and in the absence of significant mistabulation of the votecount itself, the exit poll result for the selected candidate will fall within ±1.1% of his votecount 95% of the time. In this case it tells us that we can be 95% certain that Kerry's popular vote percentage would fall in the range 49.7% to 51.9%; that is, it would fall outside that range only once in 20 times. Kerry's reported votecount of 48.1% falls dramatically outside this range.[23]

To carry our analysis further, we can employ a normal distribution curve (see Figure 1) to determine—again assuming proper poll methodology and an accurate and honest popular vote count—that the probability that Kerry would have received his reported popular vote total of 48.1%, or less is one in 959,000—a virtual statistical impossibility.[24]

---

[22] *Ibid*, p. 2, Table. Calculation of the margin of error may be checked as follows:
Calculate the standard error of a random sample using the formula $\sqrt{\dfrac{p(1-p)}{N}}$ = 0.00437, where p = Kerry percentage of the vote (0.481) and N = the sample size (13,047). The fact that an exit poll is a cluster sample, grouping respondents by precinct, rather than a fully homogenized random sample of the target venue, increases the standard error by 30% to 0.00568 (see Merkle, D. and Edelman, M. "A Review of the 1996 Voter News Service Exit Polls from a Total Survey Error Perspective," in *Election Polls, the News Media and Democracy*, ed. P.J. Lavrakas, M.W. Traugott, New York: Chatham House, pp. 68 - 72). Ninety-five percent of the time, a result predicted on the basis of a random sample will be within 1.96 standard errors, or ±0.011 (1.1%) for a sample of this size.

[23] It is dramatic because a 2.7% "miss" at these levels of precision is extremely unlikely to occur. The statistician's measure of such likelihood is known as a "standard deviation." A result which is off, as in this case, by 4.7 standard deviations is without question "dramatic:" the odds against its occurrence are 959,336 to one (see text below).

[24] Probability of a 48.1% vote share assuming an exit poll vote share of 50.8%:
P(0.481) = 1 - NORMDIST(0.481, 0.508, 0.005686, True) = 0.0000010424 (where

The Popular Vote Winner

We can proceed one helpful step further and calculate the likelihood, based on the exit poll results, that Kerry would receive more popular votes than Bush. The break-even point would be 59,024,629 votes, or 49.54% of the total.[25] This percentage lies, significantly, outside the MOE of the national exit poll and in fact we find that Kerry would receive fewer votes than Bush only 1.3% of the time. Put another way—given the exit poll results, proper poll methodology, and an accurate and fair voting process—Kerry would be the popular vote winner of Election 2004 98.7% of the time.

Is Something Wrong with The Exit Poll Results?

The clear implication of our analysis is that neither chance nor random error is responsible for the significant incongruence of exit poll and tabulated vote results, and that we must look either to significant failings in the exit poll design and/or administration or to equally significant failings in the accuracy and/or fairness of the voting process itself to explain the results. Given the dramatic implications of our analysis, we of course must consider carefully any argument that has been put forward suggesting that the exit polls failed as an accurate measure of voter intent. We examine the two least implausible hypotheses that have been put forward.

The first deals with the proportion of respondents by gender. The composition of the national sample by gender was 46% male, 54%

NORMDIST is an Excel spreadsheet function that gives the probability of obtaining 0.481 for a normal distribution with a mean of 0.508 and a standard deviation of 0.005686). 1/0.0000010424 = 959,336.

[25] Based on final election numbers from the *Washington Post*, Nov. 24, 2004.

female, which prompted a claim that females were over-represented, skewing the results towards Kerry. While it is not proven that this is in fact the case, if it is taken as stipulated and the sample is reweighted to reflect a "normal" gender breakdown of 52% female, 48% male, the effect is to increase Bush's exit poll percentage by 0.2% to 48.4% and decrease Kerry's to 50.6%. The effect on the bottom line is minimal: Kerry would be the popular vote victor 96.9% of the time.[26]

The second hypothesis put forward is the "reluctant Bush responder" hypothesis. It suggests that Bush voters were for some reason less willing to fill out an exit poll questionnaire, and therefore were undercounted in the poll results. If such a phenomenon could be proven, it would be a source of significant skewing and effectively invalidate the polls. The proponents of this hypothesis, however, have yet to offer any supportive evidence for their theory.[27] The hypothesis also does not explain the nonuniformity of the pattern of state-by-state disparities.[28] In fact, one could equally well imagine that a "reluctant

---

[26] For reference, even a clearly "male-skewed" 50% male, 50% female sample would have resulted in a Kerry victory 93.5% of the time.

[27] There is some intriguing evidence to the contrary, drawn from an analysis performed by William Kaminsky, a graduate student at MIT. Kaminsky finds that in 22 of 23 states which break down their voter registrations by party ID the ratio of registered Republicans to registered Democrats in the final, adjusted exit poll was larger than the ratio of registered Republicans to registered Democrats on the official registration rolls. In other words, the adjustments performed on the exit polls in order to get them to agree with the official tallies would, if valid, require Republicans to have won the get-out-the-vote battle *in essentially every state.* We find this requirement implausible, and indeed observational evidence pointed to just the opposite: massive new voter turnout, which virtually always cuts in favor of the challenger; huge lines in Democratic precincts; unadjusted exit poll data showing *greater* Democratic turnout; etc. Exit polls appropriately stratified to official party ID percentages, which would effectively neutralize any suspected "reluctant Bush responder" phenomenon by including the expected proportions of Republican and Democratic voters, would on the basis of Kaminsky's analysis have yielded results at least as favorable to Kerry as those upon which we have relied in our calculations.

[28] A complete analysis of all 45 states and the District of Columbia for which comparable exit poll data is available shows that four out of the 11 battleground states had exit poll/vote count disparities that were outside of a standard 5% (one-tail) margin of error, whereas this was the case for only *one* of the 35 non-battleground states. Moreover, all of these statistically significant disparities were in favor of Bush. This

Kerry responder" phenomenon was at work, and that the exit polls systematically underrepresented Kerry's vote.[29]

Conclusion

In light of the history of exit polling and the particular care that was taken to achieve an unprecedented degree of accuracy in the exit polls for Election 2004, there is little to suggest significant flaws in the design or administration of the official exit polls. Until supportive evidence can be presented for any hypothesis to the contrary, it must be concluded that the exit polls, including the national mega-sample with its ±1.1% margin of error, present us with an accurate measure of the intent of the voters in the presidential election of 2004.

According to this measure, an honest and fair voting process would have been more likely than not—at least 95% likely, in fact—to have determined John Kerry to be the national popular vote winner of Election 2004.[30] Should ongoing or new investigations continue to

---

data is at odds with claims of "systemic" pro-Kerry exit poll skew. See Baiman, R. Dec. 19, 2004 at: http://www.freepress.org/departments/display/19/2004/997 (some figures have been updated by the author to reflect more recent data). It is of course more than a little implausible that Bush voters would be reluctant to respond only in purple (i.e., swing) states (the logical targets for manipulation) but not in either red or blue states.

[29] It is by no means self-evident that either candidate's supporters were systemically more likely to be intimidating or more easily intimidated. While it might be more reasonably argued that voters finding themselves in a dwarfed minority in their communities might have been less willing to be exit poll respondents, in light of the even division of the national electorate, any such tendencies would have resulted in a wash, with no net effect on the validity of the national exit poll. We would of course welcome the release by Edison/Mitofsky and/or the National Election Pool of the data which would facilitate further analysis of these and other factors.

[30] It should be clear that more is at stake than the presidency itself. Use of computerized vote counting will only increase, as mandated by law. Vote counting is the bedrock protocol of a democracy and meaningful reform of a broken counting system is dependent on an expression of public will ultimately exercised *at the ballot box* and fairly, accurately, and honestly tabulated. If the system has broken down and is no longer counting accurately and honestly, there is no effective democratic

produce evidence that, to an extent determinative of the electoral college outcome, votes have not been counted accurately and honestly, the re-examined popular vote outcome may well be deemed relevant to the question of what remedies are warranted.

Figure 1:

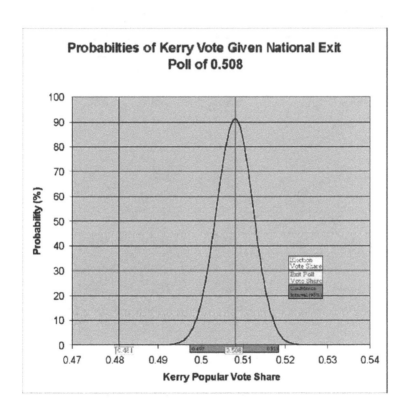

Probabilties of Kerry Vote Given National Exit Poll of 0.508

mechanism to bring pressure upon a governing majority to reform a vote counting *status quo* which is seen to work in its favor. This is, as may be seen, a potentially crippling catch-22 for a democracy.

- 163 - | C O D E   R E D

Appendix A:

CNN.com ELECTION RESULTS — AMERICA VOTES 2004

HAPPENING NOW / VIEW ALL — Posted 1:25 a.m. ET, November 3
CNN projects the Republican party will retain control of the U.S. Senate. — BREAKING NEWS

Other sections:

MAIN RACE | PRESIDENT | SENATE | HOUSE | GOVERNOR | BALLOT MEASURES | Pick state:

U.S. PRESIDENT / NATIONAL / EXIT POLL

SEARCH FOR EXIT POLLS

President: Pick state:	Senate: Pick state:	Other: Pick Other:	• How to read exit polls • Party key

13,047 Respondents — Updated: 12:23 a.m.

VOTE BY GENDER

TOTAL	BUSH 2004	2000	KERRY 2004	NADER 2004
Male (46%)	52%	n/a	47%	1%
Female (54%)	45%	+2	54%	1%

VOTE BY RACE AND GENDER

TOTAL	BUSH 2004	2000	KERRY 2004	NADER 2004
White Men (36%)	56%	n/a	40%	1%
White Women (41%)	51%	n/a	47%	1%
Non-White Men (11%)	28%	n/a	68%	2%
Non-White Women (13%)	22%	n/a	77%	1%

VOTE BY RACE

TOTAL	BUSH 2004	2000	KERRY 2004	NADER 2004
White (77%)	55%	+1	44%	1%
African-American (11%)	10%	+1	90%	1%
Latino (8%)	41%	+6	56%	3%
Asian (2%)	39%	-2	61%	*
Other (2%)	36%	n/a	56%	2%

VOTE BY AGE

TOTAL	BUSH 2004	2000	KERRY 2004	NADER 2004
18-29 (17%)	42%	-4	56%	1%
30-44 (29%)	49%	+0	48%	2%
45-59 (30%)	47%	-2	51%	1%
60 and Older (24%)	51%	+4	48%	0%

VOTE BY AGE

TOTAL	BUSH 2004	2000	KERRY 2004	NADER 2004
18-64 (84%)	48%	+0	51%	1%
65 and Older (16%)	50%	+3	50%	0%

VOTE BY INCOME

TOTAL	BUSH 2004	2000	KERRY 2004	NADER 2004
Under $15,000 (8%)	34%	n/a	65%	1%
$15-30,000 (15%)	38%	n/a	60%	1%
$30-50,000 (22%)	46%	n/a	53%	1%
$50-75,000 (23%)	53%	n/a	46%	1%
$75-100,000 (14%)	51%	n/a	48%	0%
$100-150,000 (11%)	53%	n/a	44%	2%
$150-200,000 (4%)	55%	n/a	45%	*
$200,000 or More (3%)	60%	n/a	30%	2%

VOTE BY INCOME

TOTAL	BUSH 2004	2000	KERRY 2004	NADER 2004
Less Than $50,000 (45%)	41%	n/a	58%	1%
$50,000 or More (55%)	53%	n/a	46%	1%

VOTE BY INCOME

TOTAL	BUSH 2004	2000	KERRY 2004	NADER 2004
Less Than $100,000 (82%)	46%	n/a	53%	1%
$100,000 or More (18%)	55%	n/a	43%	2%

STUDY II.

Landslide Denied:
Exit Polls vs. Vote Count 2006
Demographic Validity of the National Exit Poll and the Corruption of the Official Vote Count

Jonathan Simon, JD, and Bruce O'Dell[1]
Election Defense Alliance

Introduction: Pre-Election Concern, Election Day Relief, Alarming Reality

There was an unprecedented level of concern approaching the 2006 Election ("E2006") about the vulnerability of the vote counting process to manipulation. With questions about the integrity of the 2000, 2002 and 2004 elections remaining unresolved, with e-voting having proliferated nationwide, and with incidents occurring with regularity through 2005 and 2006, the alarm spread from computer experts to the media and the public at large. It would be fair to say that America approached E2006 with held breath.

For many observers, the results on Election Day permitted a great sigh of relief—not because control of Congress shifted from Republicans to

---

[1] Jonathan Simon, JD (http://www.electiondefensealliance.org/jonathan_simon) is Co-founder of Election Defense Alliance. Bruce O'Dell (http://www.electiondefensealliance.org/bruce_odell) is EDA Data Analysis Coordinator.

Democrats, but because it appeared that the public will had been translated more or less accurately into electoral results, not thwarted as some had feared. There was a relieved rush to conclude that the vote counting process had been fair and the concerns of election integrity proponents overblown.

Unfortunately, the evidence forces us to a very different and disturbing conclusion: there was gross votecount manipulation and it had a great impact on the results of E2006, significantly decreasing the magnitude of what would have been, accurately tabulated, a landslide of epic proportions. Because much of this manipulation appears to have been computer-based, and therefore invisible to the legions of at-the-poll observers, the public was informed of the usual "isolated incidents and glitches" but remains unaware of the far greater story: The electoral machinery and vote counting systems of the United States did not honestly and accurately translate the public will and certainly cannot be counted on to do so in the future.

The Evidentiary Basis

Our analysis of the distortions introduced into the E2006 votecount relies heavily on the official exit polls once again undertaken by Edison Media Research and Mitofsky International ("Edison/Mitofsky")[2] on behalf of a consortium of major media outlets known as the National Election Pool (NEP). In presenting exit poll-based evidence of votecount corruption, we are all too aware of the campaign that has been waged to discredit the reliability of exit polls as a measure of voter intent.

---

[2] Warren Mitofsky, the inventor of exit polling, died suddenly on September 1, 2006, of an apparent aneurysm, while fine tuning the exit polling system to be used by the National Election Pool in E2006. His successors at Edison/Mitofsky were, if anything, less cooperative in sharing information about their operation.

Our analysis is not, however, based on a broad assumption of exit poll reliability. **Rather we maintain that the national exit poll for E2006 contains within it specific questions that serve as intrinsic and objective yardsticks by which the representative validity of the poll's sample can be established, from which our conclusions flow directly.**

For the purposes of this analysis our primary attention is directed to the exit poll in which respondents were asked for whom they cast their vote for the House of Representatives.[3] Although only four House races (in single-district states) were polled as individual races, an additional nationwide sample of more than 10,000 voters was drawn,[4] the results representing the aggregate vote for the House in E2006. The sample was weighted according to a variety of demographics prior to public posting, and had a margin of error of +/- 1%.[5]

When we compare the results of this national exit poll with the total votecount for all House races we find that once again, as in the 2004

---

[3] Edison/Mitofsky exit polls for the Senate races also present alarming disparities and will be treated in a separate paper. The special significance of the House vote is that, unlike the Senate vote, it offers a nationwide aggregate view.

[4] The sample size was roughly equal to that used to measure the national popular vote in presidential elections. At-precinct interviews were supplemented by phone interviews where needed to sample early and absentee voters.

[5] We note with interest and raised brows that the NEP is now giving the MOE for their national sample as +/-3% (http://www.exit-poll.net/faq.html#a15). This is rather curious, as their published Methods Statement in 2004 assigns to a sample of the same size and mode of sampling the expected MOE of +/-1% (see Appendix 2 for both NEP Statements). Perhaps the NEP intends its new methodology statement to apply to its anticipated effort in 2008 and is planning to reduce the national sample size by 75% for that election; we hope not. It of course makes no sense, as applied to E2004 or E2006, that state polls in the 2000-respondent range should yield a MOE of +/-4%, as stated, while a national poll of more than *five times* that sample size should come in at +/-3%. It would certainly be useful in quelling any controversy that has arisen or might arise from exit poll-votecount disparities far outside the poll's MOE, but it is, to our knowledge, not the way that statistics and mathematics work.

Election ("E2004"), there is a very significant exit poll-votecount disparity. **The exit poll indicates a Democratic victory margin nearly 4%,** *or 3 million votes,* **greater than the margin recorded by the vote counting machinery.** This is far outside the margin of error of the poll and has less than a one in 10,000 likelihood of occurring as a matter of chance.

The Exit Polls and The Votecount

In E2004 the only nontrivial argument against the validity of the exit polls—other than the mere assumption that the votecounts *must* be correct—turned out to be the hypothesis, never supported by evidence, that Republicans had been more reluctant to respond and that therefore Democrats were "oversampled." And now, in E2006, the claim has once again been made that the Exit Polls were "off" because Democrats were oversampled.[6] Indeed this claim of sampling *bias* is by now accepted with something of a "so what else is new?" shrug. The 2006 Exit Poll, however, contains *intrinsic yardsticks* that directly refute this familiar and convenient claim. But before turning to the yardstick questions themselves, we need to clarify certain aspects of exit polling data presentation that have often proven confusing.

---

[6] See for example David Bauder, AP, in a November 8 article at
http://www.washingtonpost.com/wp-dyn/content/article/2006/11/08/AR2006110800403.html. Oddly enough, "oversampling" of Democrats has become a chronic ailment of exit polls since the proliferation of e-voting, no matter how diligently the nonpartisan collection of experts at the peak of their profession strives to prevent it. Of course the weighting process itself is undertaken to bring the sample into close conformity with the known and estimated characteristics of the electorate, including partisanship; so the fact that more of a given party's adherents were actually sampled, while it would be reflected in the unpublished raw data, would not in fact bias or affect the validity of the published *weighted* poll. *That is the whole point of weighting*, in light of which the hand-wringing about Democratic oversampling strikes us as misunderstanding at best, and quite possibly intended misdirection.

Any informed discussion of exit polling must distinguish among three separate categories of data:

1) **"Raw" data**, which comprises the actual responses to the questionnaires simply tallied up; this data is never publicly released and, in any case, makes no claim to accurately represent the electorate and cannot be usefully compared with votecounts.

2) **"Weighted" data**, in which the raw data has been weighted or stratified on the basis of numerous demographic and voting pattern variables to reflect with great accuracy the composition and characteristics of the electorate.

3) **"Forced" or "Adjusted" data**, in which the pollster *overrides* previous weighting in order to make the "Who did you vote for?" result in a given race match the votecount for that race, however it distorts the demographics of the sample (that's why they call it "forcing").

Because the NEP envisions the post-election purpose of its exit polls as being limited to facilitating academic dissection of the election's dynamics and demographics (e.g., "How did the 18-25 age group vote?" or "How did voters especially concerned with the economy vote?"), the NEP methodology calls for "correcting" or "adjusting" its exit polls to congruence with the actual vote percentages after the polls close and actual returns become available. *Exit polls are "corrected" on the ironclad assumption that the votecounts are valid.* This becomes the supreme truth, relative to which all else is measured, and therefore it is assumed that polls that match these votecounts will present the most accurate information about the demographics and voting patterns of the electorate. A *distorted* electorate in the adjusted poll is therefore a powerful indicator of an invalid votecount.

We examined both "weighted" and "adjusted" exit polls of nationwide vote for the House of Representatives published by the NEP. On Election Night, November 7, 2006 at 7:07 p.m., CNN.com posted a national exit poll that was demographically weighted but not yet adjusted to congruence with the votecounts.[7] We call this the **Weighted National Poll**. At various intervals over the next 18 hours, as polls closed and official tabulations became available, the results presented in the Weighted National Poll were progressively "corrected" to match the official vote totals, culminating in a fully adjusted national exit poll posted on CNN.com at 1 p.m. November 8, 2006. We call this the **Adjusted National Poll**. We will make reference to both polls in the analysis that follows.

The 2006 national vote for the House, as captured by the Weighted National Poll, was 55.0% Democratic and 43.5% Republican—an 11.5% Democratic margin. By 1:00 p.m. on November 8, the Adjusted National Poll reported the overall vote for the House as 52.6% Democratic and 45.0% Republican, just a 7.6% margin.[8] This 7.6% Democratic margin of course matched the tabulated votecount but was 3.9% smaller than that recorded by the Weighted National Poll the night before. *This was a net difference of 3 million votes fewer for the Democrats.*

---

[7] The 7:07 p.m. poll reported a 10,207 sample size and, in accordance with NEP methodology, the raw data had been weighted to closely match the demographics of the electorate.

[8] Analysts noticing the substantial increase in "respondents" between the Weighted (10,207) and Adjusted (13,251) National Polls may understandably but erroneously conclude that the shift between the two polls is the result of a late influx of Republican-leaning respondents. This is not the way it works. Since these are both weighted polls, each is in effect "tuned" to a profile of the electorate assumed to be valid—the Weighted National Poll to a set of established demographic variables and the Adjusted National Poll to the vote count once it is tabulated. The published number of respondents is *irrelevant* to this process and has significance only as a guide to the poll's margin of error. 10,000+ respondents is a *huge* sample (cf. the 500 – 1500 range of most tracking polls), and obviously an ample basis on which to perform the demographic weighting manifest in the Weighted National Poll.

Did The 2006 Exit Poll Oversample Democrats?
Cross-tabs Answer This Question

The national exit poll administered by Edison/Mitofsky for the NEP is not, as some may imagine, a simple "Who did you vote for?" questionnaire. It poses some 40 to 50 additional questions pertaining to demographic, political preference, and state-of-mind variables. Voters are asked, for example, about such characteristics as race, gender, income, age, and also about such things as church attendance, party identification, ideology, approval of various public figures, importance of various issues to their vote, and when they made up their minds about whom to vote for.

When the poll is posted, these characteristics are presented in a format, known as "cross-tabs," in which the voting choice of respondents in each subgroup is shown. For example, respondents were asked whether they thought the United States "is going in the right direction." In the Weighted National Poll, the cross-tab for this characteristic (see below) shows us that 40% said Yes and 56% said No; and further that, of the 40% subgroup who said Yes, 21% voted Democrat and 78% voted Republican for House of Representatives, while, of the 56% who said No, 80% voted Democrat and 18% voted Republican. We also see that this question is quite highly correlated with voting preference, with fully four-fifths of the "pessimists" voting Democratic.

IS U.S. GOING IN RIGHT DIRECTION?

TOTAL	Democrat	Republican
Yes (40%)	21%	78%
No (56%)	80%	18%

Cross-tabs vary greatly in the degree to which the characteristic is correlated with voting preference. The more strongly correlated, the more important the cross-tab becomes in assessing the poll's validity as an indicator of the vote.

Prior to public posting the exit poll data is weighted according to a *variety* of demographics, in such a way that the resulting cross-tabs closely mirror the expected, independently measurable characteristics of the electorate as a whole. The cross-tabs, in turn, tell us about the sample, giving us detailed information about its composition and representativeness. This information is of critical importance to our analysis because among the many questions asked of respondents there are several that enable us to tell whether the sample is valid or *politically biased* in one direction or another. These are the "intrinsic yardsticks" to which we have made reference.

Among the most salient yardstick questions were the following:

- Job Approval of President Bush
- Job Approval of Congress
- Vote for President in 2004

With respect to each of these yardsticks the composition of the sample can be compared to measures taken of the voting population as a whole, giving us a very good indication of the validity of the sample. Examining these cross-tabs for the Weighted National Poll—the 7:07 p.m. poll that was written off by the media as a "typical oversampling of Democrats"—this is what we found:

- Approval of President Bush: 42%
- Approval of Congress: 36%
- Vote for President in 2004:   Bush 47%, Kerry 45%

When we compare these numbers with what we know about the electorate as a whole going into E2006, we can see at once that the poll that told us that the Democratic margin was 3 million votes greater than the computers toted up was not by any stretch of the imagination an oversampling of Democrats. Let's take each yardstick in turn.

Presidential Approval Rating

We can compare the 42% approval of President Bush in the Weighted National Poll with any or all of the host of tracking polls measuring this critical political variable in the weeks and days leading up to the election. It is important when comparing approval ratings to make sure that we compare apples with apples, since the question can be posed in different ways leading to predictably different results. The principal formats of the approval measure are either simply "Do you approve or disapprove. . .?" or "Do you strongly approve, somewhat approve, somewhat disapprove, or strongly disapprove. . .?" We can call these the *two-point* and *four-point* formats respectively. By repeatedly posing the question in both formats on the same days, it has been determined that the four-point format consistently yields an approval rating 3-4% higher than the two-point format.[9]

Bearing this in mind and comparing the Weighted National Poll respondents' approval of President Bush with that registered by the electorate going into the election, we find very close parity. PollingReport.com catalogues 33 national polls of Presidential approval taken between October 1 and Election Day using the two-point format,

---

[9] http://www.rasmussenreports.com/public_content/politics/polling_methodology_job_approval_ratings. As Rasmussen notes, the 3-4% upwards adjustment in the four-point format impounds the virtual elimination of the "Not Sure" response obtained with greater frequency in the two-point format.

with an average (mean) approval rating of 37.6%.[10] This translates to a 41% approval rating in the four-point format used for the Weighted National Poll. A direct comparison is also possible with the Rasmussen tracking poll, which unlike the other tracking polls uses the four-point format. The Rasmussen approval rating for October 2006 is also 41%, with 57% disapproving.[11] Thus, the 42% approval of President Bush in the Weighted National Poll matches the figure established for the electorate as a whole going into the election; in fact, it is 1% "over par." As Bush approval correlates very strongly with voting preference (see below), an oversampling of Democrats would unavoidably have been reflected in a lower rating. The rating at or above the established level thus provides the first confirmation of the validity of the Weighted National Poll.

HOW GEORGE W. BUSH IS HANDLING HIS JOB		
TOTAL	Democrat	Republican
Approve (42%)	15%	84%
Disapprove (58%)	83%	15%

Congressional Approval Rating

As with the Presidential approval yardstick, comparison between the 36% of the Weighted National Poll sample that approved of how Congress was handling its job and the value established for the electorate in numerous tracking polls corroborates the Weighted National Poll's validity. The mean of the 17 national polls catalogued

---

[10] http://www.pollingreport.com/BushJob.htm. Typical of the national polls included are Gallup, AP-Ipsos, Newsweek, Fox/Opinion Dynamics, CBS/New York Times, NBC/Wall Street Journal, and ABC/Washington Post. The median approval rating is 37.4%, indistinguishable from the mean, and there is no discernible trend up or down over the Oct. 1 – Nov. 7 period.

[11] http://www.rasmussenreports.com/public_content/politics/political_updates/president_bush_job_approval. The rating combines "strong" and "somewhat" approve and is the average of Rasmussen's daily tracking polls conducted throughout the month.

by the PollingReport.com measuring approval of Congress between October 1 and Election Day (all employing the two-point format) was 27.5% approval.[12] Translating to the four-point format used for the exit poll yields a comparable approval rating of 31%, a full 5% *below* the Congressional approval given by the Weighted National Poll respondents. As with the Presidential rating, approval of what was at that point a Republican Congress correlates strongly with voting preference (see below). We would have expected an oversampling of Democrats to give a *lower* approval rating to Congress than did the electorate it was supposedly misrepresenting. Instead the Weighted National Poll yielded a significantly *higher* Congressional approval rating—indicative, if anything, of an oversampling of Republicans.

HOW CONGRESS IS HANDLING ITS JOB

TOTAL	Democrat	Republican
Strongly Approve (5%)	29%	70%
Somewhat Approve (31%)	25%	73%
Somewhat Disapprove (32%)	62%	37%
Strongly Disapprove (30%)	81%	16%

Vote for President in 2004

Edison/Mitofsky asked all respondents how they had voted in the 2004 Presidential election. The Weighted National Poll sample included 45% who said they had voted for Kerry and 47% who said they had voted for Bush (8% indicating they had not voted or voted for another candidate). This Bush margin of +2% closely approximates the +2.8% margin that Bush enjoyed in the official popular vote count for E2004.

---

[12] http://www.pollingreport.com/CongJob.htm.

VOTE FOR PRESIDENT IN 2004

TOTAL	Democrat	Republican
Kerry (45%)	93%	6%
Bush (47%)	17%	82%

While poll respondents have often shown some tendency to indicate they voted for the sitting president when questioned at the time of the next presidential election (i.e., four years out), Bush's historically low approval rating, coupled with his high relevance to this off-year election, and the shorter time span since the vote in question, make such a generic "winner's shift" singularly unlikely in E2006.

And while we present the reported 2.8% Bush margin in 2004 at face value, it will not escape notice that the distortions in vote tabulation that we establish in the current paper were also alleged in 2004, were evidenced by the 2004 exit polls, and were demonstrably achievable given the electronic voting systems deployed at that time. We note that, if upon retrospective evaluation the unadjusted 2004 exit polls prove as accurate as the 2006 exit polls appear to be, and their 2.5% margin for *Kerry* in 2004 is taken as the appropriate baseline, a correctly weighted sample in 2006 would have included even more Kerry voters and even fewer Bush voters than Edison/Mitofsky's Weighted National Poll, with a substantial consequent up-tick in the Democratic margin beyond the 3 million votes thus far unaccounted for.

These critical comparisons between measures taken of the Weighted National Poll sample and established benchmarks are presented together in the chart immediately below.

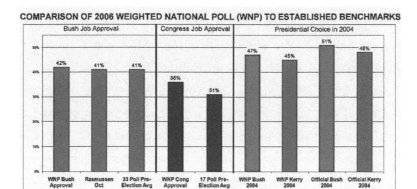

COMPARISON OF 2006 WEIGHTED NATIONAL POLL (WNP) TO ESTABLISHED BENCHMARKS

There should be little question that the three yardsticks presented above conclusively refute the glib canard that the National Exit Poll disparity was due to an oversampling of Democrats. Two additional cross-tabs are, however, worthy of note in this regard: Vote by Race and Vote by Party ID.

Vote by Race

The Weighted National Poll sample, as can be seen below, is 80% White, 10% African-American, and 8% Latino in composition, with Whites splitting their vote evenly between the parties while Latinos and particularly Blacks voted overwhelmingly Democratic.

VOTE BY RACE

TOTAL	Democrat	Republican
White (80%)	49%	49%
African-American (10%)	88%	12%
Latino (8%)	72%	26%
Asian (1%)	65%	35%
Other (2%)	59%	36%

We can compare these demographics with an established measure of the electorate published by the University of Michigan Center for Political Studies. The ANES Guide to Public Opinion and Electoral Behavior, is a longitudinal study of many aspects of the American electorate, including racial composition.[13] The chart below presents the ANES results for the past six biennial national elections.[14]

	'94	'96	'98	'00	'02	'04
White :	78	72	74	74	75	70
Black :	12	14	12	13	12	16
Asian :	2	2	1	3	2	3
Native American:	3	5	3	3	2	4
Hispanic :	6	8	9	7	8	8
Other :	-	-	-	-	2	-

As can be seen by comparing the charts above, in *none* of the past six elections was the White participation as high or the Black participation as low as represented in the Weighted National Poll.[15] The average White proportion of the electorate was 74%, 6% below the exit poll's representation of Whites, while the average Black proportion

---

[13] The American National Election Studies; see www.electionstudies.org. Produced and distributed by the University of Michigan, Center for Political Studies; based on work supported by the National Science Foundation and a number of other sponsors.

[14] The full chart, dating to 1948, may be referenced at http://www.electionstudies.org/nesguide/toptable/tab1a_3.htm.

[15] Asian and Native American voters, also strong Democratic constituencies, likewise seem to be significantly under-represented in the Weighted National Poll. The ANES results for 2006 are due to be published later this year. In *E2004* the Weighted National Poll was 77% White and 11% Black, as opposed to the ANES proportions of 70% and 16% respectively. It was this disproportionately White sample—supposedly short on "reluctant" Bush responders, but in reality overstocked with White voters who favored Bush by a margin of 11% and under-stocked with Black voters who favored Kerry by a margin of 80%! —that gave Kerry a 2.5% *victory* in the nationwide popular vote.

was 13%, 3% above the exit poll's representation of Blacks. The relative under-representation of every strong Democratic constituency in this cross-tab, in favor of the least Democratic voting bloc, hardly jibes with the "Invalid: Oversampled Democrats" label cheerfully pasted on the Weighted National Poll.

Vote by Party ID

Though Vote by Party ID generally fluctuates relatively modestly from one election to the next, it is, not surprisingly, nonetheless sensitive to the dynamics of atypical turnout battles. While we will address the E2006 turnout dynamics more fully in a later section, for the present we will simply note that a Democratic turnout romp was generally acknowledged in 2006, Republican voters having a number of late-breaking reasons for staying home.

In the Weighted National Poll, Democratic voters comprised 39% of the sample to 35% for the Republicans, as shown below.

VOTE BY PARTY ID		
TOTAL	Democrat	Republican
Democrat (39%)	93%	6%
Republican (35%)	9%	90%
Independent (26%)	58%	38%

Only 20 states register their voters by party so there is no direct comparison to be made to actual registration figures. But the ANES Guide once again proves useful. The chart below records party identification amongst the electorate as a whole on a seven-point scale, but the comparison is convincing.[16]

---

[16] The full chart, dating to 1952, may be referenced at
http://www.electionstudies.org/nesguide/toptable/tab2a_1.htm.

	'94	'96	'98	'00	'02	'04
Strong Democrat :	15	18	19	19	17	17
Weak Democrat :	19	19	18	15	17	16
Independent Democrat :	13	14	14	15	15	17
Independent Independent:	11	9	11	12	8	10
Independent Republican :	12	12	11	13	13	12
Weak Republican :	15	15	16	12	16	12
Strong Republican :	15	12	10	12	14	16
Apolitical :	1	1	2	1	1	0

In each of the past six biennial national elections through 2004, self-identified Democrats have outnumbered Republicans. The margins for 1994, 1996, 1998, 2000, 2002, and 2004 have been +4%, +10%, +11%, +10%, +4%, and +5% respectively. If Independent leaners are included, the Democratic margin increases every year, to +5%, +12%, +14%, +12%, +6%, and +10% respectively. These are very consistent numbers confirming a consistent plurality of self-identified Democratic voters from election to election.[17] The 4% Democratic plurality in the Weighted National Poll sample is seen to be at the extreme *low* end of the margins recorded since 1994, matching only the 4% Democratic margins recorded in the major *Republican* victories of 1994 and 2002. But E2006 was a major *Democratic* victory and, as will be seen, a likely *turnout landslide*.

While it would probably insult the intelligence of the media analysts who proclaimed that the E2006 Weighted National Poll was "off"

---

[17] It is worth noting that among the most suspicious demographic distortions of the Adjusted National Poll in *E2004* was the Party ID cross-tab which indicated an electorate *evenly* divided between self-identified Democrats and Republicans, at 37% apiece. Not only was this supposed parity unprecedented, but it flew in the face of near-universal observational indications of a major Democratic turnout victory in 2004: not only in Ohio but nationwide, long lines and hours-long waits were recorded at inner-city and traditionally Democratic precincts, while literally no such lines were observed and no such complaints recorded in traditionally Republican voting areas (see EIRS data at https://voteprotect.org/index.php?display=EIRMapNation&tab=ED04).

because it had oversampled Democrats to even suggest the possibility that one or more of them took the 39% - 35% Democratic ID margin in the poll to be indicative of Democratic oversampling—such misinterpretation quickly spreading among, and taking on the full authority of, the Election Night punditry—it is very difficult to comprehend by what *other* measure the Election Night analysts, and all who followed their lead, might have reached that manifestly erroneous, though obviously comforting, conclusion.

In short, there is no measure anywhere in the Weighted National Poll—in which the Democratic margin nationwide was some 3 million votes greater than tabulated by the machines—that indicates an oversampling of Democrats. Any departures from norms, trends, and expectations indicate just the opposite: a poll that likely undersampled Democratic voters and so, at 11.5%, *understated* the Democratic victory margin.

The Adjusted National Poll: Making The Vote-Count Match

In the wake of our primary analysis of the validity of the Weighted National Poll, consideration of the Adjusted National Poll is something of an afterthought, though it does serve to further reinforce our conclusions.

As we described earlier, in the "adjusted" or "corrected" poll the pollster overrides all previous weighting to make the "Who did you vote for?" result in a given race (or set of races) match the votecount for that race, however it distorts the demographics of the sample. In the Adjusted National Poll, which appeared the day after the election and remains posted (with a few further updates not affecting this analysis) on the CNN.com website, Edison/Mitofsky was faced with the task of matching the tabulated aggregate results for the set of House races nationwide. This translated to reducing the Democratic margin from 11.5% to 7.6% by giving less weight to the respondents who said they had voted for a Democratic candidate and more weight to the respondents who said they had voted Republican. Of course this process, referred to as "forcing," also affects the response to every question on the questionnaire, including the demographic and political preference questions we have been considering.

The most significant effect was upon "Vote for President in 2004." In order to match the results of the official tally, the Adjusted National Poll was forced to depict an electorate that voted for Bush over Kerry *by a 6% margin* in 2004, more than twice the "actual" margin of 2.8%, taken charitably at face value for the purposes of this analysis.

VOTE FOR PRESIDENT IN 2004

TOTAL	Democrat	Republican
Kerry (43%)	92%	7%
Bush (49%)	15%	83%

As might be expected, other yardsticks were also affected: Bush approval increases to 43%; Congressional approval to 37%; and Party ID shifts to an implausible 38% Democratic, 36% Republican.

There were, as we identified earlier, indications that the Weighted National Poll itself may have undersampled voters who cast their votes for the Democratic House candidates.[18] The Adjusted National Poll compounds such distortions in order to present an electorate cut to fit

---

[18] To the extent that weighting is based on prior turnout patterns, a significant shift in the turnout dynamic, as was apparent in E2006, would be one cause for this undersampling. A second and more disturbing cause: "actual" results from recent elections, which themselves have been vulnerable to and distorted by electronic mistabulation, fed into the weighting algorithms.

the official vote totals. If such an adjusted poll yields inaccurate and distorted information about the demographics and voting patterns of the electorate, then very basic logic tells us that the votecount it was forced to match is itself invalid. This of course corroborates the story told by the Weighted National Poll, as well as by the pre-election polls, as shown in the graph below.[19]

---

[19] The 11.5% Democratic margin in the Weighted National Poll was strictly congruent with the 11.5% average margin of the seven major national public opinion polls conducted immediately prior to the election. Indeed, this 11.5% pre-election margin was drawn down substantially by the appearance of three election-week "outlier" polls, which strangely came in at 7%, 6%, and 4% respectively. To put this in perspective, excluding these three polls, 30 of the 31 other major national polls published from the beginning of October up to the election showed the Democratic margin to be in double-digits, and the single exception came in at 9%. See
http://www.realclearpolitics.com/epolls/2006/house/us/generic_congressional_ballot-22.html.

It is also worth noting that most pre-election polls shift, in the month before the election, to a "likely-voter cutoff model" (LCVM) that excludes *entirely* any voters not highly likely (on the basis of a battery of screening questions) to cast ballots; that is, it excludes *entirely* voters with a 25% or even 50% likelihood of voting. Since these are disproportionately transients and first-time voters, the less educated and affluent, it is also a correspondingly Democratic constituency that is disproportionately excluded. Ideally these voters should be down-weighted to their estimated probability of voting, *but that probability is not 0%*. By excluding them entirely, these pre-election polls build in a pro-Republican bias of about 2-5%, which *anomalously* in 2006 appears to have been offset by the significantly greater enthusiasm for voting on the part of the Democrats, reflected in an elevated LCVM failure rate among Republicans responding negatively or ambivalently to the battery question about their intention to vote in E2006. Dr. Steven Freeman, visiting professor at the University of Pennsylvania's Center for Organizational Dynamics, has examined this phenomenon in great detail. Of course, one of the reasons for the recent shift to the LVCM—a methodology that pollsters will generally admit is distorted but which they maintain nonetheless "gets it right"—is that pollsters are *not* paid for methodological purity, *they are paid to get it right*. From the pollster's standpoint, getting it right is the measure of their success whether the election is honest or the fix is in. The reality is that distorted vote counts and a distorted but "successful" pre-election polling methodology wind up corroborating and validating each other, *with only the exit polls (drawn from actual voters) seeming out of step.*

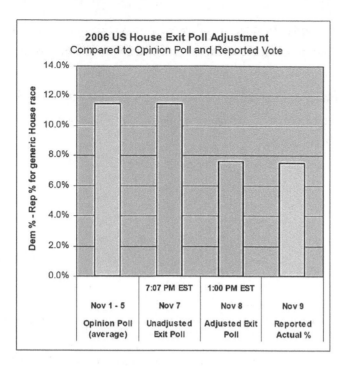

2006 US House Exit Poll Adjustment
Compared to Opinion Poll and Reported Vote

See Appendix 1 for detailed tabular presentation of the above data.

Plausible Explanations?

Since, as we have seen, the Weighted National Poll's inclusion of Democratic voters (or, better put, voters with characteristics making them likely to vote Democratic) either jibes with or falls somewhat short of established benchmarks for the electorate, there are only two possible explanations for the dramatic disparity between it and the official votecount: either Republicans unexpectedly turned out in droves and routed the Democrats in the E2006 turnout battle, or the official votecount is dramatically "off."

To our knowledge no one has contended the former. With good reason: there are a plethora of measures, including individual precinct tallies and additional polling data that we will examine in the next section, that confirm the obvious—the Democrats were the runaway winners of the 2006 Get-Out-The-Vote battle. Indeed, it is generally acknowledged that Republican voters stayed home in droves, dismayed and turned-off by the late-breaking run of scandals, bad news, and missteps.[20]

Hence it must be the reported nationwide vote tally which is inaccurate. Although this is, to put it mildly, an unwelcome finding, it is unfortunately consonant with the many specific incidents of vote-switching and mistabulation reported in 2006, with an apparent competitive-contest targeting pattern,[21] and with a host of other evidence and analysis that has emerged about electronic voting technology as deployed in the United States.

So Why Did the Republicans *Lose*?

It will no doubt be objected that if such substantial manipulation of the votecounts is possible, why would it stop short of bringing about a general electoral *victory*? While we would naturally like to credit the heightened scrutiny engendered by the untiring efforts of election integrity groups, an awakening media, and a more informed and vigilant public; an alternative, more chilling, explanation has emerged—simply that the mechanics of manipulation (software modules, primarily; see Appendix 3) had to be deployed before late-

---

[20] Indeed, once on-going analysis fully quantifies the extent of the Democrats' turnout victory, it will be time to recalculate upward the magnitude of the vote miscount in 2006.

[21] Our paper on competitive contest targeting is scheduled for publication in August 2007.

breaking pre-election developments[22] greatly expanded the gap that such manipulation would have been calibrated to cover.

To quantify the extraordinary effect of the various "October surprises," we reference below the Cook Political Report National Tracking Poll's Generic Congressional Ballot, ordinarily a rather *stable* measure:[23]

GENERIC CONGRESSIONAL BALLOT (Most Likely Voters)

Date	This Poll
Sample Size/MoE	807/3.5%

MLV	Dem	Rep
Oct. 26-29	**61**	**35**
Oct. 19-22	57	35
Oct. 5-8	**50**	**41**
Sept. 27-30	51	35
Sept. 21-24	49	41

Thus the Democratic margin among most likely voters increased from 9% (50% - 41%) to 26% (61% - 35%) during the month of October, an enormous 17% jump occurring *after* the vote-shifting mechanisms were, *or could be*, deployed.

---

[22] The powerful impact of the succession of lurid scandals (Foley, Haggard, Sherwood, et al) is clear from the Weighted National Poll responses in which voters were asked about the importance of "corruption/ethics:" 41% responded "extremely important" and another 33% "very important," *the highest response of all the "importance" questions*, outstripping even the importance of "terrorism." Iraq, another source of late-breaking negatives for the GOP, also scored high on the importance scale (36% extremely, with this category breaking for the Democrats 61% -38%).

[23] http://www.cookpolitical.com/poll/ballot.php.

It should be noted that among the various tracking polls, there were some that did not pick up the dramatic trend reflected in the Cook poll. Indeed, Cook's own parallel tracking poll of all *registered* voters (not screened for likelihood of turnout) found only a modest gain of 2% in the Democratic margin over the same period. This is indicative of the phenomenon to which we have already made reference: what most boosted the Democrats during the month of October was an extraordinary gain in the relative *motivation and likelihood of turning out* among their voters. It supports our belief that it was primarily the exceptional turnout differential, understandably missed by exit polls calibrated to historical turnout patterns, that would have given the Democrats an even greater victory than the 11.5% reflected by the Weighted National Poll, in an honestly and accurately counted election.

Implications

The 2006 Election gave the Democrats control of both houses of Congress, by margins of 31 seats (233 – 202) in the House and two seats (51 – 49) in the Senate. The Democrats won 20 House races and four Senate races by margins of 6% of the vote or less.[24] The odds are very good that the outcomes of most if not all of these races would have been reversed a month earlier, post-deployment of vote shifting mechanisms but pre-October surprises, before the resulting dramatic movement to the Democrats as reflected in the 17% Generic Ballot jump. The ballpark *sans*-October Surprise numbers: 222R – 213D in the House and 53R – 47D in the Senate.

---

[24] In the House: four races by 1%, four races by 2%, one race by 3%, five races by 4%, one race by 5%, five races by 6%, one race by 7%, five races by 8%, two races by 9%; in the Senate: two races by 1%, one race by 3%, one race by 6%, one race by 8%.

Absent a very Blue October, *which came too late to be countered by deployment of additional vote-shifting mechanisms*, we can conclude that, with the assistance of the vote-shifting mechanisms *already* deployed, the Republicans would almost certainly have maintained control of both houses of Congress.

This should be a rather sobering observation for Democrats looking ahead to their electoral future and assessing to what extent the system is broken as they contemplate the various legislative proposals for reform.[25]

Conclusion

There is a remarkable degree of consensus among computer scientists,[26] security professionals,[27] government agencies,[28] and independent analysts[29] that U.S. electronic vote tallying technology is vulnerable both to unintentional programming errors[30] and to deliberate manipulation—certainly by foul-play-minded insiders at voting

---

[25] If we are correct in our assessment that the limitations on vote shifting were more temporal than spatial—that is, had more to do with timing of deployment than with the potential size of the shift—then only extraordinary and unanticipated eleventh-hour pre-election surges *a la* E2006 will suffice to overcome future foul play. However, whatever quantitative limits may apply to electronic vote shifting, *it should obviously not be necessary to enjoy super-majority support in order to eke out electoral victories.*

[26] For instance, http://www.acm.org/usacm/weblog/index.php?cat=6.

[27] See the credentials of the interdisciplinary Brennan Center Task Force membership at http://brennancenter.org/programs/downloads/About%20the%20Task%20Force.pdf.

[28] http://www.gao.gov/new.items/d05956.pdf .

[29] See http://www.blackboxvoting.org/BBVtsxstudy.pdf , http://www.blackboxvoting.org/BBVtsxstudy-supp.pdf , and http://www.blackboxvoting.org/BBVreport.pdf .

[30] Credible reports of voting equipment malfunctions are all too common; one good starting point is http://www.votersunite.org/info/messupsbyvendor.asp.

equipment vendors, but also by other individuals with access to voting equipment hardware or software.[31]

We have arrived at a system of "faith-based" voting where we are simply asked to trust the integrity of the count produced by the secret-software machines that tally our votes, without effective check mechanisms. In the context of yet another election replete with reported problems with vote tallying,[32] the continuing mismatch between the preferences expressed by voters as captured in national exit polls and the official vote tally as reported to the public is beyond disturbing. It is a bright red flag that no one who values a democratic America can in good conscience ignore.

False elections bequeath to all Americans—right, left, and center— nothing less sinister than an illusory identity and the living of a national lie. Our biennial elections, far more than the endless parade of opinion polls, *define* America—both in terms of who occupies its seats of power and as the single snapshot that becomes the enduring national self-portrait that all Americans carry in their mental wallets for at least the biennium and more often for an era. It is also, needless to say, the portrait we send abroad.

While the reported results of the 2006 election were certainly well-received by the Democratic party and were ballpark-consistent with public expectations of a Democratic victory, the unadjusted 2006 exit poll data indicates that what has been cast as a typical midterm setback for a struggling president in his second term was something rather more remarkable – a landslide repudiation of historic proportions.

---

[31] For example, http://brennancenter.org/programs/downloads/SecurityFull7-3Reduced.pdf.

[32] Election 2006 incidents at http://www.votersunite.org/electionproblems.asp.

We believe that the demographic validity of the Weighted National Poll in 2006 is the clearest possible warning that the ever-growing catalog of reported vulnerabilities in America's electronic vote counting systems are not only *possible* to exploit, *they are actually being exploited*. To those who would rush to find "innocent" explanations on an *ad hoc* basis for the cascade of mathematical evidence that continues to emerge, we ask what purpose is served and what comfort is given by relying on a series of implausible alibis to dispel concerns and head off effective reform?

The vulnerability is manifest; the stakes are enormous; the incentive is obvious; the evidence is strong and persistent. Any system so clearly at risk of interference and gross manipulation cannot and must not be trusted to tally the votes in any future elections.

Appendix 1 – US House Exit Poll Data

1. National Generic US House Exit Poll summary

US House Exit Poll 2006	Opinion Poll (average) Nov 1 - 5	Unadjusted Exit Poll Nov 7 7:07 PM EST	Adjusted Exit Poll Nov 8 1:00 PM EST	Reported Actual % Nov 9	Reported Actual Vote Nov 9
	7 polls**	Sample size 10,207	Sample size 13,251		
Total Democrat vote for US House*	55.0%	55.0%	52.6%	52.7%	40,323,525
Total Republican vote for US House	43.5%	43.5%	45.0%	45.1%	34,565,872
Total Other Parties vote for US House		1.5%	2.4%	2.2%	1,694,392
Total US House					76,583,789
*CBSnews.com, 11/9/06 + additional sources for unopposed candidates					
Democrat - Republican spread (%)	11.5%	11.5%	7.6%	7.6%	
Variance: Exit Poll - Actual [%]	3.9%	3.9%	0.0%		
Democrat - Republican spread (count)		8,807,136	5,820,368	5,820,368	
Variance: Exit Poll - Actual (count)		2,986,768	0		
Variance from actual					
Democrat	2.3%	2.3%	-0.1%		
Republican	-1.6%	-1.6%	-0.1%		
Other	-2.2%	-0.7%	0.2%		

**Fox News, CNN, USA Today/Gallup, ABC News/Wash Post, Pew Research, Newsweek, Time as reported on RealClearPolitics.com

2. Exit Poll Screen Captures

Exit poll screen capture files will be posted at http://www.electiondefensealliance.org/ExitPollData after the release of this report.

3. US House – preliminary reported tallies by state as-of 11/09/2006, CBSNews.com

State	US House – D	US House – R	US House - Other	Dem %	Rep %	Other %
AL	224,350	351,650	3,396	38.7%	60.7%	0.6%
AK	81,408	115,062	6,236	40.2%	56.8%	3.1%
AZ	478,573	576,061	72,435	42.5%	51.1%	6.4%
AR	448,058	299,496	0	59.9%	40.1%	0.0%
CA	3,549,128	2,478,884	207,821	56.9%	39.8%	3.3%
CO	727,914	571,699	70,877	53.1%	41.7%	5.2%
CT	652,025	420,995	6,087	60.4%	39.0%	0.6%
DE	196,700	291,052	20,674	38.7%	57.2%	4.1%
FL	1,496,686	2,162,353	68,197	40.2%	58.0%	1.8%
GA	798,809	1,117,086	0	41.7%	58.3%	0.0%
HI	219,588	118,075	0	65.0%	35.0%	0.0%
ID	172,530	243,062	19,401	39.7%	55.9%	4.5%
IL	1,732,380	1,381,232	13,602	55.4%	44.2%	0.4%
IN	802,751	820,569	22,128	48.8%	49.9%	1.3%
IA	489,508	519,796	17,629	47.7%	50.6%	1.7%
KS	360,356	449,548	16,213	43.6%	54.4%	2.0%
KY	596,402	608,771	39,362	47.9%	48.9%	3.2%
LA	294,100	579,514	27,028	32.7%	64.3%	3.0%
ME	344,870	161,335	22,689	65.2%	30.5%	4.3%
MD	827,674	475,065	41,292	61.6%	35.3%	3.1%
MA	792,619	197,722	76,951	74.3%	18.5%	7.2%
MI	1,793,200	1,626,459	97,334	51.0%	46.2%	2.8%
MN	1,153,624	925,500	99,493	53.0%	42.5%	4.6%
MS	251,027	295,184	35,077	43.2%	50.8%	6.0%
MO	965,390	1,031,489	54,436	47.1%	50.3%	2.7%
MT	314,998	476,062	15,494	39.1%	59.0%	1.9%
NE	257,214	329,003	0	43.9%	56.1%	0.0%
NV	286,761	259,237	26,535	50.1%	45.3%	4.6%
NH	209,424	188,774	3,777	52.1%	47.0%	0.9%
NJ	948,740	885,007	25,070	51.0%	47.6%	1.3%
NM	304,058	241,202	0	55.8%	44.2%	0.0%
NY	2,285,026	1,268,408	8,251	64.2%	35.6%	0.2%
NC	935,490	907,236	0	50.8%	49.2%	0.0%

State	US House – D	US House – R	US House - Other	Dem %	Rep %	Other %
ND	284,242	148,728	0	65.6%	34.4%	0.0%
OH	1,970,118	1,784,993	8,052	52.4%	47.4%	0.2%
OK	372,822	517,948	14,278	41.2%	57.2%	1.6%
OR	713,441	522,846	28,446	56.4%	41.3%	2.2%
PA	2,060,969	1,705,435	48,949	54.0%	44.7%	1.3%
RI	264,101	41,753	66,176	71.0%	11.2%	17.8%
SC	466,473	592,639	13,252	43.5%	55.3%	1.2%
SD	460,946	195,736	10,470	69.1%	29.3%	1.6%
TN	860,025	797,431	54,970	50.2%	46.6%	3.2%
TX	1,783,304	2,069,491	142,391	44.6%	51.8%	3.6%
UT	234,024	282,554	31,583	42.7%	51.5%	5.8%
VT	279,170	234,442	11,110	53.2%	44.7%	2.1%
VA	810,365	1,220,073	117,870	37.7%	56.8%	5.5%
WA	802,873	498,872	6,584	61.4%	38.1%	0.5%
WV	258,438	187,895	0	57.9%	42.1%	0.0%
WI	1,001,254	836,054	15,311	54.0%	45.1%	0.8%
WY	184,454	186,394	7,465	48.8%	49.3%	2.0%
Sub-total	37,798,400	34,195,872	1,694,392	51.3%	46.4%	2.3%
Total	73,688,664					

4. Estimation of votes in uncontested US House races

Near complete election results were published shortly after November 7th for contested US House races. Most media outlets do not publish the number of votes in uncontested House races, which can be substantial. Public opinion and exit pollsters may sample voters in districts with uncontested candidates. In order to have an accurate baseline for any measurements based on the actual US House vote, it was necessary to estimate the total number of votes cast for unopposed candidates.

To estimate the number of votes in US House races with unopposed candidates:

> We identified jurisdictions, such as Florida, where uncontested candidates do not appear on the ballot at all. These races were excluded from the national aggregate US House votecount.

> For every other uncontested race we looked at historical data on ballots cast for uncontested candidates for a midterm election in exactly the same district. In most cases, the same districts were uncontested in 2002.

> In a few cases, districts with uncontested races in 2006 were not uncontested in recent elections. For those districts, we used the winning margin of the candidate of the same party in a recent midterm election.

> Our overall estimate of votes in uncontested elections – 2,525,125 votes cast nationwide for unopposed Democrats and 370,000 nationwide cast for unopposed Republicans – produces an estimated national grand total that matches quite closely the grand total vote that appears to have been used to calibrate the adjusted US House exit poll on November 8th.

Appendix 2 – NEP Methodology 2004 and 2007

METHODS STATEMENT

NATIONAL ELECTION POOL EXIT POLLS
November 2, 2004

NATIONAL/REGIONAL EXIT POLL

Edison Media Research and Mitofsky International conducted exit polls in each state and nationally for the **National Election Pool** (ABC, AP, CBS, CNN, FOX, NBC). The polls should be referred to as a **National Election Pool** (or NEP) **Exit Poll,** conducted by **Edison/Mitofsky. All questionnaires were prepared by NEP.**

The National exit poll was conducted at a sample of 250 polling places among 11,719 Election Day voters representative of the United States.

In addition, 500 absentee and/or early voters in 13 states were interviewed in a pre-election telephone poll. Absentee or early voters were asked the same questions asked at the polling place on Election Day. The absentee results were combined in approximately the correct proportion with voters interviewed at the polling places. The states where absentee/early voters were interviewed for the National exit poll are: Arizona, California, Colorado, Florida, Iowa, Michigan, Nevada, New Mexico, North Carolina, Oregon, Tennessee, Texas and Washington state. Absentee voters in these states made up 13% of the total national vote in the 2000 presidential election. Another 3% of the 2000 total vote was cast absentee in other states in 2000 and where there is no absentee/early voter telephone poll.

The polling places were selected as a stratified probability sample of each state. A subsample of the state samples was selected at the proper proportions for the National exit poll. Within each polling place an interviewer approached every n^{th} voter as he or she exited the polling place. Approximately 100 voters completed a questionnaire at each polling place. The exact number depends on voter turnout and their cooperation.

For the national tabulations used to analyze an election, respondents are weighted based upon two factors. They are: (1) the probability of selection of the precinct and the respondent within the precinct; (2) by the size and distribution of the best estimate of the vote within geographic sub-regions of the nation. The second step produces consistent estimates *at the time of the tabulation* whether from the tabulations or an estimating model used to make an estimate of the national popular vote. At other times the estimated national popular vote may differ somewhat from the national tabulations.

All samples are approximations. A measure of the approximation is called the sampling error. Sampling error is affected by the design of the sample, the characteristic being measured and the number of people who have the characteristic. If a characteristic is found in roughly the same proportions in all precincts the sampling error will be lower. If the characteristic is concentrated in a few precincts the sampling error will be larger. Gender would be a good example of a characteristic with a lower sampling error. Characteristics for minority racial groups will have larger sampling errors.

The table below lists typical sampling errors for given size subgroups for a 95% confidence interval. The values in the table should be added and subtracted from the characteristic's percentage in order to construct an interval. 95% of the intervals created this way will contain the value that would be obtained if all voters were interviewed using the same procedures. Other non-sampling factors, including nonresponse, are likely to increase the total error.

%Error Due to Sampling (+/-) for 95% Confidence Interval							
Number of Voters in Base of Percentage							
% Voters with Characteristic	100	101-200	201-500	501-950	951-2350	2351-5250	5251-8000	8001-15000*
5% or 95%	6	5	3	2	2	1	1	1
15% or 85%	11	7	5	4	3	2	1	1
25% or 75%	13	9	6	5	3	2	2	1
50%	15	10	7	5	4	3	2	1

* chart bolding ours

From National Election Pool FAQs 2007

What is the Margin of Error for an exit poll?
Every number estimated from a sample may depart from the official votecount. The difference between a sample result and the number one would get if everyone who cast a vote was interviewed in exactly the same way is called the sampling error. That does not mean the sample result is wrong. Instead, it refers to the potential error due to sampling. **The margin of error for a 95% confidence interval is about +/- 3% for a typical characteristic from the national exit poll and +/-4% for a typical state exit poll.*** Characteristics that are more concentrated in a few polling places, such as race, have larger sampling errors. Other nonsampling factors may increase the total error.

* bolding ours

Appendix 3 – Mechanics of Vote Manipulation

Practical Constraints on any Nationwide Covert Vote Manipulation Capability

Some critics of the initial draft of this paper released in November 2006 questioned whether it was possible that a systematic tabulation bias could ever be deployed to electronic voting equipment on a nationwide scale without being detected. Others claimed that if that capability truly existed, it should guarantee that one party would remain in permanent control.

The technical and logistical challenges inherent in any attempt to secretly corrupt vote tabulation on a nationwide basis are of course hardly trivial, but expert consensus is that there are multiple credible methods. We believe that the potential methods that could feasibly be used to implement widespread electronic vote manipulation on a national scale with a high probability of remaining undetected are such that a significant lead time would be required prior to the election. There is therefore a risk that any unexpected late-breaking pre-election developments could overcome a pre-programmed bias.

Voting systems risk assessment

Modern American electronic voting systems are geographically dispersed, distributed computer systems which are used intensively but infrequently. The end-to-end voting systems contain thousands of central tabulators and hundreds of thousands of in-precinct voting devices, all of which are purchased, maintained, upgraded, programmed, tested and used in actual elections in over 170,000 precincts across the United States on irregular schedules.

Through hands-on access, individual voting machines can be compromised one at a time through a variety of well-documented exploits.[33] But the sheer number of devices in use makes hands-on vote manipulation on a national scale a massively labor-intensive enterprise. The more individuals that are involved, the greater the likelihood of disclosure. The very ability successfully to orchestrate the collective behavior of tens of thousands of devices to achieve a desired outcome—election after election, without being detected—would depend on minimizing the number of people involved and so would require a significant degree of sophistication.

Undetected widespread votecount corruption would certainly be not only the greatest computer security exploit of all time, it would be the greatest—and, in terms of the ultimate stakes, most lucrative— undetected crime in history. One must presume that any individuals capable of successfully pulling off such an exploit are clever, ruthless, and utterly determined to cover their tracks. We would not expect them to display naiveté nor simplicity, but rather to act at every step to preserve total secrecy of their presence and activities.

Voting system attacks that minimize the number of people involved

The June 2006 Brennan Center report described in great detail precisely how software patches, ballot definition files, and memory cards could be used to enable just one individual to alter the outcome of an election conducted either on touchscreen DREs[34] or on optical scan equipment.[35]

---

[33] See footnotes 26 – 32 above.

[34] Brennan Center June 2006 Report: "The Machinery of Democracy: Protecting Elections in an Electronic World," pp. 34 – 40.

[35] Ibid, p. 78.

As the Brennan Center report notes:

> ... [I]n a close statewide election ... "retail" attacks, or attacks on individual polling places, would not likely affect enough votes to change the outcome. By contrast, the less difficult attacks are centralized attacks: these would occur against the entire voting system and allow an attacker to target many votes with few informed participants.
>
> Least difficult among these less difficult attacks would be attacks that use Software Attack Programs. The reason is relatively straightforward: a software attack allows a single knowledgeable person (or, in some cases, small group of people) to reach hundreds or thousands of machines. For instance, software updates and patches are often sent to jurisdictions throughout a state. Similarly, replaceable media such as memory cards and ballot definition files are generally programmed at the county level (or at the vendor) and sent to every polling place in the county.
>
> These attacks have other benefits: unlike retail denial-of-service attacks, or manual shut off of machine functions, they could provide an attacker's favored candidate with a relatively certain benefit (i.e., addition of x number of votes per machine attacked). And if installed in a clever way, these attacks have a good chance of eluding the standard inspection and testing regimens currently in place.[36]

---

[36] Ibid, p. 48.

Long-term evasion of detection

Since it is clear that the motivation exists to take covert control of electronic voting in the United States and that there are credible mechanisms for a small number of malicious insiders at voting equipment vendors to do so, long-term success boils down to evading detection—and so maintaining this power over time. One critical element of maintaining long-term secrecy would be the tradeoff of carefully calibrating the degree of vote manipulation to avoid attracting suspicion, while also ensuring the desired political outcome.

An individual in the position to introduce a covert vote manipulation software component into the operating system, firmware, device driver, or voting application itself would want to minimize risk of future detection and maximize the ease of changing the outcome of future contests. Ideally covert vote manipulation logic itself should be built into the machine as close to the factory as possible, rather than requiring redistribution of malicious program logic every election cycle; any change to the logic of a complex system could introduce new errors into the behavior of "benign" tabulation logic. And since political circumstances change, not all contests, elections and machines would be subject to the same type and degree of vote manipulation in every election, or the existence of the "Trojan Horse" itself would become all too evident.

Perhaps the easiest method to achieve both goals—long-term secrecy and long-term flexibility—is to introduce a general-purpose vote manipulation component which remains hidden within in the voting equipment for a long period of time, and which can be activated on demand by receipt of an external trigger. The trigger would not only activate the malicious software, but would also contain a parameter defining the size of the manipulation to implement. This is far from science fiction; parameterization is a basic computer software technique in use since the dawn of computing, and parameterization of voting equipment exploits is a powerful attack that is certainly technically feasible.[37]

Although of course we cannot know for certain in the absence of a proper investigation whether this was actually done in 2006, there is strong support for a hypothesis that the logistics of introducing malicious programming on a targeted nationwide basis is both technically feasible and would likely require a substantial lead time, necessitating deployment prior to this past October's "perfect storm."

---

[37] Ibid, p. 38.

STUDY III.

Fingerprints of Election Theft: Were Competitive Contests Targeted?

Comparison Between Exit Poll and Votecount Disparities in Competitive vs. Noncompetitive Contests in Election 2006

Jonathan Simon, JD, Bruce O'Dell, Dale Tavris, PhD, Josh Mitteldorf, PhD[1]
Election Defense Alliance

Abstract

In this report, we describe results from a telephone poll conducted the night of the national election of November, 2006. The poll methodology was explicitly designed to detect partisan manipulation of the votecount, and to separate evidence for manipulation from poll sampling bias. Our premise was that politically motivated tampering would target races that were projected to be competitive, while the perpetrators would be less motivated to interfere in races that were not projected to be close. Designing our poll to be maximally sensitive to such a pattern, we selected 16 counties around the country where, of the three most prominent races (Governor, Senator or US House), there

[1] Jonathan Simon, JD (http://www.electiondefensealliance.org/jonathan_simon) is Co-founder of Election Defense Alliance (EDA); Bruce O'Dell (http://www.electiondefensealliance.org/bruce_odell) and Dale Tavris (http://www.electiondefensealliance.org/about_dale_tavris) are EDA Data Analysis Co-coordinators; Josh Mitteldorf (http://mathforum.org/~josh) is a statistician, evolutionary biologist, and election integrity advocate.

was at least one competitive contest and one noncompetitive contest. In our study, the responses of the same group of respondents were compared to official election results for pairs of races, one competitive and one noncompetitive. We used paired data analysis to compare disparities between poll and official count for these matched pairs. Our results revealed much larger disparities in competitive than in noncompetitive races ($p<0.007$), suggesting manipulation that consistently favored Republican candidates. We also found a linear relationship between the size of the pro-Republican disparity and the tightness of the election ($p<0.000022$). These results corroborate analyses published elsewhere, also suggesting significant vote manipulation in favor of Republican candidates in the 2006 general election.

Background

Recent American elections have been tabulated by computerized voting equipment that has been proven through independent investigation by qualified security experts to be wide open to systematic insider manipulation.[2] This fact has been acknowledged in the mainstream American press, and indeed in government reports.[3] Nevertheless, those who, taking the next logical step, gather and present evidence to suggest that at least some recent elections may have *actually been* compromised continue to be met with skepticism and indifference.

In light of this skepticism, election forensics experts have endeavored to take the measure of recent elections from several complementary perspectives. Several methods by which systemic election theft can be

---

[2] See, e.g., http://brennancenter.org/dynamic/subpages/download_file_39288.pdf, http://itpolicy.princeton.edu/voting/ts-paper.pdf, http://www.sos.ca.gov/elections/elections_vsr.htm, http://www.blackboxvoting.org/BBVtsxstudy.pdf, or http://www.blackboxvoting.org/BBVreport.pdf.

[3] See, e.g., Government Accountability Office, Oct. 2005, at http://www.gao.gov/new.items/d05956.pdf.

perpetrated electronically and invisibly—and with high confidence of evading immediate detection—have been documented.[4] With vote-counting software and hardware both ruled 'proprietary' and off-limits to inspection—and with limited access to, and the scheduled destruction of, paper election records, where they exist—*direct* proof of an electronically-altered election outcome may well be impossible.[5] Yet although systematic electronic vote manipulation may well go undetected both during and after an election, it can still leave behind rather glaring mathematical 'fingerprints'. And when multiple analytic methods find mathematical 'fingerprints' that are all consistent with the same pattern of apparent mistabulation, the case becomes very strong— at least for anyone willing to contemplate the evidence, even though the implications are profoundly disturbing.

In *Landslide Denied: Exit Polls vs. Vote Count 2006*,[6] a study published shortly after the 2006 election ('E2006'), authors Simon and O'Dell analyzed the nationwide disparity between official votecounts and the E2006 exit polls. They concluded that mistabulation of votes reduced the Democratic margin in total votes cast for the House of Representatives by a minimum of 4%, or *3 million votes*. Based on the official margins of House races, the authors further concluded that, accurately tabulated, E2006 would have been an epic landslide, netting the Democrats a very substantial number of additional seats in Congress.

By examining in detail the 2006 US House exit poll data's underlying demographic and voter-preference questions, the authors were able to confirm both the validity of the exit poll sample and the size of the official mistabulation.

---

[4] See fn 2.

[5] To these difficulties we may add the simple-enough employment of self-deleting tabulation code, which would leave no trace of foul play even in the unlikely event inspection were permitted.

[6] http://electiondefensealliance.org/files/LandslideDenied_v.9_071507.pdf.

Past comparisons between exit polls and official results have been questioned on the grounds that sampling bias may have played a role. By comparing the national sample's responses to a variety of established demographic and voter-preference benchmarks, *Landslide Denied* established that the national exit poll certainly did *not* 'oversample Democrats'.[7] *Landslide Denied* also argued that the Republicans might have succeeded in holding on to the House and the Senate, but for the fact that the manipulation that apparently benefited them was calibrated and engineered based on pre-October polling numbers, which subsequently shifted dramatically further toward the Democrats in the final weeks before the election. If the election had been held a month earlier, the vote-shift evidenced by the exit poll disparity would have sufficed to keep the Republicans in power.

This analysis has not been rebutted or challenged, although its evidence and conclusions are clearly presented and quite straightforward. On the other hand, it has gone almost completely unreported.[8]

In the 2006 elections, the national House exit poll could provide, at most, an indication of aggregate mistabulation on a nationwide basis. Even so, in planning and preparing for forensic analysis of the 2006 elections, it was fair to assume that any damning evidence exit polls might provide would once again face skepticism in the press (as in 'as usual, the exit polls oversampled Democrats and cannot be relied upon'), and among official voices of both political parties. Therefore,

---

[7] The national sample that had allegedly 'oversampled Democrats' gave President Bush approval numbers at or above established benchmarks. Several other key indicators (such as racial composition, party ID, vote for President in 2004, and Congressional approval) all corroborated the fact that the sample leaned, if anything, to the right.

[8] *Landslide Denied* was posted on the Election Defense Alliance website on 11/17/06, and simultaneously distributed through US Newswire to hundreds of media outlets. It was picked up by *one*, a passing reference in a small publication in North Dakota. *Landslide Denied* was also submitted for inclusion in the record of Senate Rules Committee hearings on election fraud and security. It was not accepted and no explanation was offered for its rejection.

Election Defense Alliance sought to capture data from the 2006 election from a different and, we hoped, complementary angle.

Our Approach and Methodology

In order to counter the anticipated dismissal of 2006 national exit poll evidence on the basis of sample bias, we turned to an approach that would effectively remove sampling bias as a factor by measuring how *the same sample of voters responded with respect to different electoral contests.* Our study was based on the premise that vote theft would be targeted to races that were within striking distance of a shift. We hypothesized that races that appeared close in the pre-election polls would be targeted for theft, while races that were projected to be landslides would not be corrupted. We designed a study to compare pairs of competitive and non-competitive races in such a way that responses from the same polling respondents would be used for both.

Therefore, we selected counties in which we anticipated, based on pre-election polling, that there would be at least one competitive contest and at least one noncompetitive contest among the races for U.S. House, U.S. Senate, and the governorship of the state.[9] For the purpose of paired (t-test) analysis, we viewed contests decided by a margin smaller than 10% as 'competitive' and contests decided by a margin of 10% or greater as 'noncompetitive.'[10]

---

[9] Although hundreds of counties nationwide would have met these basic criteria, our selection was further constrained by budgetary considerations: with approximately $36,000 available for this project, the counties chosen had to be sufficiently small that the cost of obtaining the voter lists would not be prohibitive, and that enough counties could be surveyed to generate a statistically meaningful number of data points for analysis. Altogether 19 counties were surveyed for this project, of which 16 turned out to meet the criterion of having at least one competitive and one noncompetitive contest. These 16 counties form the basis of our primary analysis.

[10] Our 'paired' analysis of course necessitates a categorical line of demarcation. While 10% is a common-sense choice, others might be imagined. As will be seen below, the actual race margins tended to a bi-modal distribution (mean margin for competitive races = 3.2%, mean margin for noncompetitive races = 20.5%), generally distant enough from the 10% line to remove any concern about its arbitrariness. In fact, the

All contests in each selected county were sampled by a *single* Election Night survey of actual voters (whether at-precinct, early, or absentee) conducted by telephone on our behalf by the polling firm Survey USA. As a result, the *same set of respondents* was asked to indicate how they had voted in each of the contests within each selected county. This 'apples-to-apples' comparison, rather than any presumed freedom from bias in the samples themselves,[11] provided the basis for our analysis.

Hypothesis

Our hypothesis was that, although there would of course be disparities between survey results and votecounts in most (if not all) contests, in the absence of vote shifting foul play *selectively targeted to competitive races* there would be no statistically significant pattern of disparities by which competitive and noncompetitive contests could be distinguished.

Results

Table 1 on p. 208 presents our core data for the 16 counties which had both competitive and noncompetitive contests. An expanded table— showing the actual winning margins of these contests, as well as the actual votecount and exit poll percentages within the sampled counties—is presented as Appendix 1.

---

divider could have been placed at 9% or 8% without having any impact on our paired analysis.

[11] In this type of survey, calls are placed on Election Night to all voters on the county registration lists, but only those respondents who indicate they actually cast a vote are included in the survey results. Response rates are typically quite low and there is no attempt to eliminate self-select response bias (e.g., if Republicans or Democrats have a greater tendency to respond and are therefore over-represented) via stratification techniques. Such efforts are not necessary for our purposes because response bias does not adversely affect our *comparison* between competitive and noncompetitive races drawn from the same set of respondents.

Reading from left to right, Table 1 presents the county surveyed, the office contested, whether that contest proved to be competitive or noncompetitive, the disparity between votecount and survey results in competitive and noncompetitive races respectively, and the difference within each county between the disparities found in competitive and noncompetitive races (using the mean disparity when there were two competitive or noncompetitive races within a county).

'Red shift' and 'blue shift' defined

We designate an official votecount more Republican than the survey results to be a 'red shift,' and an official votecount more Democratic than the survey results to be a 'blue shift.'

TABLE 1

Comparison Between Survey and Votecount Disparities
In Competitive vs. Noncompetitive Contests In Election 2006
(All Contests In Each County Sampled By A Single
Election Night Survey of Actual Voters)

County, State	Contest	Competitive?* C/NC	Within-County Exit Poll - Vote Count Disparity Competitive Contests (R+/D-)	Within-County Exit Poll - Vote Count Disparity NonCompetitive Contests (R+/D-)	Within-County Difference Between Avg. Competitive and NonCompetitive Disparities***
Hardee, FL	Governor	C	7.5%		11.25%
	Senator	NC		-3.5%	
	House: FL-13	C	8.0%		
Okeechobee, FL	Governor	C	5.5%		12.50%
	Senator	NC		-9.5%	
	House: FL-16	C**	0.5%		
Emanuel, GA	Governor	NC		-1.0%	4.00%
	House: GA-12	C	3.0%		
Jefferson, GA	Governor	NC		0.0%	0.00%
	House: GA-12	C	0.0%		
Jefferson, IA	Governor	NC		0.5%	11.00%
	House: IA-2	C	11.5%		
Van Buren, IA	Governor	NC		8.0%	10.50%
	House: IA-2	C	18.5%		
Mower, MN	Senator	NC		-2.5%	6.00%
	House: MN-1	C	3.5%		
Pipestone, MN	Senator	NC		-1.5%	1.00%
	House: MN-1	C	-0.5%		
Cedar, MO	Senator	C	-1.5%		12.50%
	House: MO-4	NC		-14.0%	
Henry, MO	Senator	C	-1.5%		16.50%
	House: MO-4	NC		-18.0%	
Humboldt, NV	Governor	C	5.0%		-2.25%
	Senator	NC		5.0%	
	House: NV-2	C	0.5%		
Adams, OH	Governor	NC		-2.5%	8.75%
	Senator	NC		-1.0%	
	House: OH-2	C	7.0%		
Bradford, PA	Governor	NC		6.0%	-6.75%
	Senator	NC		7.5%	
	House: PA-10	C	0.0%		
Wyoming, PA	Governor	NC		-3.0%	-1.50%
	Senator	NC		-1.0%	
	House: PA-10	C	-3.5%		
Haywood, TN	Governor	NC		-2.0%	8.00%
	Senator	C	5.0%		
	House: TN-8	NC		-4.0%	
Lancaster, VA	Senator	C	-1.0%		-4.00%
	House: VA-1	NC		3.0%	
AVERAGE			3.6%	-1.7%	5.47%

* Contests decided by a 9% or smaller margin are designated competitive; 10% or larger noncompetitive.
** Contest for seat vacated by Mark Foley; shifted from noncompetitive to competitive status during October 2006.
*** Number is positive (+) where net shift is to Republican in competitive vs. noncompetitive contests.
All surveys conducted via telephone on Election Night 2006 by Survey USA.

The right-hand column conveys the overall picture. A positive percentage in the right-hand column indicates that there was more of a red shift (or less of a blue shift) in competitive than in noncompetitive contests in that county. That is, a positive percentage indicates a net shift toward the Republican candidate in the competitive versus noncompetitive contest(s) within a given county.

An Individual County Example

To take Hardee County, Florida, as an example: the competitive contests were for Governor and US House and the noncompetitive contest was for the US Senate. The competitive contests exhibited a red shift of 7.5% and 8.0% respectively: meaning the official votecounts in Hardee in those races were 7.5% and 8.0% more Republican than the survey results, an average of 7.75%.

In the noncompetitive contest for US Senate we see a blue shift of 3.5%, meaning the official votecount was 3.5% more Democratic than the survey results.

Overall, therefore, in Hardee County - *as measured by the survey responses of precisely the same group of voters* - the official votecounts in competitive contests were shifted by a net of 11.25% (that is, by 7.75% + 3.5%) to the Republican candidates, relative to the official votecount in the noncompetitive contest.

Sixteen-county analysis

We find that relative red shift toward the Republican candidate in competitive contests occurred in 11 of the 16 counties. Only four counties exhibited a relative blue shift away from the Republican candidate in competitive contests.[12] One county exhibited no net shift, red or blue.

More significantly, we found that for the 19 competitive contests, the average survey vs. votecount disparity was a red shift of 3.6%, and for the 20 noncompetitive races the average disparity was a blue shift of 1.7%. *Competitive contests were therefore relatively more red-shifted by an average of 5.3% per contest.*[13]

Statistical significance of competitive race 'red shift'

Employing the paired t-test (two-tailed) to evaluate the statistical significance of this result, we find it to be statistically significant at the $p<0.007$ level, meaning that that much of a difference between disparities in competitive and noncompetitive contests would be expected by chance only *seven in 1000 times.*[14]

According to our hypothesis, the string of positive percentages in the right hand column should not occur unless systematic election

---

[12] Interestingly, two of the four 'net blue shift' counties are located in Pennsylvania, a state which stood out in E2006 for bucking the red shift pattern in statewide US Senate races. While a total of 21 Senate races exhibited red shifts (mean = 4.2%), Pennsylvania, a state under Democratic administrative control, was one of only five states to exhibit a blue shift (2%) in its Senate race. At this point we can do little more than speculate about the possible effects of partisan administrative control upon both aggregate mistabulation and targeting patterns. (See also http://kdka.com/topstories/local_story_311194635.html)

[13] Because of the above-mentioned averaging within counties, the 16-county mean difference between disparities in competitive and noncompetitive contests was a slightly higher 5.47%.

[14] A one-tailed t-test, justifiably employed if we are testing only for the likelihood of an overall competitive contest *red* shift, would yield a p value of 0.003, a 3/1000th prospect of chance occurrence. It should also be noted that a regression analysis of magnitude/direction of shift relative to magnitude of contest margin yields an F value of 21.9, corresponding to a p value of $p<0.000022$ and strongly corroborating our finding of strong correlation using the paired testing approach. Such an analysis also dispenses with what some might consider an arbitrary dividing line between competitive and noncompetitive contests at a margin of 10%, necessary for the paired-test approach. The shift-margin correlation is powerful using either approach. Please see Appendix 2 for this analysis.

mistabulation is occurring–selectively, in competitive contests, and favoring Republican candidates. In the absence of targeted mistabulation, the mean value at the bottom of the right-hand column would be at or very close to zero.

Discussion

We have already discussed the evidence for an *aggregate* mistabulation of votes in E2006 of a magnitude sufficient to alter the outcome of dozens of federal and statewide elections.[15] The aggregate evidence is based on the quasi-official exit polls conducted by Edison Research and Mitofsky International ('Edison/Mitofsky') for the media consortium known as the National Election Pool ('NEP').

In *Landslide Denied*,[16] it is shown not only that the NEP sample of the national electorate (i.e., the aggregate vote for all House races) was of a size that makes it a virtual impossibility that the 4% poll-vote disparity could occur as a result of chance or sampling *error* but also, more significantly, that the alleged political *bias* of the sample towards the Democrats *did not exist*, as proven by the demographics of the exit poll sample itself.

Yet whenever a direct comparison between poll results (whether pre-election, exit, or post-election) and official votecounts is made and a disparity is noted, it is, inexplicably, always the *polls* that the media chorus hastens to discount and dismiss. Demonstrating the lax standards of computer security and the inadequate procedural safeguards universally applied to our electronic voting systems seems to make no impression. The present study was undertaken because we anticipated—correctly, as it turned out—that direct poll-vote

---

[15] In *Landslide Denied* (http://electiondefensealliance.org/files/LandslideDenied_v.9_071507.pdf), the authors established a net shift to the Republican candidates for US House of Representatives of at least 3 million votes nationwide.

[16] *Landslide Denied*, pp. 2 – 13.

comparisons, if they appeared to indicate outcome-determinative mistabulation, would likely face hasty dismissal, predictably on the grounds of sample bias. We therefore sought a methodology that would serve to eliminate *any* effect of sampling bias from the equation.[17]

How our study neutralizes the impact of sample bias

In the vast majority of federal and state political contests, it is possible to ascertain well in advance of Election Day the degree to which the race will be competitive. It is therefore possible to target competitive contests for fraudulent manipulation in a timeframe that allows the necessary mechanisms to be selectively deployed[18] (for example, tainted memory cards,[19] or malicious code or code parameters installed under the guise of a legitimate software distribution).

We found that we could identify such targeting patterns using poll-vote comparisons from which sampling bias had been eliminated as a factor. In the 16 counties we studied, *in the absence of fraud targeted to competitive contests*, we would expect no particular correlation

---

[17] Much of the analysis in E2004 focused on the astounding individual exit poll-votecount disparities that turned up in certain states and in the national popular vote. But some attention was also given to the telling *distribution* of disparities between states that were considered 'battlegrounds' on the one hand and 'safe' states on the other. It emerged that, of the 11 battleground states, 10 were red-shifted. It further emerged that, relative to their respective average MOEs (the battleground states were more heavily sampled than the safe states, which makes a shift of the same magnitude less likely to occur in a battleground state), the battleground states as a group were nearly three times as red shifted as the safe states. So in a sense, in E2004, there was already a rough but glaring comparative analysis of competitive and noncompetitive states, pointing strongly to targeted vote-shifting. The question raised was, if the exit poll-votecount disparity was caused by 'reluctant Bush responders', why did this very convenient phenomenon (for which no evidence was ever presented) occur so disproportionately in competitive states; that is, why were Bush voters reluctant in Ohio and Florida (where it counted) but not in, say, Utah or Idaho (where it did not)? No cogent answer was ever given.

[18] See http://brennancenter.org/dynamic/subpages/download_file_39288.pdf pages 37-39 for parameterized attacks on voting systems.

[19] See http://itpolicy.princeton.edu/voting/ts-paper.pdf for attacks on voting systems via centrally-programmed memory cards.

between poll-vote disparities and the competitiveness of the contests. Disparities would of course be expected, both as predicted by the statistical margin of error ('MOE') of each poll and as a result of any sampling *bias* independent of such pure statistical considerations.[20]

But, since we are not relying upon a direct poll-votecount comparison, but rather upon comparison between disparities, we are not concerned with the impact of either sampling error or sampling bias on the poll-votecount disparities which constitute our data set. Indeed, sampling bias in any given county survey could be very substantial *without affecting the validity of our competitive-noncompetitive comparison*, because the *same* putatively biased set of respondents would be our benchmark for both competitive and noncompetitive contest votecounts.

Take, as an example, Van Buren County, Iowa. In this county the noncompetitive Governor's race votecount margin was shifted 8% towards the Republican relative to the poll, a result on which it might be suggested that sampling bias (oversampling of Democrats) might have had an impact. But in the same county, *and with the same set of respondents*, the competitive House race votecount margin was shifted *18.5%* towards the Republican relative to the poll. We can see that sampling bias, whether or not it was in fact present, *drops out of the*

---

[20] It is important to understand the distinction between sampling *error* and sampling *bias*. Sampling error, generally reflected in a poll's stated MOE, derives from the statistical chance that a fairly drawn sample (i.e., one drawn at random and without bias) will misrepresent the whole to some quantifiable, and usually very small, degree. Sampling bias, on the other hand, extends beyond any such purely statistical limitations to impound any intentional or inadvertent biases in the sampling process that yield further misrepresentation. A classic example would be interviewers who ignore random selection instructions by choosing respondents whom they know or who look more 'like them'; another would be a differential response rate based on categorical receptivity to being interviewed or ownership of the technology (e.g., telephone, computer) used for the poll. Effects of sampling bias can be virtually eliminated by a thorough demographic weighting process such as that employed by the NEP prior to publication of their poll results. Such a process was not, however, necessary to the design of the current study, as explained in fn. 11.

equation entirely, because it would be *equally* present in both races (using the same set of respondents) and could not account for the 10.5% difference between the two shifts.

Thus, in the absence of a competitive contest targeting pattern, disparities would be just about equally likely to occur, and equally likely to be in the "red" or "blue" direction, in competitive and noncompetitive contests alike.[21]

This is not what we found. *We found a strong correlation between the competitiveness of a contest and the poll-vote disparity for the county we surveyed.* Competitive contest votecounts, taken as a group, were strongly red-shifted, with an official votecount more Republican than poll result, as compared to noncompetitive contest votecounts.

The goal of our study was not to identify particular contests, counties, or districts as having been targeted for rigging, but rather to determine whether there existed an overall *pattern* indicative of a targeting process, an indelible fingerprint of electoral manipulation.

In this we succeeded, to a high level of statistical significance.

Methodological limitations

No discussion would be complete without a frank acknowledgement of our study's limitations. We were compelled by budgetary considerations to select a small set of relatively small counties for our study. We could not afford to test any of the larger counties, where the

---

[21] "Just about equally" because the MOE decreases very slightly between a 50%-50% contest and a 75%-25% contest (most competitive and least competitive ends of our spectrum of contests). At the 200 – 300 sample sizes we are primarily working with, the MOE decrease is about 1%. This minor variation had no quantitative impact on our analysis.

cost of registration lists and survey completions would have been prohibitive.

In applying our approach to future elections, in particular to 2008, we hope to significantly expand the number and scope of counties surveyed. Should E2008 be as much a victim of targeted rigging as E2006 appears to have been, the expanded study we expect to undertake will expose and quantify the pattern to a 'DNA-level' of statistical certainty.

Or, put another way, it would appear that in light of political circumstances any effort to seize national control through manipulation of the vote counting in 2008 will have to be either of an aggregate magnitude that is truly shocking and so carries a high risk of exposure, or so well-targeted that the targeting pattern itself sticks out like a sore thumb.

To deter or expose massive electoral subversion, both modes of attack must be anticipated and monitored.

Conclusion

Our study was modest in scope because of financial constraints, but it was tightly-focused in its design. The result shines a powerful triple beam into the dark corner of secret electronic vote-counting in American elections.

> First, it detects a clear pattern indicating a wholesale shift in tallied votes. This is consistent with our study of aggregate vote shifting presented in *Landslide Denied*.
> Second, it identifies the overall direction of the shift: in favor of Republican candidates, once again corroborating our aggregate findings in *Landslide Denied*.

> Third, it confirms the common-sense notion that any group with the will and ability to secretly manipulate vote tabulation would likely focus their efforts on changing the outcomes of close contests, where the power of electronic vote-shifting would be maximized through selective targeting, while at the same time minimizing the size of the aggregate shift—and the corresponding risk of discovery.

We found evidence, in *Landslide Denied*, of an aggregate net shift of 3 million votes nationwide from Democratic to Republican candidates for the US House. If one imagines those shifted votes distributed randomly and evenly across the 435 contests, it would amount to a net shift of just under 7000 votes per contest. If we apply this model by taking 3500 putatively shifted votes from each Republican candidate and transferring them back to the Democratic candidate (for a net shift of 7000 votes), it would reverse the outcome of 15 House contests in 2006. This is not an inconsiderable effect, as it would have given the Democrats a 30-seat greater margin (248 – 187). If, however, we target and apply those same 3 million shifted votes to the most competitive Republican victories, we find it would instead reverse the outcome of 112 contests, giving the Democrats an overwhelming 345 – 90 majority in the House.

We naturally do not suggest that vote-shifting in 2006 was, or could be, targeted with such hindsight-aided precision. Our point is rather that targeting, even at the modest level of precision obtainable months in advance (from historical voting patterns and pre-election polling) can vastly increase the bottom-line effect of the covert shift of a given total number of votes or—conversely and more ominously—can enable a political control-shifting electoral manipulation that leaves only the smallest and all-but-undetectable fingerprint of *aggregate* mistabulation.[22]

In E2006, the explosive movement toward the Democrats in the month of October[23] would have overwhelmed a rational targeting plan finalized during the pre-October period, after which the logistics of further deployment or recalibration of vote-shifting mechanisms would most likely have been prohibitively problematic.[24] Such an extraordinary pre-election dynamic certainly cannot be counted on again to defeat attempts to seize political control via electoral manipulation. We submit that our findings regarding targeting in the present study, coupled with our earlier findings in *Landslide Denied*, sound an alarm for democracy, *and make a compelling case for expanded monitoring of future elections.*

We restate here the concluding sentences of *Landslide Denied*, as these latest findings only serve to increase the urgency of our warning:

---

[22] This is especially ominous in light of the fact that, in the absence of any effective system of *intrinsic* electoral audits, the only check mechanism of sufficient sensitivity and statistical power to effectively challenge the official numbers spit out by the computers is the demographically validated national exit poll (assuming that 'unadjusted' exit poll results are made available in 2008). But this check mechanism detects only an aggregate disparity. Targeted rigging allows the theft of both the Presidency and Congress with a footfall light enough to avoid setting off this sole remaining burglar alarm.

[23] See *Landslide Denied* pp. 13 – 15.

[24] See *Landslide Denied*, Appendix 2. Although the vulnerabilities of vote-counting computers make it possible to shift (or delete or fabricate) virtually unlimited numbers of votes, the size of the footprint and the likelihood of detection of course increases accordingly. The logical vote-shifting algorithm therefore remains 'take no more than you need'. A possible exception is the Presidential race, in which there is a rather compelling advantage to shifting enough votes nationwide to ensure a popular-vote victory, even though an Electoral College victory might be secured with a well-targeted fraction of those votes. A popular vote victory–as reflected in the contrasting behavior of the Democratic candidates in 2000 and 2004—plays a major role in granting or denying a Presidential candidate the standing, in the media and in the court of public opinion, to challenge even quite egregious anomalies in decisive battleground states.

'The vulnerability is manifest; the stakes are enormous; the incentive is obvious; the evidence is strong and persistent. Any system so clearly at risk of interference and gross manipulation cannot and must not be trusted to tally the votes in any future elections.'

*   *   *

Appendix 1 – Expanded Table 1

County, State	Contest	Contest Margin Statewide or CD-wide	Competitive/ NonCompetitive* C/NC	Within-County Exit Poll		Within-County Vote Count		Within-County Exit Poll - Vote Count Disparity Competitive Contests (R+/D-)	Within-County Exit Poll - Vote Count Disparity NonCompetitive Contests (R+/D-)	Within-County Difference Between Avg. Competitive and NonCompetitive Disparities***
				R	D	R	D			
Hardee, FL	Governor	7% [R]	C	49%	45%	57%	38%	7.5%		11.25%
	Senator	22% [D]	NC	50%	48%	48%	51%		-3.5%	
	House: FL-13	<1% [R]	C	51%	45%	61%	39%	8.0%		
Okeechobee, FL	Governor	7% [R]	C	45%	51%	41%	46%	5.5%		12.50%
	Senator	22% [D]	NC	44%	54%	35%	64%		-9.5%	
	House: FL-16	1% [D]	C**	45%	52%	45%	51%	0.5%		
Emanuel, GA	Governor	20% [R]	NC	59%	35%	60%	38%		-1.0%	4.00%
	House: GA-12	<1% [D]	C	59%	38%	61%	37%	1.0%		
Jefferson, GA	Governor	20% [R]	NC	50%	49%	50%	49%		0.0%	0.00%
	House: GA-12	<1% [D]	C	46%	52%	47%	53%	0.0%		
Jefferson, IA	Governor	10% [D]	NC	38%	58%	38%	56%		0.5%	11.00%
	House: IA-2	2% [D]	C	43%	54%	55%	45%	11.5%		
Van Buren, IA	Governor	10% [D]	NC	43%	55%	50%	47%		8.0%	10.50%
	House: IA-2	2% [D]	C	45%	54%	64%	36%	18.5%		
Mower, MN	Senator	20% [D]	NC	33%	62%	31%	65%		-2.5%	6.00%
	House: MN-1	6% [D]	C	33%	64%	38%	62%	3.5%		
Pipestone, MN	Senator	20% [D]	NC	55%	44%	52%	44%		-1.5%	1.00%
	House: MN-1	6% [D]	C	56%	43%	56%	44%	-0.5%		
Cedar, MO	Senator	3% [D]	C	59%	38%	58%	38%	-1.5%		12.50%
	House: MO-4	39% [D]	NC	56%	37%	43%	52%		-14.0%	
Henry, MO	Senator	3% [D]	C	46%	50%	44%	51%	-1.5%		16.50%
	House: MO-4	39% [D]	NC	40%	57%	22%	75%		-18.0%	
Humboldt, NV	Governor	4% [R]	C	65%	28%	69%	22%	5.0%		-2.25%
	Senator	14% [R]	NC	65%	30%	70%	25%		5.0%	
	House: NV-2	6% [R]	C	59%	34%	60%	34%	0.5%		
Adams, OH	Governor	23% [D]	NC	45%	52%	43%	55%		-2.5%	8.75%
	Senator	12% [D]	NC	46%	52%	46%	54%		-1.0%	
	House: OH-2	2% [R]	C	47%	51%	55%	45%	7.0%		
Bradford, PA	Governor	20% [D]	NC	48%	48%	58%	44%		6.0%	-6.75%
	Senator	18% [D]	NC	48%	49%	57%	43%		7.5%	
	House: PA-10	6% [D]	C	51%	46%	53%	47%	0.0%		
Wyoming, PA	Governor	20% [D]	NC	47%	49%	46%	54%		-3.0%	-1.50%
	Senator	18% [D]	NC	54%	42%	55%	45%		-1.0%	
	House: PA-10	6% [D]	C	59%	36%	58%	42%	-3.5%		
Haywood, TN	Governor	29% [D]	NC	20%	77%	19%	80%		-2.0%	8.00%
	Senator	3% [R]	C	30%	68%	36%	64%	5.0%		
	House: TN-8	46% [D]	NC	19%	77%	17%	83%		-4.0%	
Lancaster, VA	Senator	1% [D]	C	57%	40%	57%	42%	-1.0%		-4.00%
	House: VA-1	26% [R]	NC	60%	37%	64%	35%		3.0%	
Average								3.6%	-1.7%	5.47%

* Contests decided by a 9% or smaller margin are designated competitive; 10% or larger noncompetitive.
** Contest for seat vacated by Mark Foley; shifted from noncompetitive to competitive status during October 2006.
*** Number is positive (+) where net shift is to Republican in competitive vs. noncompetitive contests.
All surveys conducted via telephone on Election Night 2006 by Survey USA. (Hyperlinks show survey details including MOEs)

Appendix 2 – Regression Analysis

The purpose of regression analysis was to look at the correlation between vote margin and within-county exit poll-votecount disparity. We included in this analysis as a separate data point each of the 39 races in each of the 16 counties that served as the basis for our paired t-test analysis. This analysis represents a way of looking at the same data as we looked at in our paired t-test analysis, but from a different angle, with two advantages over the paired t-test analysis and two disadvantages.

The disadvantages were:

1. The regression analysis doesn't completely eliminate bias (though it eliminates the great majority of potential bias) as an explanation for our results, since some counties contributed data points to a non-competitive race without being matched by a competitive race, or vice versa. Therefore, the exact same population was not used for competitive and non-competitive races in this analysis. However, the two populations were very similar, and whereas a *potential* for a small amount of bias exists in this analysis, we see no reason to suspect that it does exist.

2. The rationale for using the paired t-test was that competitive races were characterized by the potential for fraud, whereas there would be no reason for committing fraud in non-competitive races. With that assumption, the *vote margins* would be unimportant, as long as the races could be characterized as competitive or non-competitive. If this assumption was accurate, then an analysis that included the *vote margins* of the race would include meaningless data, which could weaken the ability to detect meaningful differences between competitive and non-competitive races.

The advantages were:

1. When analyzing continuous variables (which vote margins are), regression analysis generally provides more power to detect meaningful differences than t-tests, which do not make use of the continuous nature of the variable, but dichotomize it instead.

2. To the extent that it might have been difficult to ascertain whether a race was competitive vs. non-competitive prior to the election, it would be reasonable to assume that the more competitive a race was the more likely that it would be subject to fraud. And, it is reasonable to suspect that the closer a race was presumed to be, the more susceptible it would be to fraud.

The regression analysis provided an F value of 21.85, corresponding to a p value of $p<0.000022$. That means that the correlation between vote margin and within-county exit poll-votecount disparity was so strong that it would have occurred only about one out of 50,000 times on the basis of chance alone (see graph below).

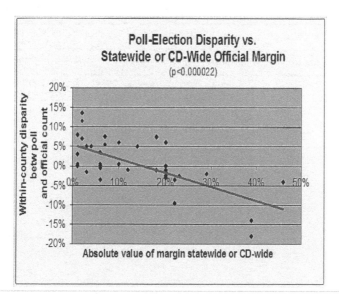

Appendix 3 – Survey USA Data Links

State	County	Link
MO	Henry	http://www.voterrollcall.com/client/PollReport.aspx?g=a6e072a1-a39e-4f6c-95e4-af1a0150bcac
MO	Cedar	http://www.voterrollcall.com/client/PollReport.aspx?g=cfd957af-bc6d-406e-b05e-23f025dd91a3
TN	Haywood	http://www.voterrollcall.com/client/PollReport.aspx?g=f5256fb4-48be-434f-a8ac-1e6c9c768e00
FL	Hardee	http://www.voterrollcall.com/client/PollReport.aspx?g=7bf59ee4-894f-43fd-9113-23bc4a8a21a8
FL	Okeechobee	http://www.voterrollcall.com/client/PollReport.aspx?g=aae0d44f-8fd7-426b-9186-cdd8d2222292
PA	Bradford	http://www.voterrollcall.com/client/PollReport.aspx?g=d3b628f5-5da3-42c7-96b9-350bc4fd11d2
PA	Wyoming	http://www.voterrollcall.com/client/PollReport.aspx?g=f04c2158-acee-4a6e-912f-14eef91303f0
MN	Mower	http://www.voterrollcall.com/client/PollReport.aspx?g=f065fa14-3452-4321-99dc-42fa8c48ee53
MN	Pipestone	http://www.voterrollcall.com/client/PollReport.aspx?g=6889cbbc-ade1-400e-a49e-c629be32bce0
OH	Adams	http://www.voterrollcall.com/client/PollReport.aspx?g=42f186df-1fdc-4f41-b5d6-b9b30026106d
GA	Jefferson	http://www.voterrollcall.com/client/PollReport.aspx?g=b962e036-0513-423b-9a5b-5d29892bf0c3
GA	Emanuel	http://www.voterrollcall.com/client/PollReport.aspx?g=dd565bbb-8dfc-4143-bd8c-016ac197203b
IA	Van Buren	http://www.voterrollcall.com/client/PollReport.aspx?g=b19fd14c-f493-406f-a18c-cf62dc1e1df6
IA	Jefferson	http://www.voterrollcall.com/client/PollReport.aspx?g=2b03ce9c-121a-45f4-a3d5-5453d177465d
NV	Humboldt	http://www.voterrollcall.com/client/PollReport.aspx?g=a36dfabf-2b31-4513-bc83-5b416056f84d
VA	Lancaster	http://www.voterrollcall.com/client/PollReport.aspx?g=70c3610b-c22e-49ed-b5a1-e102cf6ad4cf

STUDY IV.

Believe It (Or Not):
The 2010 Massachusetts
Special Election for US Senate

Jonathan D. Simon
August 27, 2010[1]

Background

On January 19, 2010 the Commonwealth of Massachusetts held a Special Election to fill the Senate seat left open by the death of Senator Edward Kennedy. It would be difficult to overstate the political implications of this election. Because the seat was the 60th for the Democrats, it carried with it the effective balance of power in the Senate: without it, in a dramatically polarized and decidedly uncooperative political environment, the Democrats would not be able to override a GOP filibuster. As the media let Americans know, everything from the shape of healthcare policy to financial regulation, from energy and environmental policy to critical judicial appointments hung in the balance.

Just as significantly, the victory by Republican Scott Brown over supposed shoo-in Martha Coakley was taken and trumpeted as a "sign:" the political calculus for the upcoming general elections in 2010 and 2012 was instantly rewritten, with the anger and unrest that apparently produced Brown's victory establishing expectations of catastrophic

---

[1] Revised October 28, 2011.

losses for the Democrats in November and beyond. All in all, the political impact of this single, under-the-radar state election was seismic, very nearly "presidential."

The Electoral System

With stakes that high, citizens not only of Massachusetts but of the rest of the United States would hope to find firm basis for *knowledge*, as opposed to mere *faith*, that the votes were accurately counted as cast and that the seating of the certified winner, along with the massive implications alluded to above, at least reflected the will and intent of the voting constituency. Instead, this is what a citizen seeking such knowledge about the Massachusetts Special Election would find:

- 97% of the ballots cast were counted unobservably by optical scan equipment ("opscan"), scanning voter-marked paper ballots; 3% of the ballots cast were publicly hand-counted.[2]
- The opscan devices were programmable computers manufactured by two corporations, Diebold/Premier Election Solutions ("Diebold/Premier") and Elections Systems and Software ("ES&S"), which together supply 80% of such equipment nationwide,[3] and 100% in Massachusetts.[4]

---

[2] Vote counting protocols identified by Massachusetts City and Town Directory at http://www.sec.state.ma.us/ele/eleclk/clkidx.htm; election returns at http://www.boston.com/news/special/politics/2010/senate/results.html.

[3] Source information at http://www.verifiedvoting.org/verifier/.

[4] Of the 280 opscan communities in Massachusetts, 223 use the Diebold/Premier AccuVote-OS scanner; 56 use the Optech Eagle scanner, originally manufactured by ES&S but whose distribution was split between ES&S and the smaller vendor Sequoia Voting Systems as a result of a court order in an antitrust action; and one employs the ES&S M100 scanner. Diebold/Premier was recently sold to ES&S for the brow-raising underprice of $5 million (about the value of *a single* large-county voting equipment *contract*), and indeed the sale was nixed by the US Department of Justice, Antitrust Division, as it would have given ES&S a virtually complete vote counting monopoly in the United States. In the absence of Diebold/Premier or any other substantial competitors, however, ES&S continues to enjoy near-monopolistic market domination.

- The vast majority[5] of the opscan devices were programmed, distributed and serviced by the highly secretive LHS Corporation, located in Methuen, Massachusetts.
- No systematic audit of the count was performed.
- No spot-checks of the count were performed.
- There was no recount of any ballots.
- There were no exit polls performed.
- No actual ballots stored within the opscan equipment were examined or are permitted to be examined.
- No memory cards, which internally direct each opscan's counting process and store the results, were examined or, as proprietary information belonging to their corporate programmer, are permitted to be examined.
- No computer code directing the recording and counting of ballots or the display of results was examined or, as proprietary information belonging to the programmer, is permitted to be examined.

The inquiring citizen or, for that matter, *public official* or *candidate* would unfortunately discover **no information** about the 97% of ballots counted by opscan equipment, other than the vote totals as displayed by that equipment after the last ballot had been scanned. That is, he or she would be reduced to 100% pure, unadulterated, blind faith that the totals displayed were accurate—fact and not fiction.

If, in fact, the vendor corporations, or any insider(s) with access to the programming and distribution processes, had chosen to serve a private political agenda rather than the public trust, *there would be nothing in the official processes of voting, vote-counting, and election certification to indicate that such a breach had occurred.* If, for example, certain memory cards had been programmed to tally any ballot bearing a stray mark as a vote for Candidate X, this single exploit might result in an

---

[5] 79.6%, or 223 of the 280 opscan communities, were serviced by LHS.

outcome-determinative shift of votes, and no one except the programmer would ever know. Or if certain memory cards had been programmed to shift every n^{th} vote for Candidate A to Candidate B, who but the programmer would know? Or again, if the "zero counters"[6] on an opscan are set to +X for the candidate whose victory is sought and –X for the candidate marked for defeat, at the end of the day the total votes recorded by the opscans will match the number of voters who have signed the poll book and the election administrator will be satisfied that the opscan has counted accurately and there has been a "clean" election, while 2X net votes have been stolen per machine so rigged.

Such vulnerability to fraud has by now been well researched and documented.[7] Unfortunately it tends to be regarded in the abstract, a technical possibility rather than an actual menace. The thinking appears to be that, *because this is America*, such things simply do not happen. Let us now set aside this comforting *a priori* conclusion and biopsy the Massachusetts Special Election with such tools as are available.

Our Analysis

We turn, in the absence of any direct validation of the opscan votecount, to the only ballots *not* counted invisibly. Just over 65,000 ballots, in 71 communities,[8] were counted by hand under public observation. Had these ballots been distributed randomly throughout the Commonwealth, we would expect the handcount results to fall

---

[6] The "zero counter" refers to the number assigned to the first vote recorded for a given candidate or proposition. Logically that number is "1" but a single line of code can be inserted into the 500,000+ lines already on the memory card to alter that to *any* number, positive or negative. There are no technical limitations to this manipulation, the only limiting concern being whether the rigged vote totals will pass the "smell test."

[7] See http://sites.google.com/site/remediaetc/home/documents/Scientific_Studies_7-20-08.pdf for a collection of such studies.

[8] See fn. 3.

within 1.0% of the opscan results with better than 99.9999% confidence.[9] Since the handcounts derive from discrete communities, however, and since Massachusetts is not politically homogeneous, an attempt must be made to quantitatively characterize and relate the two "meta-jurisdictions" which we shall call "Handcountville" (consisting of the 71 handcount communities) and "Opscanshire" (consisting of the remaining 280 opscan communities) respectively.

The first and most obvious way to relate Handcountville and Opscanshire would be by party registration. Such data is available from the Massachusetts Secretary of State, updated to October 2008.[10] It is given in Table 1.[11]

TABLE 1

Two-Party Registration - Massachusetts 2008			
Comparative Totals	GOP Reg	Dem Reg	Dem Margin
Handcount %	31.8%	68.2%	36.4%
Opscan %	23.7%	76.3%	52.6%
Differential	-8.1%	8.1%	16.2%

The two-party registration numbers paint Handcountville as significantly more Republican territory than is Opscanshire. Two-party registration is, however, a limited indicator in Massachusetts because just over half the voters in the Commonwealth (50.75%) are registered as "unenrolled" in either major party.[12] Without knowing more about

---

[9] See http://www.raosoft.com/samplesize.html.

[10] http://www.sec.state.ma.us/ele/elepdf/st_county_town_enroll_breakdown_08.pdf.

[11] Full data presented in the Appendix.

[12] http://www.sec.state.ma.us/ele/elepdf/st_county_town_enroll_breakdown_08.pdf.

the unenrolled voters in each meta-jurisdiction, reaching beyond this impression to a conclusive quantitative characterization is not feasible.

Fortunately, there exist indicators other than party registration that illuminate the political characteristics of voting constituencies. Massachusetts held contests for United States Senator in each of the two past biennial elections. The results, as broken down by meta-jurisdiction, are given in Table 2.

TABLE 2

Comparative Totals	US Senate - 2008			US Senate - 2006		
	Beatty- R	Kerry- D	Kerry Margin	Chase- R	Kennedy- D	Kennedy Margin
Handcount %	31.5%	68.5%	37.0%	31.1%	68.9%	37.8%
Opscan %	32.0%	68.0%	36.0%	30.5%	69.5%	39.0%
Handcount-Opscan Disparity	0.5%	-0.5%	1.0%	-0.6%	0.6%	-1.2%

In each of these statewide senatorial elections, Handcountville and Opscanshire exhibited virtual political congruence, much as we would expect if indeed Handcountville votes were a random sample of the state as a whole, establishing baseline expectations for the political divisions of the two meta-jurisdictions in similar contests such as the 2010 Massachusetts Special Election. In fact, when we combine the vote totals for the previous two Senate elections (2006 and 2008), we find *exact* congruence between the voters of Handcountville and Opscanshire, as shown in Table 3.

TABLE 3

Combined Vote for US Senate 2006 and 2008			
Comparative Totals	GOP	Dem	Dem Margin
Handcount %	31.3%	68.7%	37.4%
Opscan %	31.3%	68.7%	37.4%
Handcount-Opscan Disparity	0.0%	0.0%	0.0%

When we turn to the 2010 Special Election, however, we find a radically different comparative outcome. The results of the Brown-Coakley contest, as broken down by meta-jurisdiction, are given in Table 4.[13]

TABLE 4

US Senate - 2010 (Special)			
Comparative Totals	Brown-R	Coakley-D	Brown Margin
Handcount %	48.6%	51.4%	-2.8%
Opscan %	52.6%	47.4%	5.2%
Handcount-Opscan Disparity	4.0%	-4.0%	8.0%

Where votes were observably counted by hand, the Democrat Martha Coakley defeated the Republican Scott Brown by a margin of 2.8%; where votes were counted unobservably and secretly by machine, Brown defeated Coakley by a margin of 5.2%.

---

[13] The percentages exclude, for clarity, the Libertarian Party candidate, who received less than 1% of the vote, and whose inclusion does not appreciably affect the results. For a complete, town-by-town breakdown of the Brown-Coakley vote, the vote in prior Senate elections serving as baselines, and voter registration data, please see the Appendix published with the original paper, available at http://electiondefensealliance.org/files/BelieveIt_OrNot_100904.pdf.

There is no evidence that this whopping marginal disparity of 8.0% is attributable to divergent political leanings of the two meta-jurisdictions. In fact, there is strong evidence to the contrary: as the previous two Senate contests and what we can glean from party registration indicate, Handcountville is no more Democratic, and likely less so, than Opscanshire. Nor is there reason to suspect a demographic bias as cause: Handcountville consists primarily of small rural communities; Coakley, born and raised in the northwestern part of Massachusetts, had spent the past 30 years since graduation from Boston University Law School as a Boston-based, big-city attorney and prosecutor, serving from 1999 to 2007 as high-profile District Attorney of Middlesex County, home to 54 communities of which only four are in Handcountville.

Nonetheless it is incumbent upon our analysis to consider what would be the last-standing "benign" explanation for the handcount-opscan disparity and Coakley's Handcountville victory: that Handcountville impounds relatively more western towns near Coakley's old "home base," and that her Handcountville victory therefore reflects nothing more insidious than a "favorite daughter" phenomenon at work. Fortunately for our analysis, Coakley ran statewide for Attorney General in 2006, allowing us to assess whether Coakley enjoys "favorite daughter" status in Handcountville. The contest, against a Cambridge-based opponent, was, like the senatorial elections of 2006 and 2008, not sufficiently competitive to be a rational target for manipulation. The results are given below in Table 5:[14]

---

[14] Full returns at
http://www.boston.com/news/special/politics/2006_elections/general_results/attorney_general.html,
as referenced by Kathy Dopp of http://electionmathematics.org.

TABLE 5

Massachusetts Attorney General - 2006			
Comparative Totals	Coakley-D	Frisoli-R	Coakley Margin
Handcount %	72.6%	27.4%	**45.2%**
Opscan %	73.0%	27.0%	**46.0%**
Handcount-Opscan Disparity	0.4%	-0.4%	0.8%

We observe that in 2006, her only other statewide election, Martha Coakley performed just as well in Opscanshire as she did in Handcountville; in fact, she ran slightly better in the opscan communities. There was no "favorite daughter" phenomenon, no regional effect, and no Coakley advantage in the handcount jurisdictions. There was also, given the 45% margin, no incentive to manipulate and nothing at all to be gained from a "small" shift of votes on the order of the 5% shift sufficient to reverse the outcome of the 2010 Special Election.

The handcount vs. opscan disparity in the 2010 Special Election for Senate in Massachusetts stands as an unexplained anomaly of dramatic numerical proportions. We stated at the outset of our analysis that if the handcounted ballots had been distributed randomly throughout the Commonwealth, we would expect the handcount results to fall within 1.0% of the opscan results with better than 99.9999% confidence. The odds of an *8.0%* marginal disparity would be *beyond astronomical*. We have now further established that the handcount "sample" is, for comparison purposes, "better" than random: that is, based on demographics and voting patterns, the handcount voters would be more likely than the opscan voters to vote for Brown. The odds therefore of an 8.0 marginal disparity *in the other direction* would be, and there is no better way to say this, *beyond beyond astronomical*. Statisticians never say "impossible" but that is, for all earthly intents and purposes, what it is.

It remains to be noted that, as with the prior Coakley statewide race, neither the 2006 nor the 2008 Senate election which preceded it—and which we have presented as baseline contests—was competitive enough to invite manipulation: the risk entailed in shifting a net of 36% of the votes statewide is prohibitive;[15] and a shift in, say, the 5 – 10% range would not alter the outcome and would therefore garner no reward. *Such was not the case with the Brown-Coakley contest, where the risk-reward ratio was extremely favorable: a net shift of a mere 5% of the machine-counted votes would be sufficient to reverse the outcome.* As seismic as the Brown victory was, it was numerically plausible enough to pass the smell test, rendering the risk minimal. The reward, as noted at the beginning, was politically astronomical.

Not A Fluke

Should it be objected that this election somehow constitutes an isolated instance perhaps influenced by unperceived but legitimate factors peculiar to its particular terrain and moment in time, we may expand our inquiry to a neighboring time and a neighboring venue where, fortunately, both opscan and hand counting also continue to coexist. The state of New Hampshire also uses computerized voting equipment manufactured by Diebold/Premier, and is also serviced exclusively by LHS Corporation. In the 2008 general election we find Obama running significantly better in Handcountville, NH than in Opscanshire, NH—a disparity that increases to alarming proportions when party registration

---

[15] While such a massive shift of votes is technically feasible, the election result would not begin to pass the smell test, opening computerized electoral manipulation to intense scrutiny and undermining the entire enterprise nationwide.

data is used to normalize the two meta-jurisdictions, as presented in Table 6.[16]

TABLE 6

New Hampshire Statewide Vote for President 2008 Relative to Party Registration

New Hampshire Statewide E2008	Dem	Rep	Total
Opscan Presidential Vote	54.51%	45.49%	100.00%
Opscan Registered Voters	50.00%	50.00%	100.00%
Opscan vs. Party-Registration Differential	4.51	-4.51	0
Handcount Presidential Vote	56.51%	43.49%	100.00%
Handcount Registered Voters	46.69%	53.31%	100.00%
Handcount vs. Party-Registration Differential	9.82	-9.82	0
Handcount vs. Opscan Relative To Party Registration	5.31	-5.31	10.62

We see that Obama ran 4.51% ahead of (and McCain a corresponding 4.51% behind) two-party registration numbers in opscan jurisdictions but 9.82% ahead of two-party registration numbers in handcount jurisdictions. The normalized net disparity is 10.62%, comparable in eye-popping magnitude to the 8.0% disparity observed in the Massachusetts Special election.

Furthermore, in New Hampshire as in Massachusetts, we were fortunate to have a noncompetitive contest which can, as do the 2006 and 2008 Senate and the 2006 Attorney General contests in Massachusetts, function as a baseline for comparison. The results for the 2008 New Hampshire gubernatorial contest are presented in Table 7.

---

[16] Full data for New Hampshire is too extensive for inclusion in the Appendix; it is compiled from the NH Secretary of State website, at http://www.sos.nh.gov/general2008/index.htm.

TABLE 7

New Hampshire Statewide Vote for Governor 2008			
	Lynch-D	Kenney-R	Lynch Margin
Handcount %	71.76%	28.24%	**43.52%**
Opscan %	71.76%	28.24%	**43.52%**
Handcount-Opscan Disparity	0.00	0.00	0.00

Once again we find that, in a noncompetitive contest, the handcount and opscan jurisdictions exhibit political congruence (in this case, exact congruence to the second percentage decimal place), where in a presumptively competitive contest (the Presidential race), we find a glaring disparity.

Conclusion

It may fairly be objected that none of this numerical or "circumstantial" evidence, however strong, *proves* that computerized fraud has taken place or that the Massachusetts Special Election was "stolen," and we readily agree. To furnish such proof, beyond not just a reasonable doubt but any shred of doubt, we would need access to either memory cards, the code that actually ran in the opscans on Election Day, and/or the actual voter-marked ballots (chain of custody of course preserved), *all of which are conveniently off-limits to inquiry.* For anyone wondering, though, how much trust to place in privatized, concealed, and computerized vote counting—past, present and future—we suggest that the MA Special numbers scream for themselves.

And as numbers as implausible as these continue to rear their heads in high-stakes elections throughout the United States—invariably revealing a shift of votes *in the same direction*, whether measured against exit polls, pre-election polls, or observable votecounts[17]—we ask how the prevailing and irrational level of trust in invisible, unobservable vote counting can be maintained? We further ask how we can continue to employ a system that keeps software, code, memory cards, and all key aspects of the vote counting process secret, and relegates anyone seeking evidence of electoral validity to such an *indirect* quest for comparisons and baselines and numerical fingerprints as we have been obliged to undertake?

We return to the Massachusetts Special Election, which has not only dramatically altered the balance of power in Washington but has indeed ushered in a dramatically altered set of political expectations going forward into the critical elections of 2010 and 2012, as the hyper-polarization of American politics continues.[18] We cannot say with

---

[17] See generally, Charnin R, *Proving Election Fraud.* Bloomington, IN: AuthorHouse, 2010; Miller MC Ed., *Loser Take All: Election Fraud and the Subversion of Democracy 2000-2008.* Brooklyn, NY: Ig Publishing, 2008; Freeman S, Bleifuss J, *Was The 2004 Presidential Election Stolen?* New York: Seven Stories Press, 2006; Simon J, O'Dell B, *Landslide Denied: Exit Polls vs. Vote Count 2006,* (http://electiondefensealliance.org/files/LandslideDenied_v.9_071507.pdf); Simon J, O'Dell B, Tavris D, Mitteldorf J, *Fingerprints of Election Theft: Were Competitive Contests Targeted?* (http://electiondefensealliance.org/files/FingerprintsOfElectionTheft_2011rev_.pdf) 2007. Note particularly the rightward or "red" shift measured in the presidential election of *2008,* which—though it was, as a result of the Republican free-fall following the late-September crash of the markets and the general economy, insufficient to alter the outcome—was in fact of a magnitude even greater than that measured in 2004. The election of Barack Obama, contrary to the general impression, was thus anything but an "all clear" with respect to computerized electoral manipulation. It must further be noted, however, that exit polls and tracking polls alike are now weighted according to demographics drawn largely if not exclusively from *prior election* exit polls that were distorted rightward when "adjusted" to match official vote tallies. Thus, because votecounts *were* treated as sacrosanct, and all currently employed demographic baselines "tuned" to those red-shifted numbers, prior electoral manipulation clears the path for ongoing and future electoral manipulation by red-shifting the baselines against which such manipulation might be measured. With pre-election polls and exit polls so corrupted to oversample to the right, the telltale disparities between these previously reliable baselines and the votecounts disappear (making manipulated elections appear to be in line with expectations), and comparison between computer and hand counts survives as the sole reliable resource for numerical forensic investigation.

[18] It is easy enough to see how capacity to manipulate would lead to hyper-polarization: as victory becomes a given, the player is incentivized to make that victory *mean more* by moving further and further from the center; this appears to be what is occurring on a

100% certainty that the 97% of votes counted on optical scanners were subject to manipulation. But we can fairly ask: *"What evidence exists that they were not?"*

We have found *none*—no checks, audits, ballot inspections, hand tallies, exit polls, memory card or computer code examinations. Not a thing beyond pure *faith* that the corporations (and we have, for the purposes of this analysis, ignored their documented and self-proclaimed partisan proclivities) and insiders charged with the secret, unobservable counting of 97% of the votes in Massachusetts, have decided to honor the public trust at the expense of any other personal, economic, or political agenda of their own *or of anyone who would seek to influence them.* In an age of steroids and hGH, credit default swaps, Ponzi schemes, and massive institutional frauds coupled with hyper-partisan, true-believer politics, such "faith" amounts to little more than rank denial.

Nor, in the final analysis, is it evident to us that *additional* layers of technology would ultimately suffice to thwart a determined electoral manipulator—and, given the massive stakes in a politically polarized 21st Century America, we must anticipate the highest level of determination to bring about desired outcomes by any and all means. We have seen exit polls discredited, audits (Ohio 2004, e.g.) gamed, chains of ballot custody observed in the breach. Perhaps most critically, as long as it takes an expert to implement, or indeed to comprehend, a security protocol, every non-expert citizen is left on the outside looking in, never receiving knowledge, as opposed to mere *assurance*, that the bedrock protocol of his or her democracy has not been corrupted. Only transparency, *visible and observable counting by*

---

systemic level, and accounts at least in part for the bizarre politics of the computerized voting era. To wit, with rigged elections, it is not necessary to "move to the center" to win; but this newfound "freedom to be radical" is, alas, *one-sided*, and that is precisely the political dynamic we are witnessing unfold.

humans or non-programmable devices[19] *at every step*—which is just as feasible today as it was a mere generation ago[20]—can bestow that knowledge.

Computers can help us in many ways and will continue to play a major role in our lives, periodic glitches, hacks, and meltdowns notwithstanding. But to blindly and needlessly entrust our nation's *elections*—particularly its federal elections which so directly determine our national direction—to private, corporate and, it must be said, partisan enterprises operating and calculating in secret beyond our capacity to observe and validate, is, to put it with the bluntness this emergency demands, collective insanity.

---

[19] E.g., lever machines, in which each aspect of counting can be monitored.

[20] Using a parametric tool developed by Dave Berman, it has been shown that handcounting all contests for federal office (the maximum number of such races on any ballot is three) would require citizen participation averaging *one hour per voter lifetime* (one four-hour shift for which each citizen would have a one in four chance of being selected during his or her life), a civic obligation far less onerous than jury duty.

STUDY V.

The Likely Voter Cutoff Model:
What Is So *Wrong* with Getting It *Right*?

Jonathan D. Simon[1]
March 17, 2011

Logic tells us, and experience confirms, that political pollsters stay in business and prosper by predicting election outcomes accurately. Pollsters are now publicly ranked by various scorekeepers[2] according to how brilliantly close or embarrassingly far off they turn out to be when the returns come in. A "Certificate of Methodological Purity" may make a nice wall ornament, but matters not a whit when it comes to success within the highly competitive polling profession.

If election returns in competitive races were being systematically manipulated in one direction over a period of several biennial elections, we would expect pollsters to make methodological adjustments necessary to match those returns. Indeed, it would be nothing short of professional suicide not to make those adjustments, and turn whatever methodological handsprings were required to continue "getting elections right."

In the computerized election era—where virtually every aspect of the vote counting process is privatized and concealed; where study after study, from Princeton to the GAO, has concluded that the vote counting computers are extremely vulnerable to manipulation; and where statistical analyses pointing to such manipulation have been reflexively

---

[1] Jonathan D. Simon, JD, is Executive Director of Election Defense Alliance.

[2] See, e.g., the Fordham University 2008 ranking:
http://www.fordham.edu/campus_resources/enewsroom/archives/archive_1453.asp.

dismissed, no matter how compelling—it may be that the methodological contortions required for pollsters to "get elections right" constitute the most powerful evidence that computer-based election fraud and theft are systemic and rampant.

Enter the Likely Voter Cutoff Model, or LVCM for short. Introduced by Gallup about 10 years ago (after Gallup came under the control of a right-wing Christianist heir), the LVCM has gathered adherents until it is now all-but-universally employed, albeit with certain fine-tuning variations. The LVCM uses a series of screening questions—about past voting history, residential stability, intention of voting, and the like—to qualify and disqualify respondents from the sample. The problem with surveying the population at large or even registered voters, *without* screening for likelihood of voting, is obvious: you wind up surveying a significant number of voters whose responses register on the survey but who then *don't vote*. If this didn't-vote constituency has a partisan slant it throws off the poll relative to the election results—generally to the left, since as you move to the right on the political spectrum the likelihood of voting appears to rise.

But the problem with the LVCM as a corrective is that it far overshoots the mark: that is, *it eliminates many individuals from the sample who will in fact cast a vote*, and the respondents/voters so eliminated, as a group, are acknowledged by all to be to the left of those who remain in the sample, skewing the sample to the right (a sound methodology, employed for a time by the NY Times/CBS poll, would solve the participation problem by down-weighting, *but not eliminating*, the responses of interviewees less likely to vote). So the LVCM—which disproportionately eliminates members of the Democratic constituency, including many who will in fact go on to cast a vote, by falsely assigning them a *zero percent* chance of voting—*should get honestly tabulated elections consistently wrong.* It should over-predict the Republican/Right vote and under-predict the Democratic/Left vote, most often by an outcome-determinative 5-8% in competitive elections.

Instead it performs brilliantly and has therefore been universally adopted by pollsters, no questions asked, not just in the run-up to elections as in the past, but now all year round, setting expectations not just for electoral outcomes but for broad political trends, contributing to perceptions of political mojo and driving political dynamics—rightward, of course. In fact, the most "successful" LVCM models are now the ones that are *strictest* in limiting participation, including those that eliminate all respondents who cannot attest that they have voted in the three preceding biennial elections, cutting off a slew of young, poor, and transient voters. The impact of this exclusion in 2008 should have been particularly devastating, given the millions of new voters turned out by the Democrats. Instead the LVCM got 2008 just about right.[3]   Pollster Scott Rasmussen, formerly a paid consultant to the 2004 Bush campaign, employs the LVCM most stringently to winnow the sample, eliminating more would-be Democratic voters than do most if not all of his professional colleagues. A quick survey of his polls at www.rasmussenreports.com shows a nation unrecognizably canted to the right, and yet Rasmussen Reports was ranked "the most accurate national polling firm in the 2008 election" and close to the top in 2004 and 2006.

There is something *very* wrong with this picture and very basic logic tells us that the methodological contortion known as the LVCM can get election results so consistently right *only if those election results are consistently wrong*—that is, shifted to the right in the darkness of cyberspace.

A moment to let that sink in, before adding that, if the LVCM shift is not enough to distort the picture and catch up with the "red-shifted" votecounts, polling (and exit polling) samples are also generally weighted by partisanship or Party ID. The problem with this is that

---

[3] We note in passing that an extraordinary, 11th-hour Republican free-fall, triggered by the collapse of Lehman Bros. and the subsequent economic crash, produced an Obama victory in the face of a "red shift"—votecounts more Republican and less Democratic than the exit polls—even greater than that measured in 2004.

these Party ID numbers are generally drawn from prior elections' final exit polls—exit polls that were "adjusted" in virtually every case *rightward* to conform to votecounts that were to the right of the *actual* exit polls, the unshakable assumption being that the votecounts are gospel and the exit polls therefore wrong. In the process of "adjustment," also known as "forcing," the demographics (including Party ID, age, race, etc.) are dragged along for the ride and shift to the right. These then become the new benchmarks and baselines for *current* polling, shifting the samples to the right *and enabling prior election manipulations to mask forensic/statistical evidence of current and future election manipulations.*

To sum up, we have a right-shifting tunable fudge factor in the LVCM, now universally employed with great success to predict electoral outcomes, particularly when tuned to its highest degree of distortion. And we have the incorporation of past election manipulations into current polling samples, again pushing the results to the right. These methodological contortions and distortions could not be successful—in fact they would put the pollsters quickly out of business—absent a consistent concomitant distortion in the *votecounts* in competitive races.[4]

Since polls and election outcomes are, after some shaky years following the advent of computerized vote counting, now in close agreement (though still not exit polls, which are weighted to false demographics but of course do *not* employ the LVCM, and therefore still come in consistently to the left of votecounts until they are "adjusted" rightward to conformity), everything looks just fine. But it is a consistency brought about by the polling profession's imperative to find a way to mirror/predict votecounts (imagine, if you will, the professional fate of a pollster stubbornly employing *undistorted* methodology, who insisted that his/her polls were right and both the

---

[4] *Noncompetitive* races tend neither to be polled (no horserace interest) nor rigged (an outcome reversal wouldn't pass the smell test).

official votecounts *and* all the other pollsters wrong!). It is a consistency, achieved without malice on the part of the pollsters, which almost certainly conceals the most horrific crime, with the most devastating consequences, of our lifetimes.

STUDY VI.

Timeline of Events and Anomalies Associated with Computer-Based Election Fraud 2002 - 2016[1]

Jonathan D. Simon

> **2002:** Computerized voting gains a foothold in the wake of the Help America Vote Act, Mitch McConnell's brainchild, fronted by the soon-to-be-incarcerated Rep. Bob Ney and passed with the support of Democrats won over by the promise of increased turnout. The VNS (network) exit polls were withheld from the public (ostensibly because of a system glitch), masking glaring disparities in at least several key contests, including the Georgia Senate (Cleland—13% swing from tracking polls) and Governor (Barnes), where unverifiable paperless DREs had just been deployed, and where software "patches" were inserted by Diebold shortly before the election in 22,000 DREs.[2]

> **2003:** Death of Raymond Lemme, official of Florida Inspector General's Office charged with investigating the election rigging allegations made by Clint Curtis, in Georgia motel room ruled a suicide; Lemme's body photographed with bruising and slash wounds consistent with battery; investigation shut down.[3]

> **2004:** Computerized voting achieves predominance, with DREs and Optical Scanner (Opscan) equipment counting more than 80% of the votes nationally. Ohio votes "processed" in Tennessee on the SmarTech "back-up" servers set up prior to the election by Karl Rove's

---

[1] For an excellent "expanded" timeline of events, see Fitrakis R, Wasserman H: *The Strip & Flip Selection of 2016*, pp. 54 – 101, at https://www.amazon.com/dp/B01GSJLW0I/ref.

[2] See "Diebold and Max Cleland's 'Loss' in Georgia," by Robert F. Kennedy, in Miller MC, Ed., *Loser Take All: Election Fraud and the Subversion of Democracy, 2000-2008.* Brooklyn, NY: ig Publishing, 2008.

[3] http://www.democraticunderground.com/discuss/duboard.php?az=show_mesg&forum=104&topic_id=5567680&mesg_id=5567680.

IT chief, Mike Connell, after the state servers operating under Secretary of State J. Kenneth Blackwell (Honorary Chairman of the Bush campaign) "went down" just after midnight. Exit polls showed Kerry the victor in Ohio. Following the SmarTech takeover, margin flipped as Bush "surged" ahead. Exit polls were "adjusted" accordingly.

Votecounts were red-shifted, relative to exit polls, in 11 of the 12 "battleground" states. The networks and pollsters hastened to discredit their own polls, though they had been accurate enough for decades to permit early calls of even the tightest contests. It was put forward that Bush voters were more reluctant to respond to the exit polls, though careful analysis revealed that the *highest* level of exit poll response was in Bush *strongholds* and the hypothesis didn't fit the data. There was no evidence of "reluctant Bush responder" dynamics in noncompetitive states. And the pollsters, in offering the "reluctant Bush responder" excuse, ignored the fact that they had in any case weighted their polls to party ID in such a way as to neutralize any such response biases. Keith Olbermann briefly covered the uproar in several successive programs, then went on a long unannounced vacation and dropped it cold.[4]

Death of Athan Gibbs, Sr., Microsoft-backed inventor of Tru-Vote system to allow voter verification of ballots cast on computerized voting equipment. Gibbs, who was actively marketing his system, was killed when the car he was driving suddenly jumped lanes in front of an 18-wheel trailer.

> **2005:** Ohio election reform ballot proposition, leading by 28% in *Cleveland Plain Dealer* tracking poll on the eve of the election, was defeated by 25% when the votes were counted, an overnight net swing of 53% *statewide*; in the three other ballot propositions, the *Plain Dealer* poll was spot-on.

---

[4] See Freeman S, Bleifuss J: *Was the 2004 presidential election stolen? Exit polls, election fraud, and the official count.* New York: Seven Stories Press, 2006.

Death of Reverend Bill Moss, the lead plaintiff in the Ohio election challenge lawsuit *Moss v. Bush*, following an apparent stroke or aneurysm.

> **2006:** The capacity to manipulate proliferated while forensic tools grew more refined. The result is a measure of covert manipulation that was, or should have been, alarming.[5] There was a national red shift in the elections for the House of a total of 3 million votes relative to exit polls (there was a comparable red shift relative to tracking polls and a comparable red shift in competitive Senate races).[6] Of critical importance, this analysis could not be debunked on the basis of alleged exit poll sampling bias, because the sample was shown to be to the *right*, not the left, of the actual electorate.[7] The analysis was not challenged nor was an attempt made to refute it; it was simply ignored. Additional analysis revealed a "targeting" pattern, in which the more competitive a contest the more likely it was to be red shifted, a pattern pathognomonic of targeted rigging.[8]

Death of Warren Mitofsky—"father" of exit polling and head Edison/Mitofsky, official exit polling provider for US elections—of apparent aneurysm.

> **2008:** E2008 was an Obama victory and Democratic sweep. Many asked why the suspected manipulators would rig to lose? Again there was a massive red shift, in fact greater than in 2004 and 2006.[9] But, in both the 2006 and 2008 elections, unexpected 11th-hour events (in 2006 the Foley and related GOP sex scandals, in 2008 the collapse of

---

[5] See http://electiondefensealliance.org/files/LandslideDenied_v.9_071507.pdf ; also reprinted in *Loser Take All*.

[6] This exit poll-votecount red shift of course does not account for the additional impact of voter suppression tactics, as voters who stay at home or are turned away from the voting booth are not exit polled.

[7] See "Landslide Denied," cited in fn 5.

[8] See http://electiondefensealliance.org/files/FingerprintsOfElectionTheft_2011rev_.pdf.

[9] See Charnin R., *Proving Election Fraud: Phantom Voters, Uncounted Votes, and the National Exit Poll*. Bloomington IN: AuthorHouse, 2010.

Lehman Brothers and the subsequent economic crash) dramatically altered the electoral dynamics (in 2006, for instance, the Democratic margin in the Cook Generic Congressional Ballot jumped from 9% in the first week of October to 26% the week of the election, a Republican free-fall of epic proportions; a similar fate overcame McCain in the wake of the economy's collapse). These political sea changes swamped a red shift that turned out in retrospect to be under-calibrated, and they came too late to permit recalibration and redeployment of tainted memory cards and malicious code.[10] These red flags were again ignored, trampled in the Obama victory parade.

Death of US Congresswoman Stephanie Tubbs Jones, who had formally challenged the seating of the Ohio Bush electors following E2004, of apparent aneurysm while driving.

Death of Mike Connell, Karl Rove's IT "guru," in December crash of plane he was piloting. Connell had been compelled in November to give a sealed deposition in the *King Lincoln-Bronzeville vs. Blackwell* case, challenging the votecount of the 2004 Ohio presidential election in federal court, and was expected to return to complete his testimony in January. Connell's widow, combing the crash site, found the earpiece to his Blackberry device, known to contain extensive email correspondence with Rove, but the device itself was never located.[11]

> **2010:** Republican Scott Brown's victory in the Coakley-Brown special election in Massachusetts put the Tea Party on the map, took away the Democrats' filibuster-proof Senate majority, and set expectations for a major move to the right in November. There were no exit polls, no spot checks, no audits, not a single opscans memory card examined for malicious code: the result was a 100% pure, unadulterated, faith-based election, a *critical election that could have*

---

[10] Any attempt at such recalibration and redeployment on a scale large enough to be effective would have been a rather visible and highly suspicious undertaking.

[11] See Worrall S: *Cybergate: Was The White House Stolen by Cyberfraud?* Amazon Digital Services, 2012, http://preview.tinyurl.com/98ntmc6.

been stolen with virtually zero risk. In the 70 jurisdictions where ballots were hand-counted, Coakley won.[12] In fact, statewide, there was an 8% disparity from hand-count to computer-count jurisdictions, a red shift in line with that measured in 2004, 2006, and 2008, and enough to reverse the outcome and avoid a recount. Analysts asked were those hand count jurisdictions more Democratic? They weren't, they were more Republican. Were they in Coakley's part of the state? They weren't; in fact, in her only other statewide race, a noncompetitive race, she did *better* in the opscan than in the handcount jurisdictions. Ultimately analysts examined and ruled out every benign explanation for the outcome-determinative disparity.[13]

The Massachusetts special election was followed by a Democratic primary in South Carolina which pitted a known and respected candidate (Judge Vic Rawl) against a cipher (Alvin Greene) who made no campaign appearances, had no website, was threatened with indictment on pornography-related charges, and lacked the personal funds for the election filing fee, which was paid anonymously on his behalf. The contest was for the nomination for US Senate, and a November match-up with incumbent Republican and Tea Party favorite Jim DeMint, against whom Rawl had already closed to a threatening 7% in tracking polls. The votes were tallied on paperless DREs and Greene won with 59% of the vote. Rawl brought a challenge before the Democratic State Committee. Several election integrity experts testified, citing, among other gross anomalies, large disparities between early/absentee votes counted by opscan (where the ballots would at least in theory be available for comparison with the computer counts) and the DRE tallies. Greene did not appear. The Committee reacted favorably to Rawl's challenge throughout the hearing, then went into

---

[12] See http://electiondefensealliance.org/files/BelieveIt_OrNot_100904.pdf.
[13] Ibid.

closed session and voted by an overwhelming margin to reject the challenge and close the matter.[14]

The November election was a great sweep for the Tea Party and the Right, with seismic implications for the nation. It seemed that the professionals at Edison/Mitofsky and the National Election Pool (NEP) still could not figure out how to get exit polls right because, once again, the red shift turned up everywhere: in the Senate elections (16 out of 18 competitive races red shifted); the Governorship elections (11 out of 13 races red shifted); and in the House (a total red shift of 1.9 million votes). In a telling comparison with 2006—when an election-eve Democratic margin of 26% in the Generic Congressional Ballot ("Whom do you intend to vote for in the election for US House in your district?") translated into a net gain of a mere 58 House seats by the Democrats—a Republican Generic Congressional Ballot margin of 9%, and an even smaller tabulated national popular vote margin of 6.8%, in E2010 translated into a net gain of *128* seats, a completely unprecedented "efficiency" ratio, and the "epic sweep" the media duly reported at face value.

The infrastructure needed for computerized election theft has become progressively more sophisticated and efficient. The off-site "processing" that is believed to have been pioneered in Ohio in 2004, has now been deployed in other key states. This mechanism allows *real-time targeting and calibration of manipulations*, which was not possible with pre-set, memory card-based rigs. Using the off-site processing scheme, aka "man in the middle attack," votecounts can be altered surgically and elections stolen with a tidy numerical footprint. Election theft thus becomes increasingly difficult to detect—barring serious investigation of the off-site IP networks now processing many of the votes.

---

[14] See http://www.bradblog.com/?p=7902.

Compounding the forensic difficulties, forensic baselines—all except the surviving smattering of handcounts—are part of a feedback loop and are themselves being distorted to the right. The pollsters—under the imperative to *get elections right* or go out of business—have turned to a tunable fudge factor known as the Likely Voter Cutoff Model (LVCM), which skews their samples about 5-10% to the right by disproportionately eliminating from the sample members of left-leaning constituencies such as young, transient, poor, and non-white respondents.[15] Both exit polls and pre-election polls are now also weighted using demographic baselines, such as party identification, drawn from the "adjusted" exit polls of prior elections. Since these adjustments are always to the right, to bring the exit polls to conformity with the votecounts, and because they carry the demographics along to the right in the process, *current exit polls and pre-election polls are further skewed to the right.* The unadjusted exit polls—themselves red-shifted by this weighting process but lacking the LVCM to complete the distortion—remain somewhat to the left of the votecounts, but the pre-election polls, with the combined distortions of false-stratification and the LVCM pushing them well to the right, manage to accurately predict the electoral outcomes in competitive races. Logically, such methodologically contorted polls can get election results consistently *right* only if those election results are consistently *wrong*.

The US Supreme Court's party-line 5-to-4 decision in *Citizens United v. FEC*, 558 US 310 (2010), defines corporate campaign contributions as protected "free speech," gutting much of the framework for regulating or limiting such spending and opening the floodgates to a deluge of "dark money" when Congress fails to pass expected disclosure requirements.

> **2011:** In the Wisconsin Supreme Court election, another "proxy" election (cf. Coakley-Brown in Massachusetts the year before) with

---

[15] See http://electiondefensealliance.org/files/TheLVCM.pdf.

seismic national political implications, out-of-state funding poured in as Karl Rove emphasized the significance that the Republican's victory would have. In spite of the election's national significance, no exit polls were conducted. Many votes were tabulated on servers run by the storefront outfit Command Central, located across the state line in Minnesota. Apart from the 7583 votes (just enough votes to dodge a mandatory recount) discovered for the Republican candidate (found by a former employee of that candidate) the day *after* the election, there were major red-flag anomalies in returns, concentrated most strongly in Democratic Milwaukee and Dane counties, relative to established voting patterns, recent prior elections, and other races on the ballot.[16] The recount, demanded by the losing Democratic candidate, appeared to be even more corrupted than the election itself: bags of ballots were found by observers to be improperly sealed and frequently ripped open, in the very jurisdictions where the electoral anomalies had been identified. In the face of this widespread evidence that ballots had been swapped out to match the machine totals, objection after objection was lodged, duly recorded, and then ignored. The Democratic candidate ultimately bowed to pressures to concede, rather than pursue a grueling litigation before a partisan and adverse Supreme Court.[17]

There followed the State Senate recall elections in Wisconsin, and again strong anomalies emerged, this time complemented by a red shift in citizen-conducted exit polls which were admittedly of uncertain probative value. When it falls to citizen exit polls to provide the only check on secret votecounts on partisan-controlled computers, it is not surprising that the Carter Center, which monitors elections around the world, has determined that US elections don't meet the minimum standards required for such monitoring. The Republicans won exactly the number of recalls needed to keep control of the Wisconsin state senate by one seat.

---

[16] For details of the forensic analysis, see
http://electiondefensealliance.org/files/MemorandumToLegalTeamRe.Milwaukee-final.pdf.

[17] See http://electiondefensealliance.org/files/IrregularitiesinWISupremeCourtElectionandRecount.pdf.

Having gained control of key state legislatures and governorships in the 2010 rout, Republican lawmakers and administrators, guided by ALEC, wasted little time in responding to the 2010 Census by gerrymandering the states under their control; passing restrictive and discriminatory Voter-ID laws; and adding a variety of other discriminatory burdens to the registration and voting processes.

> **2012:** The recall election for Republican Governor Scott Walker of Wisconsin was dubbed "the second most important election" of this presidential election year. Corporate cash and partisan luminaries flooded into the state and all stops were pulled, particularly on behalf of the embattled, union-busting Republican Governor, who enjoyed an eight-to-one spending advantage over his Democratic opponent.

When the dust settled, Walker had won a surprisingly easy 7% victory, which was ascribed by the punditry to his massive *Citizens United*-enabled funding advantage and to the right-trending mood of the country.

What the media failed even to *footnote* was that the NEP exit poll had the race at 50%-50% (an exit poll weighted, we should not forget, to right-shifted Party ID demographics drawn from the right-adjusted exit polls of recent prior elections). This exit poll was as "official" as any conducted on November 6th for the general election: same outfit (Edison/Mitofsky), same methodology, same large sample. What was curious is that, if you had looked for it on Election Night, you would have found it in only one place: online briefly (before it was adjusted to match Walker's 7% margin) at the Milwaukee *Journal-Sentinel's* website. You would not have found it posted on any network, though the networks certainly were looking at that poll because they all came out talking about a "deadlock" and "a long night ahead." Until *about 15 minutes later* it suddenly morphed into "an easy Walker win" and "yet another triumph for the politically born-again Karl Rove," and "a grim prospect for the Democrats." The networks commissioned and paid for that exit poll and then decided, one and all, to withhold it from public view (the Milwaukee *Journal-Sentinel* either did not get the message or brazenly decided to ignore it). Because it was impossibly far "off"—at least relative to the votecount, which must be "on," else this is not America.

While the public battle has raged over Voter ID and "voter" fraud, no media attention has been accorded to continuing, indeed intensifying evidence of covert electronic fraud. An egregious but typical omission was an analysis, covered by the press in the UK but predictably ignored in the US, by Michael Duniho (retired National Security Agency analyst), Francois Choquette, and James Johnson, who examined election returns from the 2012 Republican presidential primaries. The authors found a consistent pattern: after controlling for all other factors, such as urban/rural differences, Mitt Romney's share of the vote increased, and his opponents' shares decreased, as the *size* of the precinct where the votes were being counted increased.[18]

This pattern, disclosed by Cumulative Vote Share analysis ("CVS"), is not "naturally occurring;" that is, it is not found in "ordinary" elections that would not be targets for rigging. In *those* races, when voteshare is plotted against cumulative votes cast by increasing precinct size, the slope is a flat line; there is *no correlation* between voteshare and precinct size.

The authors could find *nothing* to account for the Romney "upslope" pattern other than the selection by a rigger of larger precincts as safer places to shift votes without arousing suspicion (100 votes shifted in a precinct of 1000 total votes cast will pass the smell test; the same 100 votes stolen in a precinct of 250 total votes will not). In primary after primary throughout the bruising Romney run to the nomination the analysts found the same pattern. They then extended their analysis to suspect races as far back as 2008 and picked up essentially the same

---

[18] See http://www.themoneyparty.org/main/wp-content/uploads/2012/10/Republican-Primary-Election-Results-Amazing-Statistical-Anomalies_V2.0.pdf.

red-flag pattern for these elections, including an overall shift of up to 10% from Democratic to Republican in key contests such as the Coakley-Brown race in Massachusetts.

Obama's "reassuring" re-election victory is likely a result of covert intervention by the group Anonymous, which, having infiltrated Rove's ORCA operation, locked his operatives out of their own servers. Ohio's own official servers "go down" at 11:13 pm (cf. E2004) while Rove, in a bizarre on-air "meltdown," disputes the call of Ohio and the election for Obama by his own employer, FOX News. In addition to the actions of Anonymous, a lawsuit filed the day before the election, challenging the placement of "experimental" software patches in 44 Ohio counties and on the state's election website, has been credited by some with thwarting the planned manipulation of E2012.

> **2013:** The US Supreme Court, by a party-line 5-to-4 decision in *Shelby County v. Holder*, 570 US __ (2013), guts the restraints imposed by The Voting Rights Act of 1965, freeing nine states with a Jim Crow history of franchise discrimination to change their election laws without federal review. As in the wake of *Citizens United* (2010), Republican legislatures and administrations in these states waste no time in passing a swath of discriminatory procedural laws and regulations targeting minorities and other Democratic constituencies. Many of these provisions face legal challenge and are ruled unconstitutional by the courts.

> **2014:** Carrying a single-digit approval rating, *the lowest in history*, the Republican-led Congress *gains* seats in E2014. Of 222 Republican House incumbents who stand for re-election, *two* are defeated, a re-election rate of better than 99%; Republicans take control of the Senate and gain 12 House seats overall. This astounding result is reflexively attributed by pundits to "low turnout" among Democratic and progressive voters. Yet, across a wide swath of states, progressive ballot propositions, strongly opposed by these same Republican candidates, are passed by wide (i.e., rig-proof) margins. The question

of how these results square with the "low turnout" hypothesis is never answered. Nor is a pervasive red shift deemed at all remarkable.

The US Supreme Court, by a party-line 5-to-4 decision in *McCutcheon v. FEC*, 572 US __ (2014), removes all restrictions on aggregate corporate campaign contributions. The Court was aware, by the time of *McCutcheon*, that Congress had failed and would fail to pass any disclosure requirements that the Court had anticipated in the wake of its *Citizens United* decision. Thus the Scalia bloc decides *McCutcheon* fully aware that it is ushering in an era in American politics not just of dark (i.e., undisclosed) money, but of *unlimited* dark money.

> **2015:** The Harvard Electoral Integrity Project ranks the United State 45th among fully developed democracies in election integrity. The "Beacon of Democracy" places immediately between Mexico and Colombia.

> **2016:** Political anger, distrust, disgust, and nihilism are the hallmarks of the E2016 campaign to date. The word "rigged" is brought into common usage (and misusage) by Donald Trump, and that impression of the electoral process is bolstered by a variety of visible tactics appearing to place thumbs of significant weight on the scales in favor of certain candidates. The perception of unfairness is particularly strong among supporters of the Sanders candidacy, a nearly successful bid astoundingly funded almost entirely by individual as opposed to corporate donors. But it is Trump's warnings of a rigged November that reflect most ominously what happens when vote counting is unobservable and trust in the process has broken down.

Although Trump prevails in the Republican nomination battle, he is a witness to the Democratic battle and the uncanny numbers and patterns that accrue to the benefit of Clinton. He sees the radically divergent performance of the candidates in caucuses (where vote counting is observable and Sanders routs Clinton) vs. primaries (where vote counting is computerized and unobservable and Clinton bests Sanders);

he sees the radically divergent performance of the exit polls in the Republican primaries (where they are within expected error levels) vs. the Democratic primaries (where they are far outside expected error levels and virtually unilateral in their shift); and he may have even taken note of Oklahoma (where, in the only primary state where the voting computers are programmed by the *state itself* instead of the *vendors*, the exit poll/votecount shift is *reversed*).

Trump's alarms about "rigging," echoing those of Sanders supporters and election integrity advocates, are therefore, while undeniably both scatter-shot and self-serving, neither as irrational as portrayed by the media nor lacking in evidentiary basis.[19] We appear to be headed for a disquieting November and a disquieting electoral future. Unobservable vote counting has reached a predictable crisis of confidence and our entire political system has reached a predictable and parallel crisis of confidence after just 15 years of computerized elections. The window for reform is narrow.

---

[19] Others have begun to echo the hue and cry. See, e.g., a recent article by Roger Stone, former Trump advisor, veteran of Republican campaigns dating to the Nixon years, and NY *Times* best-selling author: "Can the 2016 election be rigged? You bet," at http://thehill.com/blogs/pundits-blog/presidential-campaign/291534-can-the-2016-election-be-rigged-you-bet. Stone writes:

> "Both parties have engaged in voting machine manipulation. Nowhere in the country has this been more true than Wisconsin, where there are strong indications that Scott Walker and the Reince Priebus machine rigged as many as five elections including the defeat of a Walker recall election. . . The computerized voting machines can be hacked and rigged and after the experience of Bernie Sanders there is no reason to believe they won't be. Don't be taken in."

I have provided this reference neither for its erudition nor for its persuasiveness, but as an arresting example of what is in store once confidence in the vote counting process breaks down.

STUDY VII.

E2014: A Basic Forensic Analysis

Jonathan D. Simon

Any comparative forensic analysis is only as "good" as its baselines. In *Landslide Denied*[1]—our archetypal post-election comparative forensics study, in which the "red shift" (the rightward disparity between exit poll and votecount results) was identified and measured—a critical component of the analysis was to establish that the exit poll respondents accurately represented the electorate. We employed a meta-analysis of multiple measures of the demographics and political leanings of the electorate to demonstrate that the exit polls in question had not "oversampled" or over-represented Democratic or left-leaning voters (in fact any inaccuracy turned out to be in the opposite direction), and therefore that those polls constituted a valid baseline against which to measure the red-shifted votecounts. In *Fingerprints of Election Theft*,[2] we went further and removed all issues of sample bias from the equation by conducting a separate poll in which we asked *the same set of respondents* how they had voted in at least one competitive and one noncompetitive contest on their ballot. The noncompetitive contests, being presumptively unsuitable targets for rigging, thus served as the baselines for the competitive contests, and the relative disparities could be compared without concern about any net partisan tendencies of the respondent group.

---

[1] See Study II.
[2] See Study III.

More recently we have commented on the feedback loop that develops between election results and polling/sampling methodologies, such that consistently and unidirectionally shifted votecounts trigger, in both pre-election and exit polls, methodological adaptations that mirror those shifts.[3] Approaching E2014, we observed that the near-universal use of the Likely Voter Cutoff Model (LVCM) in pre-election polling, and stratification to demographic and partisanship quanta derived from (rightward) adjusted prior-election exit polls in all polling, were methodological distortions that pushed both exit polls and pre-election polls significantly to the right, corroding our baselines and making forensic analysis much less likely to detect rightward shifts in the votecounts.

Indeed, given the rightward distortions of the adaptive polling methodologies, we noted that *accurate* polls in E2014 would serve as a red-flag signal of rightward manipulation of the votecounts. In effect, the LVCM and the adjusted-exit-poll-derived weightings constituted a rightward "pre-adjustment" of the polls, such that any rightward votecount manipulations of comparable magnitude would be "covered."

It is against this backdrop that we present the E2014 polling and votecount data, recognizing that the adaptive polling methodologies that right-skewed our baselines would combine to reduce the magnitude of any red shift we measured and significantly mitigate the footprint of votecount manipulation in this election. The tables that follow compare polling and votecount results, where polling data was available, for US Senate, gubernatorial, and US House elections. The exit polling numbers represent the first publicly posted values, prior to completion of the "adjustment" process, in the course of which the poll results are

---

[3] See Study V; see also http://truth-out.org/news/item/27203-vote-counts-and-polls-an-insidious-feedback-loop.

forced to congruity with the votecounts.[4] The "red shift" represents the disparity between the votecount and exit poll margins. For this purpose, a margin is positive when the Democratic candidate's total exceeds that of the Republican candidate. To calculate the red shift, we subtract the votecount margin from the exit poll margin, so a positive red shift number represents a "red," or rightward, shift between the exit poll and votecount results.

Table 1

STATE	EXIT POLL %		Margin	VOTECOUNT %		Margin	RED SHIFT
	D	R	(D - R)	D	R	(D - R)	
E2014 US SENATE EXIT POLL-VOTECOUNT DISPARITY ("RED SHIFT")							
KY	45.0%	52.0%	-7.0%	40.7%	56.2%	-15.5%	8.5%
SC(1)	41.6%	50.6%	-9.0%	36.8%	54.3%	-17.5%	8.5%
GA	48.8%	48.2%	0.6%	45.2%	52.9%	-7.7%	8.3%
WV	38.9%	58.6%	-19.7%	34.5%	62.1%	-27.6%	7.9%
ME	35.7%	64.4%	-28.7%	31.7%	68.3%	-36.6%	7.9%
KS(I)[5]	45.6%	49.4%	-3.8%	42.5%	53.3%	-10.8%	7.0%
SD	33.2%	47.8%	-14.6%	29.5%	50.4%	-20.9%	6.3%
LA	44.7%	38.4%	6.3%	42.1%	41.0%	1.1%	5.2%
NC	49.0%	45.6%	3.4%	47.3%	48.8%	-1.5%	4.9%
MN	56.6%	41.4%	15.2%	53.2%	42.9%	10.3%	4.9%
AR	42.1%	54.4%	-12.3%	39.4%	56.5%	-17.1%	4.8%
IA	46.7%	50.8%	-4.1%	43.8%	52.1%	-8.3%	4.2%
SC(2)	39.6%	59.4%	-19.8%	37.1%	61.1%	-24.0%	4.2%
IL	54.4%	42.1%	12.3%	53.1%	43.1%	10.0%	2.3%
OR	58.5%	38.1%	20.4%	55.7%	36.9%	18.8%	1.6%
VA	49.6%	47.4%	2.2%	49.2%	48.3%	0.9%	1.3%
NH	52.1%	47.9%	4.2%	51.5%	48.2%	3.3%	0.9%
TX	35.2%	61.8%	-26.6%	34.4%	61.6%	-27.2%	0.6%
MI	56.1%	42.4%	13.7%	54.6%	41.3%	13.3%	0.4%
AK	46.4%	49.1%	-2.7%	45.8%	48.0%	-2.2%	-0.5%
CO	45.8%	49.8%	-4.0%	46.3%	48.2%	-1.9%	-2.1%
AVERAGE RED SHIFT							**4.1%**

---

[4] Because these "unadjusted" exit polls, which have not yet been tainted by the forcing process, are permanently removed from public websites often within minutes of poll closings, they must be captured as screenshots or in free-standing html format prior to their disappearance. At Election Defense Alliance we archive these captures as part of our forensic operations.

[5] In the Kansas race the Republican was opposed by an Independent candidate.

Table 2

	E2014 GUBERNATORIAL EXIT POLL-VOTECOUNT DISPARITY ("RED SHIFT")						
STATE	EXIT POLL %		Margin	VOTE COUNT %		Margin	RED SHIFT
	D	R	(D - R)	D	R	(D - R)	
OH	40.4%	56.1%	-15.7%	32.9%	63.8%	-30.9%	15.2%
SD	31.7%	62.9%	-31.2%	25.4%	70.5%	-45.1%	13.9%
CA	62.5%	37.5%	25.0%	58.9%	41.1%	17.8%	7.2%
NY	56.8%	36.8%	20.0%	54.0%	40.6%	13.4%	6.6%
GA	47.3%	48.7%	-1.4%	44.9%	52.7%	-7.8%	6.4%
OR	55.0%	43.1%	11.9%	49.9%	44.1%	5.8%	6.1%
WI	49.7%	49.4%	0.3%	46.6%	52.3%	-5.7%	6.0%
ME	45.7%	44.7%	1.0%	43.4%	48.2%	-4.8%	5.8%
MN	54.2%	42.9%	11.3%	50.1%	44.5%	5.6%	5.7%
SC	44.2%	53.8%	-9.6%	41.4%	55.9%	-14.5%	4.9%
PA	57.0%	42.5%	14.5%	54.9%	45.1%	9.8%	4.7%
KS	48.6%	47.9%	0.7%	46.1%	50.0%	-3.9%	4.6%
IA	39.6%	57.4%	-17.8%	37.3%	59.0%	-21.7%	3.9%
MI	49.2%	49.8%	-0.6%	46.9%	50.9%	-4.0%	3.4%
IL	48.0%	48.5%	-0.5%	46.4%	50.3%	-3.9%	3.4%
AR	43.2%	53.8%	-10.6%	41.5%	55.4%	-13.9%	3.3%
TX	40.8%	58.2%	-17.4%	38.9%	59.3%	-20.4%	3.0%
FL	47.0%	47.0%	0.0%	47.1%	48.1%	-1.0%	1.0%
AK(I)[6]	49.5%	46.6%	2.9%	48.1%	45.9%	2.2%	0.7%
NH	52.7%	47.4%	5.3%	52.5%	47.3%	5.2%	0.1%
CO	49.2%	47.2%	2.0%	49.2%	46.1%	3.1%	-1.1%
AVERAGE RED SHIFT							5.0%

---

[6] In the Alaska race the Republican candidate was opposed by an Independent.

Table 3

2014 US HOUSE EXIT POLL - VOTECOUNT DISPARITY ("RED SHIFT")			
	D %	R %	Margin
GENERIC CONGRESSIONAL BALLOT	43.2%	45.4%	-2.2%
US HOUSE NATIONAL EXIT POLL	48.1%	49.9%	-1.8%
US HOUSE NATIONAL VOTECOUNT	45.2%	50.7%	-5.5%
RED SHIFT			3.7%
Total Votes Counted		77,564,577	
Net Votes Red Shifted		2,897,414	
Maximum Contests Reversed		89	

To summarize the data presented in Tables 1 – 3:

- The US Senate red shift averaged 4.1% with a half dozen races presenting red shifts of over 7%. Of the 21 Senate elections that were exit polled, 19 were red-shifted.
- The gubernatorial red shift averaged 5.0% and 20 out of the 21 races were red-shifted.
- In US House elections, which are exit polled with an aggregate national sample,[7] the red shift was 3.7%. This is the equivalent of approximately 2.9 million votes which, if taken away from the GOP winners of the closest elections, would have been sufficient to reverse the outcomes of 89 House races

---

[7] The sample size of the House poll exceeded 17,000 respondents, yielding a Margin of Error (MOE) of less than 1%.

such that the Democrats would now hold a 120-seat (277 – 157) House majority.[8]

- Although the thousands of state legislative contests are not exit-polled, it is fair to assume that the consistent red shift numbers that we found in the Senate, House, and gubernatorial contests would map onto these critical (as we have seen) down-ballot elections as well.

These red shift numbers, well outside applicable margins of sampling error, are egregious even by the dubious historical standards of the elections of the computerized voting era in America. Although it is an *indirect* measure of mistabulation, the red shift has been, with very few exceptions, pervasive throughout that era, and it is not reflective of the impact of any of the overt tactics of gerrymandering, voter suppression, or big money. It represents a very telling incongruity between how voters indicate that they voted and the official tabulation of those votes. While it is not "smoking gun" proof of targeted mistabulation, it is, in the magnitude and persistence we have witnessed over the past half-dozen biennial election cycles, just about impossible to explain without reference to such fraud. It is simply too much smoke for there not to be a fire.

We relied as well on pre-election polling averages as a corroborative baseline,[9] and found that the red shifts from these predictions were comparable, though somewhat smaller than the exit poll-votecount red shifts (3.3% vs. 4.1% for the US Senate races; 3.5% vs. 5.0% for the

---

[8] Of course I am not suggesting that vote theft can be targeted with such infallible precision. But it would make no sense at all *not* to target vote theft to the closest races and shift enough votes to ensure narrow victories. When one couples the evidence of a nearly 3 million vote disparity with even a modestly successful targeting protocol, the result is easily sufficient to flip the balance of power in the US House.

[9] The pre-election polling numbers represent an average of all polls available from the two-months prior to Election Day (Source: RealClearPolitics at http://www.realclearpolitics.com/epolls/latest_polls/elections/. See also www.ballotpedia.com, a very flexible and useful resource).

gubernatorial races; and 3.3% for the Generic Congressional Ballot[10] vs. 3.7% for the US House Aggregate Exit Poll). We suspect that these differences can be accounted for by the impact of the Likely Voter Cutoff Model in pre-election polling, which pushes samples even further right than does the use of prior elections' adjusted exit poll demographics to weight the current exit poll sample, thereby further reducing the poll-votecount disparity.

The standard arguments have of course been put forward that all these exit polls (and pre-election polls) were "off," that essentially every pollster in the business (and there are many), including the exit pollsters, overestimated the turnout of Democratic voters, which was "known" to be historically low because the official votecounts and a slew of unexpected Democratic defeats tell us it was. In response to this entirely tautological argument, there are two non-jibing realities to be considered. The first is that the sampling methodologies of the polls were *already* distorted to impound the anticipated low turnout rate of Democratic voters in off-year elections, a model which has been grounded on the official votecounts of this century's three previous suspect computerized midterm elections, E2002, E2006, and E2010. The second is what would have to be termed the apparent schizoid behavior of the E2014 electorate, in which—from county-level referenda in Wisconsin backing expanded access to healthcare and an end to corporate personhood, to state-level ballot proposals to raise the minimum wage across America (see Table 4)—voters approved, by wide margins, the very same progressive proposals that the Republican candidates they apparently elected had violently opposed.

---

[10] The Generic Congressional Ballot is a tracking poll that asks a national sample of respondents whether they intend to vote for the Democratic or Republican candidate for US House in their district.

Table 4

E2014 - Ballot Propositions	Margin of Passage	Status
AK Minimum Wage Increase	38.7%	Pass
AK Legalized Marijuana	6.4%	Pass
AK Protects Salmon vs. Mining	31.8%	Pass
AR Campaign Finance Reform (Lobbyist Regulation)	4.8%	Pass
AR Minimum Wage Increase	31.8%	Pass
FL Water and Land Conservation	50.0%	Pass
FL Medical Marijuana (60% required)	15.2%	Pass
IL Right To Vote (anti-VOTERID)	45.4%	Pass
IL Minimum Wage Increase	32.8%	Pass
IL Birth Control Inclusion in Prescription Drug Insur.	31.8%	Pass
IL Millionaire Tax Increase for Education	27.2%	Pass
NE Minimum Wage Increase	19.0%	Pass
NJ Funds for Open Space and Historic Preservation	29.2%	Pass
NM Student Included On Board of Regents	29.4%	Pass
NM Public Library Bond	25.9%	Pass
NM Education Bond	19.6%	Pass
OR ERA	28.4%	Pass
OR Legalized Marijuana	12.0%	Pass
RI Clean Water, Open Space, Healthy Communities Bonds	41.8%	Pass
SD Minimum Wage Increase	10.1%	Pass
SD Health Provider Inclusion (anti insurance corps)	23.6%	Pass
SD Minimum Wage Increase	10.1%	Pass
WA Unlversal Background Checks for Gun Purchases	18.6%	Pass
Average Margin of Passage	**25.4%**	
CO "Personhood" (Anti-Abortion)	-29.6%	Fail
ND Life Begins at Conception	-28.2%	Fail
WA Gun Rights (pro gun owner)	-10.6%	Fail
Average Margin of Failure	**-22.8%**	

The wide margins are significant because they tell us that, unlike the key contests for public office, these ballot propositions were well outside of smell-test rigging distance. Thus, even had defeating them been an ancillary component of a strategy that appears riveted on seizing full governmental power rather than scoring points on isolated issue battlefields, these ballot propositions would have failed any reasonable risk-reward test that might have been applied, and thus were left alone.[11]

Table 5

CONGRESSIONAL APPROVAL RATING		
Approve	Disapprove	Margin
8%	89%	-81%
OBAMA APPROVAL RATING		
Approve	Disapprove	Margin
47%	52%	-5%
OWN REPRESENTATIVE DESERVE REELECTION?		
Yes	No	Margin
29%	41%	-12%
HAS CONGRESS PASSED ANY LEGISLATION THAT WILL IMPROVE LIFE IN AMERICA?		
Yes	No	Margin
11%	69%	-58%

Source: Rasmussen Reports (Week Preceding E2014)

With so much not making sense about E2014 it seems hardly necessary to add that it makes no sense at all for an historically unpopular Congress to be shown such electoral love by the voters that exactly

---

[11] As was the state of California, the one place in America where Democrats actually made US House *gains* in E2014. This perpetuates a pattern we have noted in several previous elections that may speak to the deterrence value of a well-designed audit protocol and a higher level of scrutiny from the (Democratic) Secretary of State's office than is found in the vast majority of other states.

TWO (out of 222) incumbent members of the Republican House majority lost their seats on November 4, 2014, while the GOP *strengthened* its grip on the House by adding 12 seats to its overall majority, and of course took control of the US Senate, 31 governorships, and 68 out of 100 state legislative bodies.

It would seem to require magicianship of the highest (or lowest) order to pull these results from a hat known to contain a Congressional Approval rating in the single digits (See Table 5). In handing over vote counting to computers, neither the processes nor the programming of which we are permitted to observe, we have chosen to *trust the magician*, and we should not be at all surprised if for his next trick he makes our sovereignty disappear.

VI. FOR FURTHER REFERENCE

These are the days of miracle and wonder and don't cry, baby, don't cry, don't cry, don't cry.

-- Paul Simon, "The Boy In The Bubble"

Books:

Charnin, Richard: *Matrix of Deceit: Forcing Pre-Election and Exit Polls to Match Fraudulent Vote Counts.* 2012, ISBN 1480077038
http://preview.tinyurl.com/97xgb7r

Charnin, Richard: *Proving Election Fraud: Phantom Voters, Uncounted Votes, and the National Exit Poll*, AuthorHouse 2010, ISBN 9781449085278   http://preview.tinyurl.com/8anvvbr

Collier, James M.; Collier, Kenneth F.: *Votescam: The Stealing of America,* Victoria House Press 1992, ISBN 0963416308,
http://www.amazon.com/Votescam-Stealing-James-M-Collier/dp/0963416308

Conyers, John; Miller, Anita; Vidal, Gore: *What Went Wrong in Ohio: The Conyers Report On The 2004 Presidential Election*, Academy Chicago Publishers 2005, ISBN 089733535X
http://preview.tinyurl.com/9e7jpzh

DeLozier, Abbe W.; Karp, Vickie (eds): *Hacked! High Tech Election Theft in America*, Truth Enterprises Publishing 2006, ISBN 9780615132556

Fitrakis, Robert J.; Rosenfeld, Steven; Wasserman, Harvey: *What Happened in Ohio? A Documentary Record of Theft and Fraud in the 2004 Election*, The New Press 2006, ISBN 1595580697
http://www.amazon.com/What-Happened-Ohio-Documentary-Election/dp/B005HKT4JQ/ref=pd_sim_b_2

Fitrakis, Robert J.; Rosenfeld, Steven; Wasserman, Harvey (eds): *Did George W. Bush Steal America's 2004 Election? Essential Documents*, CICJ Books 2005, ISBN 0971043892
https://www.amazon.com/dp/B01GSJLW0I/ref

Fitrakis, Robert J.; Wasserman, Harvey: *The Strip & Flip Selection of 2016: Five Jim Crows & Electronic Election Theft*, CICJ Books 2016, ISBN 9781622493364

Freeman, Steven F.; Bleifuss, Joel: *Was the 2004 Presidential Election Stolen? Exit Polls, Election Fraud, and the Official Count*, Seven Stories Press 2006, ISBN 1583226877

Harris, Bev: *Black Box Voting; Ballot Tampering in the 21st Century*, Talion Publishing 2004, ISBN 1890916900

Kreig, Andrew: *Presidential Puppetry: Obama, Romney, and Their Masters*, Eagle View 2012, at http://www.lulu.com/shop/andrew-kreig/presidential-puppetry/paperback/product-20479955.html.

Miller, Mark C.: *Fooled Again: How the Right Stole the 2004 Election*, Basic Books 2005, ISBN 0465045790

Miller, Mark C. (ed): *Loser Take All; Election Fraud and the Subversion of Democracy, 2000-2008*, Ig Publishing 2008, ISBN 9780978843144

Palast, Greg: *Billionaires & Ballot Bandits; How to Steal an Election in 9 Easy Steps*, Seven Stories Press 2012, ISBN 978609804787

Palast, Greg: *Armed Madhouse*, Dutton 2006, ISBN 0525949682

Parks, Sheila: *WHILE WE STILL HAVE TIME: The Perils of Electronic Voting Machines and Democracy's Solution: Publicly Observed, Secure Hand-Counted Paper Ballot (HCPB) Elections.*
http://www.amazon.com/dp/1479156531/ref=rdr_ext_tmb

Raymond, Allen: *Confessions of a Republican Operative: How to RIG an Election,* Simon & Schuster 2008, ISBN 9781416552239

Rosenfeld, Steven: *Count My Vote; A Citizen's Guide to Voting,* Alternet Books 2008, ISBN 9780975272459

Steele, Marta: *Grassroots, Geeks, Pros and Pols: The Election Integrity Movement's Rise and Nonstop Battle to Win Back the People's Vote, 2000-2008*, The Free Press 2012, available at
http://freepress.org/store.php#a2012.

Tavris, Dale: *Democracy Undone*, Bitingduck Press 2012, ASIN B009KR7MCI. http://preview.tinyurl.com/8sqv682

Ventura, Jesse (with Russell, Dick): *American Conspiracies*, Skyhorse Publishing 2011, ISBN 1616082143

With, Barbara: *Steal This Book Not My Vote,* 2012
http://barbarawith.com/stealthisbook.html

Worrall, Simon: *Cybergate: Was The White House Stolen by Cyberfraud?* Amazon Digital Services, 2012,
http://preview.tinyurl.com/98ntmc6

Selected Evidentiary and Analytical Studies:

Choquette, Francois; Johnson, James: *Republican Primary Election 2012 Results: Amazing Statistical Anomalies* (2012) http://electiondefensealliance.org/files/PrimaryElectionResultsAmazin gStatisticalAnomalies_V2.1.pdf

Clarkson, Elizabeth: *How trustworthy are electronic voting systems in the US?* (June 2015)
https://www.statslife.org.uk/significance/politics/2288-how-trustworthy-are-electronic-voting-systems-in-the-us

Common Cause, Rutgers School of Law, Verified Voting Foundation: *Counting Votes 2012: A State by State Look at Election Preparedness,* (August 2012) http://www.countingvotes.org/

Fries'dat, lulu; Sampietro, Anselmo; (in collaboration with) Scheuren, Fritz: *An Electoral System in Crisis,* (July 2016)
http://www.hollerbackfilm.com/electoral-system-in-crisis/

O'Dell, Bruce: *Testimony for Hand-Counted Paper Ballots, Texas Legislature,* (4/4/2007)
http://electiondefensealliance.org/print/book/export/html/1269

Simon, Jonathan; Baiman, Ron: *The 2004 Presidential Election: Who Won the Popular Vote? An Examination of the Comparative Validity of Exit Poll and Vote Count Data* (2004)
http://freepress.org/images/departments/PopularVotePaper181_1.pdf

Simon, Jonathan; O'Dell, Bruce: *Landslide Denied: Exit Polls vs. Vote Count 2006, Demographic Validity of the National Exit Poll and the Corruption of the Official Vote Count* (2007)
http://electiondefensealliance.org/files/LandslideDenied_v.9_071507.pdf

Simon, Jonathan; O'Dell, Bruce; Tavris, Dale; Mitteldorf, Josh: *Fingerprints of Election Theft: Were Competitive Contests Targeted?* (2007)
http://electiondefensealliance.org/files/FingerprintsOfElectionTheft_2011rev_.pdf

Simon, Jonathan: *Believe it (Or Not): The Massachusetts Special Election for US Senate*
http://electiondefensealliance.org/files/BelieveIt_OrNot_100904.pdf

Simon, Jonathan: *The Likely Voter Cutoff Model: What Is So Wrong with Getting It Right?*
http://electiondefensealliance.org/files/TheLVCM_0.pdf

Various Authors: *Compendium of Studies of Electronic Voting Prepared for New York Litigation (2008).*
http://sites.google.com/site/remediaetc/home/documents/Scientific_Studies_7-20-08.pdf

Related Published Papers and Articles:

Ananda, Rady: "Fatally Flawed Systems Await Voters," (9/1/2008)
http://www.opednews.com/articles/Fatally-Flawed-Systems-Awa-by-Rady-Ananda-080909-59.html

Anderson, Pokey: *Peering Through Chinks in the Armor of High-Tech Elections by Pokey Anderson* (2007)
http://www.votersunite.org/info/PeeringThruChinks.pdf

Bernstein, Jessica: "How Progressive Media Won't Let Us Talk About Election Fraud," *HIGHBINDER* (7/19/2016)
http://highbinder.org/progressive-media-election-fraud/

Campbell, Denis; James, Charley: "Retired NSA Analyst Proves GOP Is Stealing Elections," UKProgressive.co.uk (10/26/2012) as reprinted at
http://www.dailykos.com/story/2012/10/26/1150485/-Retired-NSA-Analyst-Proves-GOP-Is-Stealing-Elections

Collier, Victoria: "How to Rig an Election," *Harper's Magazine* (10/26/2012) as reprinted at http://readersupportednews.org/opinion2/277-75/14198-focus-how-to-rig-an-election

Collier, Victoria: "The 'Shocking' Truth About Election Rigging in the United States," Truthout (9/6/2016); http://www.truth-out.org/op-ed/item/37486-the-shocking-truth-about-election-rigging-in-america

Collier, Victoria; Ptashnik, Ben: "A National Call to Link Arms for Democracy," *Truthout* (5/31/2014); http://www.truth-out.org/opinion/item/24033-a-national-call-to-link-arms-for-democracy

Friedman, Brad: "Diebold Voting Machines Can Be Hacked by Remote Control," *Salon* (9/27/2011)
http://www.salon.com/2011/09/27/votinghack/

Hommel, Teresa: "Does Touchscreen Voting Violate The 5th Principle?" (6/27/2009)
http://www.wheresthepaper.org/DREsViolate5thPrinciple090627.pdf

Kennedy, Robert F. Jr.: "Was The 2004 Election Stolen?" *Rolling Stone* (6/1/2006), as reprinted at
http://www.commondreams.org/views06/0601-34.htm

Perlman, Diane: "The Silence of the Scams," *OpEdNews* (4/21/2005) as reprinted at
http://www.truthisall.net/Diane_Perlman/diane_perlman.html

Pynchon, Susan: "Election Dirty Tricks: Business as Usual or Treason at the Ballot Box?" (5/1/2006)
http://votetrustusa.org/index2.php?option=com_content&do_pdf=1&id=1249

Thiesen, Ellen: *Vendors are Undermining the Structure of U.S. Elections* (2008)
http://www.votersunite.org/info/ReclaimElectionsSumm.asp

Ungar, Robert: "Romney Family Ties to Voting Machine Company That Could Decide the Election Causing Concern," *Forbes* (10/20/2012)
http://preview.tinyurl.com/9yemp4a

Compendium: "ELECTION FRAUD Beginner's Guide: A Broken Democracy Crash Course"
http://www.organikrecords.com/corporatenewslies/beginner_v2.htm

Websites:

www.CODERED2014.com

www.ElectionDefenseAlliance.org

www.democracymovement.us

www.Votescam.org

www.BlackBoxVoting.org

www.electiondefense.org

www.Bradblog.com

www.OpEdNews.com

www.VotersUnite.org

www.TrustVote.org

www.michiganelectionreformalliance.org

www.ElectionsAtRisk.org

www.bethclarkson.com

www.RichardCharnin.org

www.MarkCrispinMiller.com

www.WheresThePaper.org

www.HandCountedBallots.org

www.thealliancefordemocracy.org

www.FreePress.org

www.solarbus.org/election

www.bbvforums.org

www.ElectionJusticeUSA.org

www.VerifiedVoting.org

Facebook Groups:

Black Box Voting

Documenting Democratic Primary Election Fraud: 2016

Election Defense Alliance – WI

Election Integrity Project

Election Integrity

ElectionJusticeUSA

Election Nightmares

HCPB FAQ

MA Occupy Hand-Counted Paper Ballots

Occupy Rigged Elections

PDA Clean Fair Transparent Elections Team

WI Citizens for Election Protection

Wisconsin Counts! Protecting Wisconsin's Elections

Videos and DVDs:

Stealing America: Vote by Vote, Dorothy Fadiman, director;
http://www.stealingamericathemovie.org/

Uncounted – The New Math of American Elections, David Earnhardt, director; http://uncountedthemovie.com/

Murder, Spies & Voting Lies: The Clint Curtis Story, Patty Sharaf, director; http://votinglies.com/

I Voted? Jason G. Smith, director; http://www.ivotedmovie.com/

The Best Democracy Money Can Buy, David Ambrose and Greg Palast, directors; http://www.palastinvestigativefund.org/?id=69

Dan Rather: *Das Vote, "Digital Democracy in Doubt,"* HDNetTV http://www.huffingtonpost.com/dan-rather/digital-democracy-in-doub_b_774137.html (see link to iTunes video download at end of article)

Electile Dysfunction, Penny Little, director; http://www.electile-dysfunction.com/

No Umbrella, Laura Paglin, director; www.noumbrella.org

Hacking Democracy, Simon Ardizzone, director; http://tinyurl.com/8vqrd6u

Stephen Spoonamore, cybersecurity expert, interview; http://www.velvetrevolution.us/electionstrikeforce/2008/08/worlds_leading_computer_securi.html

Princeton hack demonstrated; http://www.youtube.com/watch?v=OJOyz7_sk8I

ACKNOWLEDGEMENTS

I want to begin by gratefully acknowledging every individual who has ever made even a single phone call or written even a single email or letter or Post-It note, or spoken even once to a friend, partner, co-worker, or stranger on a train on behalf of election integrity. You have been willing to be bothered, to bother others, in many cases to take some measure of risk. Thank you for doing the daily work of citizenship and patriotism: it is on you that a happy ending will ultimately depend.

Thank you to all my colleagues in the Election Integrity movement who, having been barred from the endzone, nevertheless line up for play after play, even if it's just a bruising three yards and a cloud of dust.

With especial appreciation for the collaborative forensic work of Josh Mitteldorf, Steve Freeman, Dale Tavris, Bruce O'Dell, Kathy Dopp, Beth Clarkson, Richard Charnin, Francois Choquette, Ted Soares, Dave Griscom, Richard Hayes Phillips, J.Q. Jacobs, Howard Stanislevic, and Ron Baiman.

For the tireless efforts and eloquent voices of Professor Mark Crispin Miller, Dorothy Fadiman, Bradblog's Brad Friedman, OpEdNews's Rob Kall and Joan Brunwasser, Jeannie Dean, Bev Harris, Bob Fitrakis, Harvey Wasserman, Cliff Arnebeck, Greg Palast, and ElectionDefense.org's Vicki Collier and Ben Ptashnik.

For Election Defense Alliance co-founders Dan Ashby and Sally Castleman, and for Sally's devoted and continuous collaboration, friendship, and support over the past eight years in the trenches.

For my former spouse and always friend Julie, who endured and understood.

And for the generous support of The Threshold Foundation, The Silicon Valley Community Foundation, and EDA's many individual donors, who have made possible much of our forensic work and election integrity advocacy.

Thank you to Arlene Montemarano, Mike Ferriter, Judy Alter, Jacqueline Janecke, Bob Koehler, Ethan Scarl, Heleni Thayer, Andrea Novick, Avi Green, Toni Serafini, David Moore, Dick Russell, Dana Jill Simpson, Mimi Kennedy, Keith Thomson, Jim Fadiman, Jenny Clark, Marta Steele, Kathleen Campbell, Avi Rubin, Ed Felten, Harri Hursti, Ron Rivest, David Earnhardt, lulu Friese'dat, Nancy Tobi, Mike Hicks, John Brakey, Jim March, Lori Grace, Stephen Caruso, Joe Libertelli, Kat L'Estrange, Linda Pinti, Sheila Parks, David Frenkel, Simon Worrall, Ginny Ross, Pokey Anderson, Laura Pressley, Vicki Karp, Abbe Delozier, Karen Renick, Sherona Merel, Paul Lehto, Rady Ananda, Gail Work, Craig Unger, Dave Lewit, Roy Lipscomb, Lowell Finley, Victoria Lovegren, Joanne Lukacher, Bob Fleischer, Teresa Hommel, Emily Levy, Andrew Appel, Alex Shvartzman, Kate Scott, Laura Wigod, Desi Doyen, Jack Gordon, Mary Magnuson, Jim Mueller, Jen Miller, Sierra Nolan, Maggie Thomas, Grant Petty, Brett Kimberlin, Summer Rose, Lee Camp, Deb Lusignan, Lucius Chiaraviglio, Jessica Bernstein, Fritz Scheuren, Anselmo Sampietro, Dan Wallach, Jeremy Epstein, Perry Adler, Bruce Underhill, Ray Beckerman, Peter Peckarsky, John Zogby, Jennifer Brunner, Kevin Shelley, Dennis Kucinich, Cynthia McKinney, Stephanie Singer, Joel Simpson, AJ Vicens, Leonard Carpenter, Steve Scalmanini, Annie Esposito, Jesse Ventura, Lynn Landes, Alex Halderman, Pat Leahan, Shyla Nelson, Pete Johnson, Susan Pynchon, Laura Paglin, Ellen Brodsky, Marge Creech, Mark Adams, Rebecca Mercuri, Spencer Gundert, Laure Gaussen, Paul Velleman, Andrew Kreig, Ben Wofford, Michael Collins, Michael B. Green, David Swanson, Dennis Karius, Ben Manski, Bob Wilson, Nancy Matela, Mike Hicks, Mary Howe Kiraly, Joyce McCloy, Jim Soper, Michelle Mulder, Michael Richardson, Bennie Smith, John Ervin, Chris Hood, Casey Reed, Kevin Zeese, Garland Favorito, Nancy White, Jack Evans, Bernie Ellis, and the late Rev. Bill Moss, Raymond Lemme, Andy Stephenson, Tom Courbat, Athan Gibbs, Beverly Campbell, Harold Lecar, Stephanie Tubbs Jones, and John Gideon. All have worked selflessly and given greatly of themselves to defend our democracy.

Especially meaningful have been the work and voices of Paul Craig Roberts, Chuck Herrin, Stephen Spoonamore, Clint Curtis, and the late John Washburn. Each set aside his political partisanship to honor the truth and pursue the evidence wherever it might lead. And I salute the courage and integrity of Virginia Martin and Jason Nastke, Co-commissioners of Elections, Columbia County (NY); Ion Sancho, Supervisor of Elections, Leon County (FL); and former California Secretary of State, Debra Bowen; whose care and responsibility have gone far beyond the surface appearance of things.

With appreciation for the efforts of Keith Olbermann, Dan Rather, Robert Kennedy, Jr., and Thom Hartmann, who have all anteed up powerfully at the Election Integrity table. This is one hand that, however bad, deserves to be played to the last card, all-in.

For the late Jim and Ken Collier, who saw this coming before any of us, who did go all-in, and who never got up from the table.

To all the journalists, pundits, politicians, opinion leaders, and institutions in the Bystanders' Brigade, who have responded to our entreaties to join us in speaking out about computerized election theft by wishing us good luck in our work: thank you for the encouragement. I hope one day you will simultaneously find the "bandwidth" and the courage to leave the Bystanders' Brigade and actually do something to rightfully earn both a more genuine appreciation and your place in history.

With great appreciation for the able (and infinitely patient) assistance of Carin Handusn (iwebresults.com) with CODE RED's cover, website, and all things PR.

Finally, many thanks to my partner Carla who, besides her own election integrity efforts and editorial contributions to this book, has been in my corner all the way, keeping us both in relatively good cheer on this trip down the rabbit hole and on through Wonderland.

ABOUT THE AUTHOR

Jonathan Simon is Executive Director of Election Defense Alliance (www.ElectionDefenseAlliance.org), a nonprofit organization founded in 2006 to restore observable vote counting and electoral integrity as the basis of American democracy.

As a result of his prior experience as a political survey research analyst in Washington, Dr. Simon became an early advocate for an exit poll-based electoral "burglar alarm" system, independent of media and corporate control, to detect computerized vote shifting in Election 2004. In the absence of such a system, he was nevertheless able to capture and analyze official exit poll data briefly posted on the web prior to its Election-Night disappearance, realizing as the following day dawned that he was in fact the only person in the world in possession of this critical data, which went on to serve as the initial basis for questioning the validity of the 2004 presidential election.

Dr. Simon has gone on to author, both individually and in collaboration, numerous papers related to various aspects of election integrity. He has worked in cooperation with many Election Integrity organizations; appeared in several election integrity-related films, including *Stealing America: Vote by Vote* and *Uncounted: The New Math of American Elections,* and as an interviewee on several dozen live broadcasts. He tweets @JonathanSimon14 and invites all interested in corresponding to connect with him through LinkedIn or the *CODE RED* website www.CODERED2016.com.

Dr. Simon is a graduate of Harvard College, New York University School of Law, and New York Chiropractic College. He is admitted to the Bar of Massachusetts and since 1993 has directed an interdisciplinary healthcare facility in Cambridge, Massachusetts.